UP 'TIL NOW

*A collection of short stories and anecdotes
of growing up in Newfoundland,
becoming a Registered Nurse,
pursuing a Nursing career in Nova Scotia,
retiring and returning home
to Newfoundland and Labrador in 2000.*

by

BONNIE JARVIS-LOWE, RN. Rtd.
Graduate, Class 1969
Grace General Hospital School of Nursing,
St. John's, NL

TRAFFORD

Canada ▪ England ▪ Ireland ▪ United States of America

© Copyright 2004 Bonnie Jarvis-Lowe. All rights reserved.

No part of this publication may be reproduced, stored in a retrieval system, or transmitted, in any form or by any means, electronic, mechanical, photocopying, recording, or otherwise, without the written prior permission of the author.

Printed in Victoria, Canada

In some cases the names have been changed to protect the identities of the characters and their circumstances.

Cover design by the author.

A cataloguing record for this book that includes the U.S. Library of Congress Classification number, the Library of Congress Call number and the Dewey Decimal cataloguing code is available from the National Library of Canada. The complete cataloguing record can be obtained from the National Library's online database at: www.nlc-bnc.ca/amicus/index-e.html
ISBN: 1-4120-1821-8

TRAFFORD

This book was published *on-demand* in cooperation with Trafford Publishing. On-demand publishing is a unique process and service of making a book available for retail sale to the public taking advantage of on-demand manufacturing and Internet marketing. **On-demand publishing** includes promotions, retail sales, manufacturing, order fulfilment, accounting and collecting royalties on behalf of the author.

Suite 6E, 2333 Government St., Victoria, B.C. V8T 4P4, CANADA
Phone   250-383-6864   Toll-free   1-888-232-4444 (Canada & US)
Fax   250-383-6804   E-mail   sales@trafford.com
Web site   www.trafford.com   TRAFFORD PUBLISHING IS A DIVISION OF TRAFFORD HOLDINGS LTD.
Trafford Catalogue #03-2198   www.trafford.com/robots/03-2198.html

*This work is dedicated to the
Graduating Class Grace General Hospital
School of Nursing 1969, and
in Memory of the Classmates we have lost.
YOU WILL NEVER BE FORGOTTEN.*

'A PRAYER'

Let me do my work each day, and if the darkened hours of despair overcome me, may I not forget the strength that comforted me in the desolation of other times. May I still remember the bright hours of my childhood when a light glowed within me, and I promised my early God to have courage amid the tempests of the changing years.

Spare me from bitterness and from the sharp passions of unguarded moments. May I not forget that poverty and riches are of the spirit. Though the world knows me not, may my thoughts and actions keep me friendly with myself.

Lift my eyes from the Earth, and let me not forget the uses of the stars. Forbid that I should judge others lest I condemn myself.

Let me not follow the clamor of the world, but walk calmly in my path. Give me a few friends who will love me for what I am and keep burning before my vagrant steps the kindly light of hope.

And though age, and infirmity overtake me, and I come not within the sight of the castle of my dreams, teach me still to be thankful for life and for times' olden memories that are good and sweet, and may the evenings' twilight find me gentle still.

Anonymous

TABLE ON CONTENTS

PART ONE
STORIES OF A LIFE
BEFORE, DURING AND AFTER A NURSING CAREER

A SOMEWHAT SHORT AUTOBIOGRAPHY	11
LABRADOR ROSE, LABRADOR LOVE	14
A NEWFOUNDLAND RANGER AND A LABRADOR ROSE	15
CAPPING OFF A CHALLENGING AND FULFILLING CAREER	19
ILLNESS, PERFUME AND BLACK CHIFFON	22
AS I SEE IT, AND SEE IT I DO!	25
SANTAS' MAGIC	29
THE SCHOOL PICTURES	32
A COMMAND PERFORMANCE	35
LIFETIME ACHIEVEMENT AWARD FOR BRAVERY AND PERSEVERANCE!	38
SPECIAL BURGEO SATURDAY AFTERNOONS	41
WILL YOU SAVE ME THE CORE?	45
FRIENDSHIP, ONE OF LIFES' GREATEST GIFTS	49
THE UGLY BLUE COAT	53
A STRANGER IN THE CHURCH	56
MY STRANGEST AND BEST JACK 'O LANTERN	58
MY HERO, MY REBEL	61
BERYL AND THE BUDGIE BIRD	64
THE MOUNTIES' ORIGINAL HAIRDO	68
I CAN'T LET YOU GO ALONE	71
THE PERFECT CHRISTMAS TREE	75

PART TWO
SAYING FAREWELL TO NEWFOUNDLAND
APRIL 1970

MOVING AWAY-1970	81
THE YELLOW STRIPES AND THE BLACK BANDS	83
MY FATHERS' EYES	86
IT'S THE LITTLE THINGS	89
THE TIMES YOU ASK 'WHY, WHY, WHY!	93
DOLORES	96
OF NURSES AND COMETS	99
JAKE	102
MY APRIL LOBSTER	106
CHERYL P., AND HER RECYCLING PROGRAM	109
NURSE KAREN, 2032***	112
THE QUIET COURAGE OF A NURSE NAMED SARA	114
THAT'S FUNNY. HOME WE CALLS 'UM FLOWERS!	117

OOOOOHO BABY	122
ONE SIZE DOES NOT FIT ALL!	126
ROOTS AND WINGS	129
THE HOSPITAL ROOM BEDSIDE TABLE-COURSE–101	132
THINGS YOU CAN BE SURE OF	134
IT'S JUST A BAG OF BIRD FOOD!	136
MICHAEL AND VALERIE-A LOVE STORY	139
LISTEN TO YOUR NURSE!	145
WHEN THE LIGHT OF THE NURSE FLICKERS AND DIES	147
THE TALE OF THE NIGHT OF THE WINE!	151
JENNYS' SONG	154
JOEY AND THE CHRISTMAS SMILE	158
THIS LITTLE LAMP	162
KEEPING THE WATCH ON CHRISTMAS DAY	165
THE MATRONS' EXPERIMENT	169
A MAD COW IN STITCHES	174
THE SKUNKS OF SUMMER	177
BECKY	180
BEVS' BATTLE	184
JANINES' JOURNEY	189
THE 1973 DODGE DART	195
ONE OF LIFES' BIGGEST DECISIONS, KNOWING WHEN TO QUIT	199
WORKING THE LAST DAY	202

PART THREE

'THE YEAR 2000'

COMING HOME TO NEWFOUNDLAND AND LABRADOR

A SPECIAL VISIT TO THE 'KYLE	207
THE OLD LILAC TREE BY THE SEA	210
THE LITTLE BOATS OF NEWFOUNDLAND	215
SO, EXACTLY WHAT IS A BOILUP?	219
MY SEA ROSES	223
A VISIT TO A SPECIAL PLACE, SHOAL HARBOUR, NL	226
YOU'RE DARN RIGHT, I'M GOIN' FISHIN'!	231
A LETTER TO MY BELOVED NEWFOUNDLAND AND LABRADOR	234
BECOMING A LONG DISTANCE NANNY	238
HOW SWEET IT IS, A DAY ON THE BAY	241
A WILD GOOSE CHASE	244
POPPYS' WORKSHOP	249
THE LITTLE PINK RUBBER BOOTS	252
MY QUEST FOR THE WONDERFUL PARTRIDGEBERRIES	255
IN SEARCH OF OCEAN JOY	259
THROUGH MY LENS	262
HOPSCOTCH BY GOSH!	266
A GIFT WITHIN THE GRIEF	270
THE CAPTAINS NEW RECIPE	274

PART FOUR
MY ATTACHMENT IS GROWING

THE GARDEN	285
JOHNS' JOBS	289
THE PERFECT PROM DRESS'	293
SIMON, MY CHRISTMAS CAT	298
IT'LL BE GOOD FOR YOU, YOU'LL LIKE IT!	300
NO CHANGING SCHOOLS FOR ME!	303
MOMS' SPECIAL COOK BOOK	306
TEENAGERS, YES, TELL ME ABOUT IT!	310
DO ANGELS MAKE PICKLES?	313
THE MARIPOSA AND THE BOSSA NOVA	317
THE KEEPER OF THE ISLAND LIGHT	321
LEST WE FORGET	324
A MEMORY FROZEN IN TIME	328
HOOKED ON COD CANDY	331
FOR THE LOVE OF BOATS	335

PART FIVE
QUIRKS AND QUARKS COLLECTED ALONG THE WAY
THE END...OR IS IT? DID I EVER TELL YOU THE ONE ABOUT...

A JARRING EXPERIENCE	343
QUITTING THE COLOR BOTTLE	345
HOW MUCH COLD DO YOU WANT?	347
PATIENCE PATIENTS!!	349
THE SURGEON AND MY 'SEEMORE	350
JUST CALL IT THE I/V	352
POOR TIMING OR NOT??	353
WHERE'S THE KEY?	354
THE PERCEPTIVE PATIENT	355
WHAT WAS SHE THINKING?	357
RETIRED AREYA?	358
WHO WAS SHE?	360
REMEMBER YOUR HELMET	362
A MAJOR BUM CHECK	364
THE SHORT EXPLANATION!	365
A MOST EMBARRASSING MOMENT	367
MIXED MESSAGES	369
I CAN'T BELIEVE I DID THAT!	371
WANT A REFERENCE?	373
HOW WINDY WASIT ANYWAY?	374

NURSING RESUME ... 377

PART ONE

Stories of a life before, during and after a nursing career

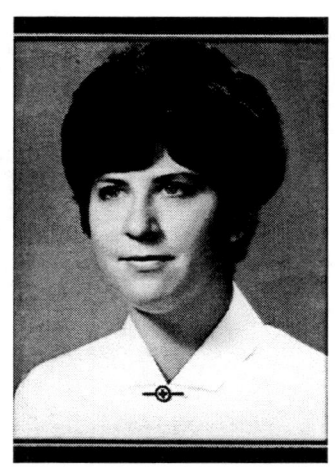

She wears a Black Welver Band 1969
Finally a Registered Nurse

'A Childhood Dream came true'

A SOMEWHAT SHORT AUTOBIOGRAPHY

Yvonne (Bonnie) Jarvis-Lowe

I was born in Marys' Harbor, Labrador, in 1948. My father was a Newfoundland Ranger stationed at Port Hope Simpson, so in a few weeks I took my first boat trip on the 'Kyle', one of the coastal boats that serviced the Newfoundland and Labrador coasts. The 'Kyle' took Mother and I home to my father at the Rangers Quarters in Port Hope Simpson, and that was the first in what was to be a long list of boat trips and moves. My family moved to Twillingate when I was just a year old. After that came Burgeo, Port Saunders, Grand Falls, Clarenville, (where I met my husband the summer he joined the RCMP), and Bell Island. My father had merged from the Ranger Force into the RCMP with a confederation so we, as a family, of course went where his work took him. The family later moved to Labrador City, Goose Bay, and then back to Mount Pearl. I had left home and was beginning my own family by then.

I attended many schools obviously, graduating from Grand Falls Academy, Grand Falls, NL. in 1964. However the problem was that to enter the Grace Hospital for Nurses training one had to be seventeen years and seven months old. I was just fifteen. My parents enrolled me in the Commercial course at St.Catherines High School in Grand Falls, and after graduating I worked as a stenographer with Harvey Dawe Ltd. in Grand Falls until Fathers' transfer in 1966 to Clarenville. In October of 1966 I entered training at the Grace General Hospital School of Nursing, graduating in 1969, and after a short trip to England, went to work in Grand Bank, NL, for a short time.

In April, 1970, I married and moved to Nova Scotia where my husband served in many areas in his role as an officer in the RCMP, Dartmouth, Sydney Mines, Halifax, Lunenburg, Windsor, and then Halifax again. We lived in Windsor, Nova Scotia, for the longest time that I have lived anywhere- 23 years. So therefore the major part of my life and career was in the little town of Windsor, Nova Scotia, living in the small village of Falmouth, just a few kilometers away. Many lifelong friendships were developed in Nova Scotia and have stood the test of time to this very day. It is a beautiful province, and we have wonderful memories of our time there.

We have two children, a son and a daughter, my daughter is in Calgary and my son in Fort McMurray. Both well educated and self-sufficient. And now we have the supreme pleasure of being grandparents to a beautiful little girl. My daughter and her husband are Kylees' parents.

The year 2000 brought a big change to our lives when we made the move back to Newfoundland, giving in to the call of the sea, back to where our roots lay, and our families lived. It was not something we had ever planned, but it was necessary to do. The call was too strong to ignore.

So now we are both retired, enjoying our various pursuits, having a little grandchild adds to our lives even though they are far away, it is somewhat easier than it was for me leaving home and keeping the lines of communication open, because the age of technology has made it so. Communication is quicker and accessibility of travel is a far cry from the way it was thirty years ago.

So, that is me. I am 54 years of age now, love photography, writing, books, music and of course my beautiful cat. Newfoundland and Labrador is a beautiful and inspiring place to be at this time in our lives, and being able to see the ocean every day is a dream come true. I have finally adjusted to being out of the loop of hands on nursing, a difficult adjustment at first but health considerations played a part in my decision to leave while at the top and still actively nursing. Travel is big on the agenda now, as is family.

Story Telling is a passion that has always been with me. I recall a team mate on night duty saying "Bonnie, I am so tired, tell me one of your stories!" and it would start a great laugh, and of course, bring forth a story.

'Do No Harm', is the pledge we took in 1969 when we began our nursing careers as the 'Class of 1969, Grace General Hospital School of Nursing Graduates'. I do hope throughout my life that I did no harm, and if I did, it certainly was never intentional. I am proud of the fact that in the face of some terrible behavior by people, I never ever said a mean word to a patient. And frankly I don't know how I did that. I think a special force looks over little Newfoundland girls who are pursuing their dreams, and showing they care.

Bonnie Jarvis-Lowe

PS: Although my given name is Yvonne, I had a Welsh godmother, and I was born the same week as Prince Charles. She said he was another 'Bonnie Prince Charlie' and I was a 'Bonnie little Princess', I believe she was vastly misled on the 'Princess' part, however the name 'Bonnie' stuck and is used by one and all to this day . . .

LABRADOR ROSE, LABRADOR LOVE

A NEWFOUNDLAND RANGER AND

A LABRADOR ROSE

*'Dedicated to Newfoundland Rangers and their
wives, then and now'*

My mother is a Labradorian, born in the little community of English Point in Forteau Bay. She was the youngest of a large family, and at the tender age of seven years she lost her mother to a fatal illness. For years after that while her father fished, and tried to survive, she spent time with older sisters, and then a sister-in-law or two who became her surrogate mothers. She still dislikes and avoids the color purple because she associates it with her mothers' death, but she has a grand daughter Laura Belbin, who is named after her great-grandmother Trimm, and she loves the sound of her mothers' name when somebody calls to Laura. All those years later the loss is still felt profoundly by my mother, that loss of a mother-daughter relationship as a young, very young child. Her name was Ethel Trimm in those days.

Mother was feisty, stubborn, but beautiful and charming, with a gorgeous mane of long dark wavy hair. Her keen wit and will to carry on in the face of adversity shaped and steeled her for life, and they are characteristics she passed on to her five children, thankfully so. In the midst of a bout of ill health she tries to maintain her routine, but many days she cannot do it, and it upsets her terribly.

    Mother had left the Labrador coast and gone to Ontario to work when she was very young. On a visit back in 1947 to see her family she met my father. This was at the time of Commission of Government and the Newfoundland Ranger Force was the police force that enforced the laws, made sure families were taken care of, and generally were the mainstay of rural Newfoundland and Labrador.

Very unexpectedly they met. My uncle had befriended the young Newfoundland policeman, and brought him home, and in so doing of course he met my mother. She was nineteen years old, with a captivating smile, he was a few years older and handsome and fit. She says he had the most brilliant blue eyes she had ever seen. And after that initial meeting the young policeman used every excuse he could to visit her. The snow was very deep, and she would sit with her embroidery, by the fire and wait for the first glow of the lantern coming toward the house. And the lantern and Logan boots would walk past the window, making a great idea for a painting I am sure.

So, mother never returned to Ontario. She couldn't go without her heart and she had given that to the handsome Ranger, Stephen Richard Jarvis. And Stephen Richard Jarvis had given his heart to her, so in due time they married, and began what was to be a very interesting, sometimes difficult, but always challenging life together.

I am the first child of this marriage. There were four more children to follow, and many transfers, and milestones along the way. So, in actual fact, I am a Labrador girl too. Born in Marys' Harbour, and taken back to the Rangers post in Port Hope Simpson by the Kyle.

My father had just returned from overseas and World War Two where he served in the Royal Navy throughout the whole war. He joined the Newfoundland Rangers after he returned and served in various outlying places, fit for anything, and though quiet by nature, not likely to take guff from anyone. Mother describes his eyes as 'wild' during that time. In those days bad dreams, overreactions to situations, and all the things that we now associate with Post Traumatic Stress Disorder plagued him. Most of those young men had suffered so much, seen so many terrible things, but the only thing to do to deaden the pain was to turn to the good old rum, something we now know makes this disorder worse. The women were the steadying influence, the enforcers, the lovers, the nurturers that helped them survive the inner turmoil during the busy days and the dark, cold nights. And for most of them, their wives were their anchors in the storm and they freely admit that. I know my father, Ranger #176 would wholeheartedly agree.

The confederation with Canada came in 1949, and changes were in the wind. Father was transferred to Twillingate, three children were in the family by the time they left Twillingate six years later. Father went to Ottawa, did the course in federal law enforcement, and the RCMP was now in our lives. Ranger #176 was in a different uniform, and had a different number after that. Mom was young, and I recall a photo of her taken in Twillingate, in the garden in Robins Cove, and she looks like she would be the teenage babysitter. She withstood the challenges of raising a family, my meningitis illness, a transfer to Burgeo, stormbound in St. John's and spending Christmas at the Newfoundland Hotel, then getting to Burgeo where, when Dad was on patrol, she handled the problems and crises that arose. The Asian Flu outbreak caused her to deliver my sister three months prematurely, almost too tiny to live, but live she did, and with gusto. She herself is a nurse in Nain, Labrador now.

Then there came Port Saunders, Grand Falls, Clarenville, Bell Island, Labrador City, Goose Bay, and then back to St. John's again. Mother became active in her church again, supported us through all our teenage angst, organized weddings and graduations, welcomed grandchildren, and indeed lived a full life.

The days of detachment living gave way to owning their own home, no cells to care for, no prisoners to feed, or office attached to the house. They traveled a little and enjoyed a lot. Then disaster struck in the form of major cardiac surgery for Father. Then her energies had to be directed toward getting him back on his feet. And a good job she did too. Father had the very best that could be had to help him get well.

Mother was a strong woman, one of the strongest I have known. She suffered through transfers, teenagers, illnesses, and with every transfer Mother would be so organized and have the organization of the household down to a science in no time. She says she was raised poor but was never hungry, dirty, and never jealous, and I believe her.

Mother herself is ill now, and it is Fathers' turn to step up and help her. On one of my past visits to Mount Pearl to visit them, Mother stroked my arm and said "I was strong like that one time wasn't I?"

Yes, Mom, you were. I made a joke and she smiled but her eyes had a faraway look, as if remembering days of old. We can just support and say thanks, "Thanks mom, for all you did, gave, made happen, supported and taught. It is small wonder that Fathers' favorite song is "Labrador Rose "because that is indeed what my mother was, a strong Labrador Rose, the sweetest of flowers. Together with her Ranger they tackled the world, and handled all the dramas and ups and downs together.

Hopefully, in time, Mother will have a return to health. Meanwhile we say thank you, and thank you to all of the other strong women who were part of a pair, a team, a policeman and his wife, people the communities relied on and looked to for direction. The women had strength and resourcefulness, supported their husbands in their work, and in so doing served their country, and expected little in return. May you all, including my mother, be remembered for your many contributions and may your days be filled with love, laughter and good health. And most of all, may you be really appreciated for all your devotion through the years, and remembered for years to come.

You served our country, as did your Ranger husband, and we should, and will never forget that!

CAPPING OFF A CHALLENGING AND FULFILLING CAREER

It was October 1966, my parents drove me to the Grace Hospital Nurses Residence in St. John's, Newfoundland. My three year nurses' training had begun. I loved it and I never looked back. I had waited so long for this day. Not quite eighteen years old and full of vim and vigor I wanted to get started. I wanted to become a nurse. In October of 1969 that dream became a reality as I walked away from the Grace General Hospital with the initials 'RN' after my name. Little did I know that the major part of the learning process was just beginning. And that learning process continued to a day in June 2000, in a little Nova Scotia hospital where I had worked for so long, and where I had made the biggest decision of my adult life, to set Nursing aside and pursue other interests and dreams and to move back to Newfoundland. At the age of 51 a new stage of my life was about to begin.

At the same time I could not leave Nova Scotia until I had registered as a nurse in Newfoundland again. Obviously a second thought and a nagging doubt was lingering in my mind. It was so very hard to let go, so hard to walk away, but I knew in my heart of hearts that it was time. As my mentor and friend, Marilyn, used to tell me "the hardest thing in life is knowing when to quit!"-and oh how right she was.

Wanting to be a nurse went back to childhood days, and it never occurred to me to do anything else, to have any other career. Nursing was my dream, and that was that!

After three years at the Grace I worked in Grand Bank, Newfoundland for three months in 1969. Then I returned to the Grace General Hospital to work, and to be in St. John's made it easier to prepare for my wedding. I married Alvin John Lowe, known to many as 'Joe' in April 1970. He was a member of the RCMP, and at that time members of the force were not permitted to be stationed in their home province. So we left a week after our wedding to set up housekeeping in Nova Scotia where we lived and worked, raised our family, and made lifelong friends over the next 34 years. We have fond memories of Nova Scotia, but it was time to come home.

In Nova Scotia I worked in Sydney Mines, North Sydney, Lunenburg, Halifax and Windsor. The major part of my life in Nova Scotia was spent in Windsor, gateway to the magnificent Annapolis Valley. I worked at Hants Community Hospital in Windsor for many years.

I have three sisters and a brother. My three sisters are nurses as well. My brother is an Electrical Technologist. My sister Margie works in Urodynamics at the Health Science Center in St. John's, NL, Beryl has been a nurse in Northern Labrador for more than twenty years, and Kathy, the youngest sibling is teaching at the School of Nursing Studies in St.John's, NL. My brother works in St. John's as well. Five siblings, with RNs, BNs', and Masters Degrees combined with very diversified acquired skills keeps a family conversation very lively indeed. My brother David watches in quiet amusement from the sidelines.

I have often been asked what it takes to be a nurse. My first reaction is to say "sheer grit and determination, a good strong back, and the ability to suffer the human condition, both the good and the bad."

But a nurse also needs the ability and strength of mind and body to be able to cut down a teenager who has hung herself, and deal with the gut-wrenching heartache when she finds the child who has decided to die is a baby she delivered sixteen years before. It takes the fortitude to tell a woman in labor that her baby is dead, and it takes the dedication to stand in the Operating Room in the middle of the night for an emergency and see a young mans tuxedo lying in pieces on the floor with blood seeping into it, as the surgeon works frantically to save his life, knowing his life will never be the same after this accident that brought him to us.

But Nursing has its' rewards, and I would not change the career I chose but there is much more to it than meets the eye. Mathematics, physics, psychology, and good old-fashioned stamina and common sense are total necessities. The sadness of a grieving family is often offset by the birth of a beautiful healthy newborn, the smile of the stroke patient as he does something by himself for the first time, the young diabetic who has mastered self-injection and is so proud, and so much more positive happenings enable the sadness to be absorbed and allows the nurse to continue on. Nursing is an art if done well, and a gift as well.

Retiring was a word that was difficult to say for a long time. I could not believe I did not have a Nursing job, but the system is in chaos now, the workloads extremely heavy, and the hours long. I knew that in order to do other things I would have to forge ahead into uncharted territory and begin anew.

And lo and behold I did find that there is life outside of the hospitals and Nursing, and I also discovered that once you are a 'Nurse', you are always a 'Nurse'.

I had a wonderful fulfilling career, with all the ups and downs that go with working with people who are experiencing great highs and awful lows in their lives, but there is and was fun and laughter, teamwork, friendships that will last forever, and self satisfaction that I did my best, as I am sure most, if not all nurses do.

I was always known as the 'Newfoundland Nurse' while working in Nova Scotia, and it was a pleasure. I wanted to be the Newfoundlander who showed how we can laugh at ourselves in spite of it all.

And in spite of it all, a few days ago a cashier at a grocery store asked me as I turned to go if I was a 'Grace Hospital Nurse'. She had noticed my graduation ring.

"Yes," I answered proudly, "I am a NURSE!"

ILLNESS, PERFUME AND BLACK CHIFFON

A mother expressed her disappointment to me that her honor roll daughter had not made any plans for furthering her education and seemed content to 'go with the flow' as she put it. She went on to say that there was nothing in our small community to offer the young people and her daughter should be using this time to do something toward building a future.

I had nothing more to offer the conversation. I could empathize to a degree, but not totally. This was mainly because making a career choice was never something I had to think about. I know the decision is a difficult and complex one in today' world, and maybe it always was that way for some but for me my career choice was made and engraved on my heart when I was six years old. I wanted to become a nurse. That was it, I always knew it, and geared myself toward it.

It all started for me in the middle of the night in a darkened hospital room in Twillingate, Newfoundland. I was six years old and my father was posted in Twillingate with the RCMP. This would have been in the Mid 1950s'. I clearly remember as if it were yesterday, waking up, surrounded by those metal edged hospital screens, and through the gap in the screens seeing a lighted room in the distance. I could hear soft voices in conversation, and I cried out to them, what I said I do not know, probably a cry of a frightened child, calling for 'Mom' or 'Dad'. Where was I? What had happened to me?

Soon the light came on and the room filled with people, all dressed in white, and I remember the terror I felt. Apparently I had been incommunicative for some time. I don't know for how long. I only know that it caused quite a stir and hustle and bustle when I woke up that night. Prior to this waking the last thing I remembered was lying on the couch in our home suffering from an earache, and feeling very unwell. Then I vaguely recalled my parents being alarmed, saying something about a hospital, doctors and so on. After that there was nothing.

A long illness followed that earache. I had developed Bacterial Meningitis. After the waking up I sure had memory, memories of injections, of being very weak, my clothes being too big, having difficultly in walking, and all the other things that accompany a long bout of sickness. I ate meals lying or standing, my childs' hips too sore to sit from all the injections, the injections that saved my life.

It is an old wives' tale that meningitis leaves you with something or takes something away. It left me with a burning desire to become a nurse. I suppose part of it was the memories of the nurses who cared for me, cuddled me after each painful procedure, and generally and gradually brought me back to health.

But most of all there is the crystal clear memory of one special young nurse, a young lady whose name I never did know. She was pretty, with dark eyes and dark hair, and she had a special touch that accompanied her bounty of kindness. She would drop by the ward to visit me in the evenings after she was off duty and read me stories, she knew my love for books.

But one evening in particular she scurried into the ward, wearing the most beautiful black chiffon dress and lovely shiny high heeled shoes and was a picture to behold. The wonderful fragrance of her perfume shut out the hospital smells. She made her quick visit, said she was late for her party and rushed off blowing a kiss as she went.

That young nurse was the epitome of kindness, charm and unconditional love, wrapped in a beautiful package. She would never know the impact she had on one little six-year-old girl.

And so it went. I grew up, geared myself toward the goal of being a nurse and finally had achieved it. No year off or break for me, I was in a big hurry. Then at the age of twenty-one I had made it. Now 33 years later I have to let go of my nursing career, the structured part of it anyway. Once a nurse, always a nurse they say-and I am a nurse. But the time has come to move on to other things, other interests-not an easy decision to make for me.

It is not for me to decide if I touched lives in a special way, I hope I did.

Only my patients can determine that. In the Operating Room, behind a cap and mask, I always tried to make contact. Often somebody would walk up to me and say, "I know your voice, but I don't know why!" And finally they would figure it out. It was proof that they remembered some sort of connection with me during their difficult time.

The last five years before retiring I spent working with Palliative and Cardiac Care patients. I was always referred to as the 'Newfoundland Nurse'-couldn't and wouldn't hide that accent!

I hope they know I cared. I really hope I was as kind as the young nurse who cared for me when I was so sick. The decision made in my childhood became my vocation and I loved it. And on any particularly difficult day I could escape by closing my eyes and see the wisp of black chiffon and smell the most wonderful perfume of a young woman from so many years ago!

Bonnie Jarvis-Lowe, RN.Rtd.

AS I SEE IT, AND SEE IT I DO!

There were only three or four steps but I stumbled, the way you stumble when you misjudge the distance from one step to another. Strong arms reached out and broke the fall and after that I was on my way! The gravel on the road looked so clear, I could see each little rock, see the letters on the sign outside the church, it was nothing short of an actual miracle for me.-I could see!! You would think I was the only one whoever had such a wonderful miracle happen to them and I didn't know whether to talk about it or not. I would have so much to see now, so many books to look at over and over, and I would never have to squint at things and get a sore head because it was so hard to see. Yes, the man my parents took me to had changed me and my life forever, and I was in absolute awe!

The man in the building where my parents took me had tested me and found the problem, and he fixed it. I needed eyeglasses! So he wrote on some papers after he had me do all sorts of things, and that day my parents had brought me back to see the man again. And I had been fitted with the eyeglasses. Never mind I couldn't pronounce what the word was that was wrong with my eyes, never mind the other kids called me 'four-eyes' and never mind the strange looks, I loved those little eyeglasses. I was just four years old and I think that on that day my life changed forever. In my childs' mind I was so delighted that I can remember to this day the feeling of sheer bliss. I remember the little case they came in and were so carefully placed in at bedtime, and I remember being shown how to place them with ear pieces down so as not to scratch the lens, and I did whatever it took to help me care for those wonderful things they called spectacles.

Before my glasses I could see 'TIME' on the Time magazine, and sometimes the bigger letters inside but I could never see the regular size letters because they were all fuzzy and so were the pictures. I knew the alphabet at that age so my parents could easily test me with letters and they came to realize that I had a definite problem with my vision. Dad would read the magazine and I would marvel that he could do that and I worried that I was never going to be able to read on my own, and I loved books. My favorite thing to do was to sit beside Mom or Dad and have them read and help me to read, but it was so difficult. What if I could never do it by myself? The imaginings of a child are very real and very scary and I remember those fears so well. The day the eyeglasses came- all was put to rest, I could actually see all sorts of things I had never seen before. And see and read I did, and I never looked back. Even writing about it makes me tingle inside with the joy I felt that day. I could see, and see clearly! Wow!

It appears the problem was astigmatism, a condition of the eye that caused its' victim to see things smaller than they actually are, which explained my stumbling, and the fact that I could see the Big Letters but not the same exact letters in a smaller case. Astigmatism crippled my ability to enjoy anything in a book, made me stumble and fall, caused all sorts of minor problems , but the reading was the worst of all. Now that I had the glasses, I could see the pictures in the magazines, the numbers on the calendar, and even the writing on the nickels and dimes. I tell you I truly believed I had been given a miracle. Never once would I have to be reminded to wear my spectacles, and never once did I whine about having to wear them. Not once, not to this day and I am fifty three years old now. I still love my glasses, love keeping up with the latest in fashion frames, and over the years I had all sorts of lovely in-style frames, a concession from my parents for being such a trooper I think. And once I got on my own I could go hog wild with frames, and go hog wild I did! Some of those frames of the sixties are downright ugly but we thought they were divine way back then.

Yes, new glasses every year, flying from outpost communities to Corner Brook to see the eye doctor, and the dentist of course. New glasses coming in a little box by mail, developing a habit of always pushing up on the nose piece, but always grateful to have them and always grateful for all kinds of books to study and learn from. I became a 'readaholic', and still have that condition to this day. Always have to have a book ready to read when one is finished.

The contact lens became the thing to have, but not for me. Thankfully I had a great excuse not to bow to peer pressure because the eye doctor said contacts for me would be like putting a 'Frisbee on a football', so to heck with that. I was off the hook, and continued to get the new specs as needed; Always keeping an extra pair, then getting the prescription sunglasses, another miracle for me.

What an amazing thing when you stop and think about it! A pair of a manmade lens to help out your own imperfect eye lens, and your life can go on as usual. We take if so for granted now, but it is wonderful when you consider it all. My terrible childhood fears of never being able to read all put aside with a visit to a doctor who knew what to do, and did it! Now I have astigmatism and another correction, the one that comes with age, so two corrections in one pair of glasses. It is wonderful! And so many books I have studied, so many I have read for just plain interest, so many stories I have written, so many of the worlds' wonderful sights I have seen and so truly grateful I am.

When I see the cataracts of the elderly, of the people in the tropics who have their eyes damaged by the bright sunlight ,or the little girl helping her blind dad cross the street, or the cute little babe with his little spectacles kept on with elastic around his head I still marvel at how much can be done now. Cataract surgery is so safe now, people so in a tune with what their needs are, teachers so aware that they know an eye problem in just a day or two with a child, such advances from years ago. People still suffer visual impairments and my heart aches for them but the technical aids available are so many, so varied, and so available. As for me, I type this and I can see it clearly, every word, every comma, but if I remove my glasses it is nothing but a blur- how could I not love those little black-framed lenses? Yes, to me it has always seemed like a miracle. I am so grateful to my parents and that young Twillingate eye doctor. The young doctor who was visiting our town so long ago. I still think his doctors black carry bag was a big bag of MIRACLES!

SANTAS' MAGIC

'A very different Newfoundland Christmas'

As Christmas stories and memories go, this childhood Christmas memory of mine is as different as it is magical. It is the story of how two young parents turned a hotel room into an amazing Santa Land in St.John's, Newfoundland in the mid-fifties.

My father was a member of the RCMP and was transferred to Burgeo, so our family was moving from Twillingate to Burgeo, Newfoundland. It was the middle of December, and of course the only means of travel was by coastal boat.

We reached St. John's by middle of December, my father and mother, one three-year-old sister and a toddler brother, with me, the all-knowing six-year-old.

The fog was thick, the weather 'down' and we were stuck. We had been booked into the Newfoundland Hotel for what was to be, to my parents' dismay I'm quite sure, a lengthy stay, which included the Christmas Holiday Season.

For us children, who understood, it was a dream come true to be able to roam the halls of this fine big building. I'm not so sure it was that much fun for my parents. It was probably more of a nightmare to them, having to spend Christmas with three active children in a hotel suite. My sister and I were scared Santa wouldn't know where we were and Mom and Dad constantly consoled us that all would be well. Santa always knew these things they said. My brother had a fuzzy stuffed dog that absolutely terrified him if he was startled by it, so our entertainment was making him scream. On those nights we got room service, we were considered to be too 'savage' to take to the big fancy dining room.

Then the hotel held a Christmas party for their staff and families and were kind enough to invite us as well. It was wonderful. We got to tell Santa where we were, and what we would like, received treats, and saw other children. So for a time we were content and satisfied.

Christmas morning came at last. Our stockings were stuffed, games of checkers and dominos, toys and books, shiny decorations, licorice all-sorts, our favorite candy, were all magically in place. Santa did remember. It was splendid. And for a time the fuzzy dog disappeared, our baby brother was happy, as we all were. The snow was falling and Christmas magic was in the air. Dad even stopped his history lessons of old St. John's for a day or two. I learned more about St. John's in those rooms at the age of six than I would for years to come as my father used every opportunity to teach us new things.

My uncle was in the city and joined us for Christmas dinner. We were dressed in our new and best clothes, the baby even looked angelic, as we dined in the sparkling clean big dining room of the Newfoundland Hotel, with the Christmas lights reflecting on the snow outside. I clearly recall seeing the tiny margarine balls, the white linen napkins, and hearing the Christmas music. We were for a time princesses in a magic kingdom. Our parents chatted to our uncle and we looked around and took it all in, especially me, being blessed with an outrageous need to know 'how' and 'why' about everything. It was mind-boggling that Santa had found us, and even found Mom and Dad. I wouldn't understand until years later how hard Mr. and Mrs. Santa worked that year.

For a short span of time the "steamer report" was not an issue, the long days in the hotel room were forgotten and we had a glorious Christmas Day.

Boxing Day came, a day of playing our games, being allowed to keep our pyjamas on later than usual, and stuffing ourselves with chocolate and licorice.

Yes, it was certainly a Christmas to remember, and I have remembered it always. Every time I drive by the Fairmont Newfoundland I think of that time of my childhood. And that building will always be called the Newfoundland Hotel by me, and my sister. I smile to myself at how much fun we had after Boxing Day when we found the fuzzy dog and took turns sticking him through the rungs of my brothers' crib, and hearing him screech. And you know the strangest thing of all, he still has that darn dog!

THE SCHOOL PICTURES

Oh, sure, there it was, the notice that school pictures would be taken on such a day at such a time and the butterflies would start and everyone would be talking about what they should wear. Half of us dreaded the day, the other half could take it or leave it, and I am sure some secretly loved it, but I sure didn't. I would be in the first category. Dread, disgust, and downright rebellion would start, I did not, and still do not, like having my picture taken.

It mattered not that we were in schools in isolated communities, difficult to access, it mattered not that we were in a one room or two room school, those photographers would find us and point that camera at us and a few weeks later the brown envelopes would start arriving and I did not like it one little bit.

Often I wondered where they came from, why it had to be done, how those people with cameras could get to us in little schools, and I also wondered if I could escape, but it was all for naught. I would be photographed come what may, along with the rest of my school mates. I understood later in life that it was so nice to have school photos of my own children, so nice to compare my grade three photo with that of my daughters' grade three photo, and the only difference people could tell was that mine was black and white and hers was colored. I could accept it by then, and by then I had become somewhat of a photographer myself. But back in those little schools with our home cut hair styles, or school girl 'perms' that turned my hair into a dark brown brillo pad, I just could not get it! Why did we have to go through this? My mother must have turned a deaf ear because I am sure I never shut up about it from the time of the notice until the pictures were taken. Then there would be a little down time, and then when they started arriving I would start up again. My parents would go on about how beautiful they were and I knew darned well that with freckles, glasses and a brillo pad on my head there was no beauty there that any human could see!! My sister had straight flaxen hair and her school photos were so sweet and mine were atrocious. One or two years I think may have been acceptable but for the most part I hated those school photos. And as I grew up I methodically destroyed all I could find.

But then I would be with my parents visiting a relative and there would be one of those photos, there was no end to it! So I finally gave up, and grew up, and could accept the photos by the time Graduation time came. But I still didn't like them.

Let me tell you the typical drill of the picture taking day. First of all you would know the photographer was in the community as he would have had to come by steamer or plane, and he, it was always a 'he' in those days, would be staying at such and such a house. That much we would pass around. Then the parents, who had been two weeks preparing us for the photos, what to wear, haircuts and hair styles etc. had it all decided on, and the dreaded day would dawn. I would wake and wonder how long he would wait around if I hid away, then would decide I couldn't do that, so I would get up and shuffle to the bathroom, staying away from mirrors! Then mirror time would be upon me, and oh, for sure, there was the pimple that was as big as a second nose, the hair stuck up or out or someway it shouldn't be at all and had never been before, and then the glasses would be crooked. Dad would steam the earpieces of my glasses, I would put them on and make another trip to the mirror! Yikes! The brillo pad hair was ten inches deep and the pimple was spreading- mother would shuffle my behind out the door and off we would go toward the lens, into the light, whatever you call it!

After the drill and the photos were taken I would relax slightly, the rest of this I could handle. Then the camera man would start deciding on retakes, yes, one of them would be me for sure. And off I would go. Then it would be over like a miserable bout of flu, and life would go on. Some of those photos are floating around my relatives homes to this day. And I stay behind the lens as much as I can, right to this very day, even though the freckles are gone now.

But on a recent visit to my parents house I took out all the old albums and looked back at the photos of us all, little children growing into teenage years, then into young adulthood. Photos of Primary delight up to proud graduations and achieved goals, and they really are not so bad, seeing as how I managed to get rid of the worse ones. Now they are memories captured, stories remembered and laughter shared. It wasn't so bad after all. All the angst and rebellion I went through seemed nothing and so far away when I looked at the school pictures of the five of us, now all adults, with graduation portraits on the piano, and also the grandchildren of my parents are having their University graduation portraits displayed. And I have my sons' and daughters' photos to enjoy. A wonderful marvelous thing those school pictures aren't they? Now I don't know why I went through such misery, that is until I remember the school girl brillo pad hairdo, and thankfully that photo, I think, was totally destroyed, quite strangely the envelope caught fire. I don't know what happened there-you just never know sometimes how such things happen, and then again sometimes you do!!!

A COMMAND PERFORMANCE

The big night had finally arrived. I was sitting in a little nook just off the stage in a big room, praying and hoping the earth would open and swallow me whole, never to surface again. It was a school concert that night and all the students in our little school in Burgeo, on the south coast of Newfoundland had been preparing and rehearsing for weeks for this night. In a tiny isolated community in the 1950s' this held the prestige of a Broadway musical, and often performers were just as talented as those professional actors and actresses.

My problem was I was painfully afraid of speaking in front of a crowd.I could hold skits, perform songs and poems and dance it up for my friends and family, but I hated command performances and having to be up on a stage in front of a crowd.My anxiety level would be so high I would be sick. And I felt sick sitting in that little nook that night. I will never forget the feeling. I could hear chairs scraping the floor, hear the voices of our parents all talking at once, the piano player doing her scales, and I was going over my recitation, as they called it, in my head. There was no escape, as we were one of the first groups to go on. I was eight years old, and dressed in a plaid jumper, and a pretty blouse, with navy knee socks, and mother had placed a lovely barrette in my thick dark hair. But the sweat ran down my back and I felt trapped. Our teacher was rushing about with her face flushed and putting the finishing touches on everything. Finally, the music to the 'Ode to Newfoundland',and the concert was off to a start. I was relieved in a way, to get it over with after three weeks of misery, and to get on with my life would be such a relief.

Knowing my lines was not a problem, there were only four,

and I could remember fifty if I had to, I just had a phobia of being on a stage. We were soon due to go on, when I felt the barrette slipping out of my hair, my shoes were beautiful patent leather, and would be fine if I had one less toe, and I wanted to go to the bathroom, fast! But all of a sudden I was ushered onto the stage in a moment of sheer terror it seemed, and as I stood ready to say my lines I felt my left knee sock slowly slipping down my leg. Was there no end to this punishment?? I glanced at the teacher, she was urging me to speak, but my usual overused voice was gone, I tried again, and this time the recitation came out. It went like this "Here I stand upon the stage, A tiny little figure, If the boys don't like me now, they will when I grow bigger!" Bow, back up, bow again, and get the heck out of there. Applause was heard but not by me. I felt sick, wanted the bathroom, my hair was in my eyes, my sock slipped to my ankle, my feet hurt and I was sweating. Terror and a panic still stayed even after it was over. And I felt sick for days after. Gradually the feeling left but I never forgot it. Not ever.

First of all, nobody in their right mind would have a child say those lines today, and secondly I could have recited the Ancient Mariner if they wanted me to, but I had the humiliation of those stupid four lines. And it stayed with me always. In nurses training I would use any excuse to perform, had fun doing so, had no problem with stages or crowds, I couldn't understand it, and I couldn't forget those four little lines. I stood on the nurse's desk at work one day holding a bouquet of dead flowers and recited the lines, the hilarious laughter of my co-workers brought the supervisor running in our direction. She took one look at me, silence fell over everyone, but I think she had just about had enough of me. All she said was "Jarvis, don't forget to wipe the desk when you're through making a fool of yourself!" And she left. And we laughed even harder. And we knew she was laughing too.

I did the recitation standing on the fireplace hearth for my kids, dressed as an eight-year-old with one sock down over my shoe, I did it for my friends at parties, and I still do it from time to time just for fun! Well, why, if you hated it so much, do you still do it you ask? I think it is because I just like the feeling of doing it without being commanded to do it and because in this day and age the lines are so dreadfully silly. And even sillier coming from a grandmother dressed as a child with a bouquet of dead dandelions. That's why!

Yessirree, I am nominating myself for an Emmy for that Burgeo performance, no, on second thought, I think I will go for the lifetime achievement award, because I have been doing it for a lifetime. I was eight years old, I am now fifty-four, and I still can't get it out of my head.

'HERE I STAND UPON THE STAGE,' sorry gotta go, my sock fell down!!

MY ORANGE COW

Years ago, while still a student nurse, I became the proud owner of an 'Orange Cow'! She was three feet tall, with a gorgeous set of little brown horns, and had a large daisy stuck in her mouth. So, of course, she was named 'Daisy', and Daisy went wherever I went. I dragged her from room to room at the Grace Hospital Nurses Residence, and after graduation Daisy accompanied me to Grand Bank Cottage Hospital, where I had my first job as a brand new Registered Nurse. My friend and I had gone to England right after graduation for a two or three week trip, and Daisy was cared for by my parents who were used to me and my strange characters, living or stuffed. When I returned from England I took Daisy and we set off to stomp out illness and eradicate disease, with all the missionary zeal of the young. We went to live in the little nurses' residence up over the hospital in Grand Bank, Newfoundland.

Daisy had been given to me by a young man, the same young man who was to become my husband. I knew nothing about becoming the owner of this cow until she was delivered to me, and to this day I have no idea where he found her or why he bought her, but he did. And she was so soft and fluffy, and her large eyes so endearing I would never be able to refuse her, so we became a team, Daisy and Me. She sat on or beside my bed, listened to my grumbles, my problems, my laughter, and sat beside me when tears came and after awhile she was just part of me. If I got in a huff or full of anger, I would never stomp off without my Orange Cow, and that is the way it went for years. I always had to take her, I don't know too many people who want an overstuffed bright orange cow to adorn their homes.

The night I was given this endearing creature, this stuffed

bovine, I was late arriving back at the residence. Curfew broken again, and my mind conjuring up ways to get back to my room without being noticed. Now, what never occurred to me was that carrying a large orange cow is going to get you noticed in New York City, where anything goes, much less our very restricted living quarters as students. I managed to get to the elevator, pushed the floor button that I knew would land me on the floor where there was a kind of secret route to the residence. However, before I reached that floor the elevator stopped, as I am sure my heart did also. On the elevator stepped the night supervisor. I figured I had just gone too far, and this was it this time.

"Jarvis," she said, eyeing me with a squint over her glasses, "I am not seeing this, I do not want to see this, I do not want to deal with this, and I am ignoring you with all the control I can muster. And the quicker you and that thing you are dragging get out of my sight the better off we all will be. Do you understand?"

Yep, I understood all right. And mumbled something akin to thank you, and stepped off the elevator, heaving a sigh of relief. I know that Mrs. Supervisor had all of my pranks she could stand and getting out of her sight would be a great relief to both of us. So I did! This was quite a stroke of luck indeed. So Daisy got to my room and she cowered there for the remainder of my training days,(no pun intended).

I married and left Newfoundland several years later. Daisy had to stay behind in the care of my parents again. Father said he figured she wouldn't cost much to feed so she could stay. And every year I came back for vacation and there Daisy would be, her coat gradually fading to a color somewhat more yellow than orange.

However, I could not give her away. There were too many memories between us. I remarked to Father that Daisy was getting old and he commented we all were, and that was that. I had no idea of the prank he was to pull on me that year.

On our way back across Newfoundland in our camper van we stopped here and there and at one stop we proceeded to prepare lunch. I came close to dying of fright when I reached under the bunk of the van for dishes and felt this soft furry material. I screamed, the kids came running, and together we pulled Daisy out from under the bunk. Father had done it again! He felt it was time Daisy came with me and he sent me off carrying a stowaway, not showing a bit of emotion as he did so. I called him collect to say "Very Funny, Father!" And his laughter was endless.

The rest of the trip Daisy spent stuck up in one van window or another, the kids waving at passing motorist, and they would wave or toot their horns at them.

We arrived back in the Annapolis Valley late in the day after the ferry crossing, and while unpacking we realized we did not have my Daisy. Well, I was a wreck!

Finally the children decided that Daisy did not want to leave Newfoundland and had escaped while we slept. And I had to agree, and the matter was put aside.

So, Daisy is a lot older now, and probably all yellow. If anyone is traveling across Central Newfoundland anytime and the children start yelling that they saw a "yellow cow, Mom, really!"Just do the parental, 'Yes dear, now let's see how many different license plates we can identify." That usually fixes any travel problem. Because Daisy is where she wants to be, and probably is enjoying immense freedom from being jolted, insulted, carried, dragged and bundled up by me and others, and is enjoying her freedom.

Yes, she is probably all yellow by now, and is most likely avoiding people, especially those leaving Newfoundland, the place she wants to be.

Just do the license plate thing-works every time!

SPECIAL BURGEO SATURDAY AFTERNOONS

Oh, indeed, I could hear my fathers' voice loud and clear coming from the office at the end of our house, the RCMP detachment in Burgeo, Newfoundland. Dad was doing his routine call and report.

"XJL20 CALLING XJD97, come in please, over!"This was followed by the familiar sound of radio transmission static as he waited for an answer. Over and over he would call until he got through to Corner Brook, the head office for the Burgeo area.

That was the way it was deemed necessary to be in those days of the fifties and sixties, the Mountie and his family lived in the detachment living quarters, the offices, exhibit lockers, a bedroom for any visiting member, and a large room filled with a jail cell occupied the other half of the building. We lived in that little town, and in that building for three years in the late 1950s. Father did his work, Mother was a busy mom with four little children .I was the oldest at the age of nine or ten. We would play house in the jail cell, using a satin bedspread if we wanted to be a princess, a queen or the bishop. Wild imaginations, lots of fun, and playing in a jail cell, making it a house, a church, school, recital hall or dance floor was common place in our lives as strange as it may sound now. We loved it, and we carry the memories with us.

But on Saturday afternoons in good weather, or at least reasonable weather, I had a special job, I would take the stroller and my siblings for ice cream at Webbs' store. It was a long walk pushing a stroller but we loved it. So on this particular Saturday the baby, David, was ready to go, and little Margie was getting anxious and Dad had the quarter. We needed that quarter because that was the money for the ice cream. I would buy three cones, seven cents each, which left me with four coppers (pennies) and for them I would buy four jelly candy, peppermint nobs or barrels, one for each of them and two for me. Yes, two for me, I was pushing the darned stroller and I should have the bonus candy. And that routine was set in stone for Saturday afternoons.

Finally Mother opened the door to the inner sanctum and came forth with the shiny quarter, and a big smile. We were off for our adventure after all. We had a new baby sister at home, much too young for ice cream, so it was a break for Mother, and good exercise for us to have our little 'treat trips'. I don't remember how far we walked on those gravel roads but it usually took two or three hours to complete the round trip. David called ice cream by his own special name, and we always had vanilla. He would be a sticky baby boy, and Margie a tired little girl, as we approached home at the end of the trip. She was just little and it was a long walk for her tiny legs, so we would stop here and there, no rush, no fuss.

The little ones loved the special walk, with ice cream and candy as a treat. We examined every rock, flower and insect ,as we dodged along. Stopping to talk to people we knew, going into someone s' shed at their invitation to see new kittens or puppies, and generally sizing it all up, taking in the world around us. I think my stop and go, stop and sight see style of hiking and traveling is learned behaviour from those Burgeo days, and it is a pattern of behaviour that has been known to get friends a tad angry with me at times. But I wanted to see it all then, and I want to see it all now.

After we bought our treats at Webbs we would turn around and start the trek back toward home. All sorts of mishaps could befall us on the way back, from dropping cones, which David called "Ni-Ni," for what reason we never would know, to losing a wheel off the stroller. A nap time would overtake one of the young ones and I would get the ice cream they didn't eat, another bonus! That is until they would wake and scream and kick and bawl for their treat that was long gone. Just in time our home would come into view, I would be totally exhausted, Margie would be so sleepy she could scarcely keep her head up, and David, the baby, would be starry eyed, having had his nap and being propelled all the way by me. Yes, quite a routine we had then, no Riverboat serial film for us, we had a 'cone date' to keep on those afternoons.

Such a simple and innocent way of life. Claire Mowat in her book "Outport People' described Burgeo vividly. When I read it, I could close my eyes and see the detachment with the flag flying high overhead, the hospital, the shoreline, the wharf, and I could pick out the characters and know who was who. I read it while living in Nova Scotia and I could hardly keep the tears back, as my hectic life at the time was a far cry from the 'ice cream Saturdays in Burgeo'.

Burgeo was fun, lots of fun. We played game after game of baseball with one of those red, white and blue rubber balls that would bounce for miles if you weren't quick enough to catch it. The sand of the Sandbanks was so soft and silky, the Doctors beautiful Newfoundland Dogs, our little Beagle that we had to give away ,but yet-so many memories of happy days.

And then there was the hilarious and unforgettable memory of the man who lived next door and some of his antics. One of them causes me to chuckle even now.

He was such a nice man, and so good to us children. One day however, he mistook a package of Rinso detergent for Cream of Wheat, put it in the boiling water to prepare his breakfast and of course the house started filling with bubbles, lots and lots of bubbles, coming out the door and open window. A frantic yell to Mother sent her flying and we all went flying chasing her although we were not allowed past the gate. The adults all gathered to help the poor gentleman clean the mess but forever after I would call him 'Sudsy.' Mother did not approve and I would be chastised, although on occasion I saw her turn her head as a smile came to her face. Father would out and out laugh at it all and run his fingers through his thick dark hair. Nothing ever upset Father too much. He said he had seen a world at war and all he wanted in his life was 'peace, my dear ones, just peace,' a line he uses to this day.

So that was our Burgeo, isolated and fogged in for periods of time, but happy making our Jack o Lanterns out of turnips as we recovered from chicken pox, getting in trouble for turning around in church, and laughing at it all, riding a brand new Elswick bike head first into a concrete wall and surviving, and nothing too much bothered us. We were free and happy children who played make-believe in a jail cell and had Saturday 'cone dates', and we had free and happy friends who joined us often.

So many times when the heaviness of life is overwhelming and the road ahead seems unsure and dark, I just need to sit back and remember Burgeo, our life there and most of all the 'three cones and four candy for a quarter.'

And then will flow in the sweet memory of a young mans' voice saying "XJL20 calling XJD97, can you copy?"

Yes, XJD97 I have taken you with me since those days, and I certainly can copy.

"Over, but not out!"

WILL YOU SAVE ME THE CORE?

*'Sharing the wonderful taste of an apple
becomes a lifelong memory'*

It was recess time again, and the teacher always insisted we go outside for fresh air. My sister and I were attending a small school in Northern Newfoundland where my father was posted as a member of the Royal Canadian Mounted Police. He was the only 'Mountie' for a big area and drove a Land Rover Jeep. That little Jeep stands out in my memory to this very day, as does that little outport town. We made lifelong friends in that town, friendships that continue to this day.

The wood stove in the Parish hall that was our Senior School was smoky and the smell of books, drying woolen mittens and rubber boots, wasn't good for us all day our teacher said! He was right. The air outside was bitterly cold but better than the air in the stuffy classroom. Mr. Power was a great teacher, and we all loved him. I still have a letter of encouragement he wrote me a few years later when he heard I was having trouble adjusting to a bigger school. Yes, he was a truly dedicated teacher and we all knew it.

And just as an aside I should probably be honest and tell you that we must have wanted to be in school that day because any day we wanted off class we would have one of the boys gently kick the stove every few minutes, long enough to get the pipe loose and smoke would billow out and everyone would be sent home. The other trick was for the girls to sharpen crayons and casually toss the shavings on the hot stove, and that would also cause enough smoke and dismay to have us dismissed. Nothing to it, off for the day, the harbor frozen solidly, the ice showing that lovely shade of pale blue with the occasional seal wandering about, big white fluffy clouds looking like cotton wool against the blue Newfoundland sky, and if the conditions were fit for skating we would get the day off. But it must have been an unfit day to find us all in school, we guessd we may as well pass the day together with Mr. Power as be outside in the cold wind, that was usually our collective thinking.

I remember the recess times in winter particularly because of the big apple I would have, my sister would have one as well. We were in Port Saunders, my little enchanted community where I believe most of my life was shaped, the road not yet opened down the peninsula, a community where we lived a free and wonderful four years during my fathers' posting there. Father would get a barrel of apples, a barrel of this and that it seemed, from the produce boat that came in the late fall, and the apples would be 'Kings', a huge late ripening apple. But every recess when the apple came out of the lunch bag some little boys or girl, usually much younger than I, would approach with several others in tow and finally would ask the familiar question 'Can I have the Core?"

It always made me feel terrible that I had a big apple and they did not, so the apple would get passed around, everyone would have a bite, a practice that soon stopped when my parents found out that we were practicing a 'germ spreading activity'. So my parents said 'Bring your friends home for an apple so they can eat it properly." And we did. Some of the children were afraid to come to our home, it was the 'Mounties' House' and they knew it had the office and jail on one side, our living quarters on the other. However, when they got to know us four children, realized we were the same as they were, they would visit. Once they cleared that hurdle they would come home with us often, their fear being long pushed aside.

I don't think our classmates were hungry least I hope not! There always seemed to be good food cooking anytime I would visit their homes. I think they just had the longing for the taste of fresh fruit in the middle of winter. The barrel of apples was big, but I also think it was magical! We never ever go to the bottom of that barrel until springtime. I would be headfirst down the barrel with my legs kicking in free air getting the biggest apple I could find, the big 'King' to share around, and the barrel always had more apples in it. Mother would tell Father he should eat more fruit, he would say that he wanted the children to have it, and so it went, every year. Of course with all the kindness my parents spread around I remain constantly amazed that they didn't end up destitute or living in a tent in the middle of a bog somewhere. They are living proof that kindness is returned ten fold.

So we fast forward twenty years, and I am living in the Valley of the Apples, in Nova Scotia. By then I am with another Mountie, my husband, and posted in Windsor, Nova Scotia. The Annapolis Valley farm market I visited often had Cortlands, MacIntosh, Spy, Gravensteins, Bishop Pippins, Russets and best of all an enormous bin of Kings, the famous 'Recess Time Apple' of long ago.

It took a whole day to eat one of those King apples, and they were great for cooking, making apple sauce, and anything else apples flavored. Apples surrounded us, from the blossoms in the spring, to the special pointed ladders of the apple pickers in the fall, all things my children took so for granted.

Wolfville and Acadia University was just a fifteen minute drive from our village of Falmouth, and I spent quite a bit of time in Wolfville. Great shops, farm markets, library, and lots of second hand stores to browse if one had the time. And in the fall the town would fill with three thousand University students, many of them from Newfoundland and Labrador. It was wonderful to see those Newfoundland license plates on the vehicles, and the excited students running around downtown.

And a lovely phenomenon would happen around late September or early October if you drove 'up the valley', as we called it. Probably not noticeable to many, but it sure was to me. And I would silently cheer them on when I saw it. It was the 'gathering of the windfalls' as I would come to call it. A small vehicle with Newfoundland license plates would be parked on the side of the road and the orchard next to it would be full of students filling their pockets and backpacks with the windfalls of the apple orchard. I enjoyed seeing this many times until finally the harvest was done. The fresh faces of the young people, their smiles and sunburned noses, was all food for the soul. And I would think "Yes, get the apples, get them before they rot, make amends for every little boy and girl that didn't have an apple at recess time." And the day I saw the Ford Escort full of apples with only room left for the driver and passenger and the car sported Newfoundland license plates, I knew they would be OK. They would not have to ask for 'the core.'

A simple thing perhaps, but surely a lesson to be learned. That dispensing of the apples taught me to share, to give, and to be kind, to do a random act of kindness once in awhile, to shine a big red apple to a glossy sheen and have it ready should someone want it. And the day I saw a ten-pound bucket of apple cores thrown out at an apple pie baking contest I thought my heart would break as I remembered the little faces in the school yard years ago that looked up at me and asked "Can you save me the core?"

FRIENDSHIP, ONE OF LIFES' GREATEST GIFTS

A poem in one of our school books years ago had two very significant lines in it which have always remained with me. I can clean out the cobwebs of my mind but those lines refuse to leave. They seem to be engraved on my brain to this very day. The lines read 'True friends are like diamonds, precious and rare, false friends like autumn leaves, found everywhere'.

One of our teachers in a small two-room schoolhouse in Northern Newfoundland made us memorize the whole poem, but those lines stood out in my mind and have continued to hang onto my memory all of my life.

I have used the lines often, especially when raising two great kids who seemed to have such soft and easily hurt hearts. When rebuffed by somebody they thought was a 'friend' their tears would flow, and they would be broken hearted. And it would be time for the famous lines of that long ago poem, and it always worked. Gradually they came to realize that there really are true friends, and there are false friends. Most of us have had both in our lives at one time or another.

Memory is a marvelous gift, but sometimes it brings back the bad times as well as the good. It makes us more appreciative of the good times I think.

When I was thirteen years old, I had a friend I'll call Joy. She was a joy to me as a friend, confidante, classmate and all-around soulmate. Our birthdays were just two days apart, and we discussed everything. She wondered about our Protestant church, I wondered about her Roman Catholic church. We both read Nancy Drew books-devoured them, actually. We became known as a pair for the few years I lived in her tiny outport home.

I really don't remember when I didn't know Joy, and I don't

remember how we met-it just seems to me she was always there from the day we arrived in the little community.

Joy had black glossy hair and a slim build, and one heck of an imagination. Our imaginations were one of the first of our characteristics to click and we were off on one of the best trips of our lives.

We would spend countless hours sitting with our legs dangling over the end of the 'government' wharf, probably having to keep an eye on either one of her younger siblings or one of mine.

It was during those times, with the sun beating down on our tanned skin and scraped knees that we had the most exquisite discussions. We talked about the latest Nancy Drew mystery, the other girls at school, our dreams for the future and whether or not the man wandering the beach was a 'crook' like in one of our books.

Once in a while, we wouldn't be able to stand it any longer and we would take her fathers' punt out in the harbour, causing quite an uproar from shore once we were spotted and our parents notified.

The sleep overs we had gave us the opportunity to create all kinds of imaginary dramas, our flashlights flickering on the dark bedroom walls.

Joy, as far back as I can remember, wanted to become a teacher, and she did. I always knew she would because her determination was so strong even way back then.

Sneaking a little turnip from somebodies' garden, we would sit in the sun and peel it with our little pocket knives, the ones with the Mountie on them, and munch on the vegetable between words. Our conversations were endless, our love for each other so innocent and deep. But it was all to come to an end. My father was transferred away from that little lovely community and my times with Joy would come to an end at the close of school.

The tears we shed were limitless. What would we do without each other? How could I go and leave her behind? But it had to be, heartbreak or not.

And a heartbreak it was. I dreaded the packing, and I dreaded the days that I would be in a new school, a bigger school, without Joy. I didn't know if she would be OK without me. We worried about each other. Then the moving day came. We drove through the little community, my father purposely leaving Joys' house until last-because, I'm sure, he dreaded what the scene would be. 'We soon arrived at the gate that led to those familiar steps I had run up so many times, or had seen Joy come running down breathless, eager to start another adventure. The tears flowed and flowed on this day, so much that the steps were difficult to see.

Her parents came out to greet mine, Joy came out and we stayed off to one side, unable to let each other goes. We were fractured, hurt, and so incredibly sad. No reassurance from our parents helped, no promises of trips back down stopped the tears. Somehow we knew it would never be the same.

I see the scene now as clearly as if it were yesterday. We hugged tightly and would not let go, crying and crying. Our hearts were splintered. But it came time to go and Joys father put his arm around her and my father led me to the car. I glanced back and saw a distraught Joy, with her fathers' strong arm around her slim shoulders. That picture is engraved on my mind to this day.

We were right. Things would never be the same. I moved to a bigger school and had much trouble adapting. My father drove down that Northern Peninsula Highway as often as he could, so we could see our friends and make an easier transition. That was the year of Grade nine for us, and I sank into a deep adolescent depression, Joy was gone, and the joy was really gone from my life.

But time heals, and gradually I made the transition, meeting a few new friends. I never, since that experience, wanted to grow too attached to any one friend. The months passed, we moved on with our lives, the letters we wrote to each other became less frequent. It was time to let go.

We met again years later, I called her on her fortieth birthday and on both of those occasions, time slipped away, the years melting and bringing us back together.

We have not seen each other for years, many years. But if I ever had a true 'friendship' it was the one I had with Joy.

We are both in our fifties now, Someday our paths will cross again, of that I am certain. The years will fall away again, and maybe she'll have the latest Nancy Drew mystery with her. Now that would be divine! Joy, you were a Joy to me, and you still are.

THE UGLY BLUE COAT

If I ever despised anything in my life more than that blue coat, I am a loss to think of what it could be, except maybe creamed green peas on toast, a dish that is served in some institutions.

A blue coat came into my life when I was ten years old and thoughts of it haunts me to this day, forty years after the dreadful experience. It was simply so ugly and unattractive I can't wipe it from my memory bank.

I cannot really remember how it found its' way to me. I was living in Burgeo, Newfoundland, and at the time most of our things came from a catalogue order so that was possibly how the rag found me. Unlike Josephs' coat of many colors, this ugly thing was just a soft blue color. When I first tried it on I felt like I had been wrapped in a table cloth, had a few buttons pinned on me, and the whole thing just hung there.

I hated it from the first five minute wearing and I pleaded, cried, yelled and sulked, all to no avail. That was my summer coat for wearing to Sunday school and church. It could have better served some sailboat well as its' main sail. The coat engendered such hatred in me that it lives on as a family story, much to my dismay. I had to wear it because I needed a coat and you could not just go to a store and try on a dozen or so and decide what you liked best. And it was an understanding that every spring and fall we got new coats to keep up with our growing.

Well, this coat could well have waited ten years, and it still would not have fit me properly. As a matter of fact the thing would not have fitted me at any point in my life because I firmly believe to this day that it wasn't really a coat, but a piece of rag left at the end of the bolt of material that gave it birth! But I was stuck with it. My parents said how wonderfully it fit, how lovely the color, and all in all how very beautiful this garment was and I should be proud to own it. Bull! Off to church I would go, one of my siblings in tow, and even they were brainwashed into telling me how much they liked my mainsail .And for them to be complimenting my clothing I knew they had been bribed to do so.

Over time, my mother and father took pictures of all of us, and each of us alone, and throughout the years I gradually, quietly and methodically got rid of all those photo reminders of the ugly coat. Still the photos would appear from time to time, from where I do not know, but the images seemed endless, but I managed to very subtly destroy them all.

Now, the strange thing about it all is that I could never remember in later years what finally happened to the monstrosity. Maybe my parents gave up the fight, maybe I outgrew the coat, I just did not know. My selective memory wiped out all traces of the coat. And as long as it was gone from my life-that was my main goal. And I just wanted to forget all about the traumatizing experience of wearing a sail.

But how could I forget? Year after year, when home on vacation, I would wait, and sooner or later, unable to resist the temptation of getting a reaction of wrath from me, my father would have to mention that darned coat, and he did it casually, but relentlessly throughout the years.

If I happened to be looking for my coat, he could never resist, or control his bringing up the ugly blue coat. He would say quietly "Why don't you wear the blue coat? It's a lovely coat, and it matches your eyes!"I, of course, unable to control myself either, would go into the usual rant causing Father to go into gales of laughter. And his laughter was contagious, so soon everyone would be laughing at my unfortunate experience. I failed to see the humor of it.

Then I caught him! Over dinner at my parents' house one summer vacation day, the conversation, as usual, turned to childhood days, memories that stood out in our minds of certain special events and, of course, the blue coat had to come up-not mentioned by me, always brought into the conversation by my father. As he was strolling through his bottomless memory bank in his quiet thoughtful way, he suddenly spoke out loud, and to this day I don't think he ever meant to say what he did. It just flew from his brain to his tongue and that was it! He was caught!

"Ah, yes," he mused to himself, "that blue coat was one ugly garment."

The silence that followed that statement was deafening. Nobody moved. I was as speechless as my father, who was wondering how to cover this one up. All I could manage to say was "Yes, it was ugly, darn ugly, and I bloody well knew it!" And all of this was followed by the usual gales of laughter, and teasing from my siblings.

So goes the story of the infamous piece of rag called a 'coat'. Father finally admitted it, I always knew it, and now it could be put to rest.

And then I had what one would call a 'flashback'. I remembered what happened to the disgusting garment and in silent retaliation I am keeping the secret to myself forever.

However I will say it is strange that the blue coat gave off such a bright flame, something it never did for me while wearing the thing!

A STRANGER IN THE CHURCH

One sunny Sunday afternoon in June 1963 I was living in Grand Falls, Newfoundland, now known as Grand Falls-Windsor. And I was enjoying the usual teenage activities of the time. One of those activities was being a member of the AYPA, the Anglican Young Peoples' Association, and taking part in its various meetings, functions, and field trips.

On this particular Sunday afternoon the AYPA was planning an outing and we were to meet at the back of the Anglican church parking lot, and we did. It was learned that some material we needed for this particular pursuit was not with us. It was left inside the church and I was sent to gather it up.

I had not lived in Grand Falls for long at that point, and was eager to please the group. I headed for the church, just meandering along with no special thoughts, enjoying the day and looking forward to the field trip. However, when I reached the big doors of the brick building I felt somewhat uneasy, as for some reason I did not like to be alone in a church.

I entered the building through its' heavy double doors. It was empty and still, the sun was streaming in through the stained glass windows, and I felt anxious as I knew I would. My plan was to fetch the items and get out of there as fast as humanly possible. Then I was startled by a noise, and I looked to see a very dashing gentleman walking toward me, his hands resting behind his back, his face wearing a warm smile. He wore dark rimmed glasses and a dark suit, and my first thought was that he was a visiting clergyman. He stopped next to me and in a very kind voice asked my name, and why was I in such a hurry? He continued to ask numerous other questions, including the name of my school, how my grades were, if I liked living in Grand

Falls, and how many brothers and sisters I had. He then noted what a lovely church it was we were standing in, pointing out various features of the building as he talked.

As the chat continued I had time to really look at him and his features became familiar to me. He was quite the conversationalist, and after ten minutes he bid me goodbye, and told me how he had enjoyed our chat. As he left through the first door he turned around and told me I must remember to do my best in school.

I watched him walk away, his hands still behind his back. I then noticed he was holding a black hat in one hand. I followed him to the door, and as he left through those big double doors I peered through the window, watched him put on his hat, while a huge, black car pulled up and he opened the door and disappeared into the back seat.

As he drove away, it struck me who he was- he was none other than our Newfoundland Premier Joseph R. Smallwood. I had seen photos of him, and studied about him in school, and about his role in the provinces' confederation with Canada. I could hardly believe I had spoken with the premier.

When I returned to my group, I excitedly told them about the encounter in the church. Some of the group laughed and snickered at my story, so I left it at that and never mentioned it again. After a few days had passed I told my father about my meeting with the man in the church the previous Sunday, and he also laughed, but with delight.

Yes," Dad said, "It would have been Mr. Smallwood. He was in town for meetings on the weekend. I believe you." And he was happy to know I had spoken with the premier. I was so relieved. My mother also believed me, but my siblings would not, and they teased me mercilessly.

Almost forty years have passed since my chance encounter with Joey Smallwood. He was a busy man, but he took the time, not only to visit local buildings, but also to stop and spend a few minutes chatting with a young girl who would remember the experience for the rest of her life. I had talked with the premier, and it was truly a 'premier experience'.

MY STRANGEST AND BEST JACK 'O LANTERN

One time, many sleeps ago, as the children say now, I attended a two-room school. It was in Newfoundland, in a little place called Port Saunders. I loved my pets, friends, school, and talk of that little community often. Not too long ago my sister and I had quite a discussion about our different Halloweens, the one when we had the chicken pox, the one of the snowstorm, the one where our brother made himself sick on the sweets, but there is one Halloween that is by far the most memorable.

In our little school one October Thanksgiving came and went and we were into drawing pumpkins, most of us never having seen one. We had over the years carved oranges, turnips, and all sorts of things to make our Jack O' Lanterns. It was accepted that this was what we used and nobody questioned it at all. Until one memorable Halloween when we had a new teacher in our little school.

The young man was so young, barely out of school himself, and full of all sorts of stories of the world outside our community, and had many ideas, creative and interesting ideas. We adored him, even got to school on time to see him. If anyone could become a good teacher, it was he, and he did, he went on to become a professor at a university.

About a week before Halloween the teacher suggested we have a Halloween competition, a competition to see who could make the best Jack O'lantern, and we would compete with the other classroom. Our minds took off in various directions, hands shot up, everybody had suggestions, but the teacher raised his hand.

"Now this will be an indoor contest, and what do you think

we can use that will not cause a fire, is hard to work with, but will last forever?" he asked the class.

Well, everyone had an answer but not the one he wanted. He reached under the desk and brought up a tin can, similar to those that vegetables came in, "What do you think of this?" he asked our wondering and questioning faces. Yes, we agreed, we could use tin cans, and light the candles inside, this would be fun!

The teacher set out the guidelines. The can had to have a wire handle, a certain size candle, and we were allowed to have one adult help us. And it couldn't be him, as he and the other teacher were the judges.

So for a week we had parents, neighbors, older friends, the grocery store man and anyone else we could commandeer, helping us with our tin creations.

My sister remembers using a bean can, I remember the 'corn' can, and we both remember scratches on our hands, and most of all we remember hiding our cans from each other.

The day of the Halloween party came, our mothers baked, and all our Jack O'lanterns were lined up on a table. There were no names on them as they were ready for judging. The afternoon was dark, and we waited until it was twilight almost, then the teacher lit each candle in our cans, and put a piece of dark cloth up to our one front window.

It was truly an awesome experience, as we stood, or sat in our seats, and looked at the transformation of the tin cans into beautiful Jack O'lanterns, all glowing, all reflecting off one another. Teacher finally said he just couldn't choose, so we all were winners, and we all got a special little prize he had made up for us. We sat in silence in that little school room as the heat of the stove died down, and the tin cans lit up the room, with beauty and reflected light. I will never forget it. They all had such grand smiling faces.

Then the lower school room joined us. Their teacher could not choose either, and they all had a prize. They filed into our larger room and placed their creations on a table on the other side of our classroom.

What a sight to behold, a memory to savor for a lifetime, and a lesson in creativity never to be forgotten. The room was ablaze with lights, it got dark outside, it always got dark early, but it just seemed so much darker that day with so much light inside. We had our Purity syrup, our cupcakes, and left the school with our little candle-lit tin cans. Our very special Jack O' Lanterns. What a wonderful lesson, what a wonderful afternoon, and what dedicated teachers!

It is just those sorts of moments that shape our lives, and we never forget them. We had little comforts at school, but we had our marvelous teachers and their creativity, something they passed on to us almost every day.

I have a pumpkin to carve if I want, but I think this year I will make a tin can Halloween light. The tradition should live on, the tradition of sharing, caring, and most of all, creating and making the most of what we have. Thank you teachers of Port Saunders, Newfoundland .May all your Jack O' Lanterns still be burning bright!

MY HERO, MY REBEL

For most children, especially when they reach the adolescent years, there usually appears in their life a person that causes them to open their mouths in awe and wonder, and stories of this person are listened to and stored with care, and they never ever forget this special person. It may be a person in authority in the school or justice system, or somebody who has always been in their lives but just on the boundaries, and now they discover them for the first time through older eyes and more intense scrutiny.

Such was the case in my life.Surveying the world over the top of a book usually, and hungry for adventure, a trip to the coast of Labrador, to Forteau Bay, and the little settlement of English Point, led me to all sorts of different excursions in boats and cars, with friends and cousins, because English Point was the home of my mother.Usually once a year we would make the coastal boat trip back for mother to visit her family, and for father to visit old friends, now some of them family, that he became acquainted with when he served on the Labrador coast as a Newfoundland Ranger.My mothers' brothers became friends of his and consequently he married my mother.So they had a great affinity for Labrador, and still do.

All of a sudden one year Uncle Stan, my mothers' oldest brother, became the focal point of my attention.I had heard story after story about Uncle Stan Trimm , and his exploits , but the summer of my twelfth year it seems like a light came on and I really watched Uncle Stan, followed him around, and his constant chatter and story telling that he was famous for made him larger than life to my adventuresome mind. But with Uncle Stan you didn't need too much of an imagination, because many of his exploits were really true happenings, and his devil-may-care attitude would drive my Aunt Elsie to distraction, but nobody ever attempted to change the ways of Stan Trimm, he had a history that proved it was pointless, so he carried on as he always did, and was never happier than when he was in his fish shack, standing next to a barrel of seal blubber, telling stories well into the night. Yes, he was my Uncle, and I shadowed him for that summer, and a few summers after that, learning a lot more than I should probably, but in retrospect it was fun, and most enlightening.

Uncle Stan figured the rules of society were made for others, he didn't comply with most of them. If he did, he did it reluctantly. His shirt tail was always half way out of the top of his belt, he played the fiddle until he cut the top of one of his fingers fixing a motor of something , and that really irked him.He bought a snow machine when they first came out, had all sorts of trouble with it, so threw a temper tantrum and hooked the snow machine to the dog team and dragged it in the woods anyway, muttering that the thing was 'goin' in there one way of the other'. He took my father for a boat trip fishing sea trout, they ran out of gas and rowed all the way home, and pulled the boat up onto the slipway , only to discover there was a can of gas underneath their supplies in the cuddy of the boat. Well, that causes a jump up and down, kick the boat fit that caused quite a commotion.He was darned mad at that!!My father laughs until tears come when he tells the story.

There was another facet of this Uncles' personality that people knew about and knew they could depend on, and that was kindness. He fed the hungry, gave away equipment, lent his truck, sheltered the travelers, and was just an all around good Samaritan, but he did not want you to know that.He also was so impatient that Aunt Elsie would put the pie out for the night lunch and if she was too long getting the plate he would pull out his trusty pocket knife and cut the section of pie, lift it out, and drag it along the table, causing us all to hold our breath.But Aunt Elsie would just yell for a minute or so then look at the bystanders and say "See what I gotta put up with?" We would just nod,

Uncle Stan would laugh, and continue on with his ever present storytelling.

His life continued on this way well into his senior years, and illness took its' toll, the hard life of the Labrador fisherman had done nothing to help his arthritis, but he remained obstinate to the end. When he left us, I felt a big part of me had gone too, even though I was an adult, living far away. My rebel Uncle was an institution in my mind, and I was always a little girl in his, always. And that was nice to have someone think of you that way.

Yes, he was a rebel, he did it his way, he did what he wanted, and he gave what he could. The story is told of an unkind act a merchant did to him when he went to purchase his special brand of cigarette that he smoked constantly. He asked for his brand, but the merchant handed him another.

"These aren't what I want, now give me what I asked for!" Uncle Stan yelled at the man who obviously was in his bad books anyway.

"Pretend they're your kind, Mr.Trimm," the merchant answered.

So Uncle Stan opened the cigarettes, lit one, and turned to walk out the door.

"Just a minute, you never paid for those!" yelled the storekeeper.

Uncle Stan turned and squinted at him over his cigarette smoke and said in a condescending voice 'PRETEND THEY'RE PAID FOR!"

And he left.

Yes, that was my colorful, unforgettable Uncle Stan. A man who worked hard, was important to so many and in his own way taught us the lesson that you have to be your own person, and it is good to be a story teller.

The Rebel Uncle became a Hero to me. I think he was terrific, and I think I inherited some of his traits. I can't tell you what they are, Uncle Stan wouldn't like that! Pretend you know!!

BERYL AND THE BUDGIE BIRD

I opened the door to our house just in time to see Mother staring into the bird cage. My sister Beryl had a budgie bird named 'Pete', and this bird was the household treasure for the month. Mother had the dishcloth in her hand and her hands on her hips, not a good sign, and she was doing quite an inspection of the cage.

She beckoned me over and said "Now, look at him and tell me what you think!" I dropped my packages, purse, keys and books and hastened to see why in the world my mother was so distraught. I did a short five-second visual inspection, then opened the cage door and stuck my hand inside to touch the little bird lying at the bottom of the newly cleaned little bird home. Yes, sure enough, he felt just like one of the little bird ornaments on the Christmas tree. A beautiful little bird had met his demise.

"Well, what do you think?" asked Mother.

"He's dead," I replied.

"No, he can't be, not now," Mother moaned, her hand over her mouth.

"Well, my dear mother, this bird is no more, he has ceased to be, he has shed his mortal coil, he is, in fact, quite dead," I managed to say, my mind by this time thinking this was very much like a 'Monty Python' skit that I liked and laughed about so much, the unforgettable John Cleese and the Parrot Sketch.

I looked up and smiled, I had made the worse move possible. I smiled. Mother was not happy. What were we going to do and whatever it was had to be done while my baby sister Kathy, just two years old, was having her nap?

This fuss was so unlike Mother, who accepted the life and death of our pets, cried with us and explained that we had to have our cry and then get on with our lives. This was the woman who put up with every kind of pet we brought home, stayed up all night with sick mommy cats and kittens, and believe it or not had suffered the unbelievable experience of having a cat go for the goldfish, the dog go after the cat, the previous budgie to this one, Jacko, got out of his cage and in all the fuss the water from her scrub bucket went everywhere, the fish went under a radiator and the bird had a heart attack and fell into her scrub bucket. Didn't faze her. The heart attack was the kids' theory, but the bird did fall from the ceiling into her bucket. Yes, she had seen it all with five offspring and here she was crumbling over Pete the deceased budgie bird.

Finally she found enough breath to tell me what the major problem was, and explained it in detail. She ended by saying, "You remember when Hortoise the Tortoise fell off the coffee table and died, well that was Beryls' pet too, and she was in the middle of exams and she went down in her average over that. And she is in the middle of exams again now. So she cannot know this happened!"

Enough said. Beryl was my sister, fourth in the family of five, beautiful and smart, kind and soft-hearted, and was protected quite a bit as she had been just a three-pound bundle of crying flesh at the time of her birth in a little hospital in Southern Newfoundland. But she survived. And Mother and I knew she would agonize over Pete, and she would possibly mess up on her exams. And messing up on exams was not acceptable to our parents. So something had to be done fairly quickly.

I was due at work as a Registered Nurse on a busy unit in about two hours so we set to work to fix the situation. We had to dispose of the body of Pete, the cage, food, and anything else around that could ever prove he existed in the household. That was my brilliant scheme! Kathy was due up from her nap, I had to get ready for work so we wasted no time and in less than an hour there was not a tidbit of evidence that there was ever a bird in our house. Absolutely everything was taken care of, furniture rearranged to hide where the cage sat, Kathy woke up, I went to work, and Mother prayed! So the daily routine of our lives continued on as usual. Beryl never mentioned Pete. David, our one brother, couldn't care less, so he was no problem, and everyone else was sworn to secrecy. Great plan, everything was left well enough alone. That is until a week later when Beryl finished her exams. My wedding plans were the big issue of the time, so we thought we were on easy street.

But one could never, and still should never underestimate this sister of mine. She was born small, but lived big. Her big smile, her happy-go-lucky nature, quick wit, and ability to be forgiven for the most awful clumsy accidents she would have, was a family story that went on and on. Beryl has a love of life that brings out the best in all those whose lives she touches. One year on a summer vacation to my mothers' home on the Labrador coast she got herself invited to go trout fishing. Of course all the fishing rods were lying crossways in the van, which was Ok until Miss Beryl decided to stand up, the van rounded a turn and down Beryl went, breaking off every single fishing rod!! And got hit with a fit of uncontrollable laughter and very quickly forgiven for breaking the gear. That would not happen to anyone but Beryl. Such was the way her life went. Always forgiving, and always forgiven! We would just stare in wonderment with our mouths open at how she could do it, we wondered how to get so lucky.

But for some reason, she did not notice the missing 'Pete' or the cage, and went on about her life. The bicycles were getting out of winter storage and she was all caught up in that for a time. Mother and I stayed silent, hoping all would go well.

And then it happened. I noticed my sister standing in the area where the cage had been hanging, obviously deep in thought. We distracted her, but soon she was back in the same spot.

"There's something missing here," she announced. "Seems strange!"

Nobody spoke. Those who could, slipped away. Those who stayed just watched with nervous anticipation, fearing the jig was up-and it was!

"Didn't I have a bird here?" she asked. No answers were forthcoming.

"Yes, I did. I had a bird. His name was Pete. Where is he?" She was becoming a little more demanding now.

"The cage and stuff are upstairs," I finally coughed the words out.

"Why would you put him upstairs? I didn't see him up there!"she yells. And that is one thing she could do really well, and still can, is yell!

By now, Mother was expecting the worse.

"I said we put the cage upstairs. The bird is not in it. And besides it took you long enough to miss it," says I!

"Where's Pete? Where's my bird? Moooooooooooo-mmmmmmmmm!" Here we go I thought "Pete is dead, he is no more, he is gone, and it took you two weeks to miss him, so give it up," I yelled back. Mainly because that is how sisters are sometimes.

"You mean to tell me he died two weeks ago? I never knew that. That's a riot " and with that she started to laugh, and she laughed for half an hour, rolled on the floor, and of course the whole scene was hilarious, and soon we were all laughing.

In time she gathered herself together, told all her friends about her dead pet, passed her exams and provided in doing so another story for our list of crazy family antics. As for Pete, hopefully he is in Birdville, finally out of a cage and enjoying his freedom!

THE MOUNTIES' ORIGINAL HAIRDO

Many years ago, on a large rocky island in the sea, there existed an enchanting little outport community that was an intriguing place to live as a child. It was a most delightful place to grow and learn. This small community was a land of constant exploring, fishing with bamboo rods, playing endless pool games, boiling mussels on the beach, usually with the mussels in a large can over an open fire, picking all sorts of berries, and beach combing for star fish and other delights the ocean would offer us.

Just as the season for many activities ended, a new season, with a new set of adventures, would begin. Winter would bring the ice, and the seals would come into the harbor. We would observe them for hours under the bright blue Newfoundland winter sky. But then we would have an activity that was exciting but dangerous which was called 'jumping pans'. As the ice broke into large pieces we would practice jumping from one piece to another, and the wrath of our parents would be fast and furious once we were discovered. And on and on the activities went, the cycle of carefree childhood days.

Port Saunders was the little community that so captivated us as children. It was our home for four years while my father was posted there as a member of the Royal Canadian Mounted Police, in the late 1950s and early 1960s. We lived in a Cape Cod Style 'detachment', as it was called. The family residence was on one side and the office for the Mountie, the prisoners' cells, and tiny rooms for strange and various things that Mounties collected was on the other side.

Through a common front door, there was a little entryway with the office door to the right, and the residence door to the left-a fact crucial to this story.

Four of us children, our friends, a dog, a busy father who worked day and night in all kinds of weather, and a mother overseeing us all, would make one think that we would be less inclined to mischief than children with less to do. But mischief was frequently astir, and the Mounties' children started it all. This childhood creativity could cause quite an uproar at times. However sometimes it got overlooked and everyone heaved a big sigh of relief. On the occasion I am about to relate I've never been really sure what the aftermaths was, but I can guess.

Fathers favorite time of day was after supper. He would, when time permitted, lie down on the sofa and turn the radio on. There was no television then and the radio was our link to the outside world. Inevitably in a short time Father would be asleep. I swear he never removed his uniform in those days, and he was on call day and night for any and all strange happenings. The Mountie carried a heavy load in those small isolated communities around the Newfoundland and Labrador Coasts.

As soon as he drifted off to sleep, and shall we say, unresponsive, my sister and I would change the radio station to one with singers such as Bobby Darren, Paul Anka, or Elvis Presley crooning, and Father never ever noticed. As in most crimes, the more you get away with, the braver you get. One foggy, rainy evening we were stuck inside. Father was having his nap, and Mother was upstairs with the new baby. Life seemed rather dull.

Enter the elastic bands, confiscated from the office of course; a crime was in the making already! We tuned in the rock and roll music, and with our little brother watching in astonishment we went to work to give Father a new 'hairdo'. He never moved as his thick, dark, shiny hair slowly became about one hundred little spikes, each held tightly by a stolen rubber band. It was sort of like the 'punk rock' look that was popular forty years later.

Because he was so compliant, we placed elastic bands on his ears, rolling them down to look like lips. Poor Dad, nobody deserved this, least of all him-but it was such fun we could not stop. Thankfully Mother had not appeared to witness this transformation.

Then horror struck with the ringing of the doorbell! Father was programmed to that doorbell and he made a leap off the sofa, and sprinted to open the door into the entryway. And of course he swung the outside door wide open to face two men who must have been quite shocked!

We were dumbfounded as we heard the dreaded "Good Evening Sir!"

This greeting was followed by mumbling of mens' voices, then my father took the two gentlemen into the office. They left shortly after and Dad walked back to the sofa and assumed his horizontal position, oblivious to how he looked.

We held our breath. Mother still had not appeared. Maybe we had time to fix it!

"Dad, can we play with your hair?", my sister asked him quietly.

"Sure," he said. It was one of my sisters' favorite activities to comb Dads' hair, and he never minded it at all.

So we set to work and one by one we removed those elastic bands and combed his wonderful shiny hair back into place. Boy, that was a close!

Now, so many, many years later I can imagine how many stories that event must have generated. I can see the two men going back to their friends and saying "Yes, now, b'y, the Mounties after crackin' up! He looks like he's gettin' a perm or somethin'-too bad, he was a nice fella too b'y!"

Then my imagination reaches to the next generation. I picture a group of men sitting around in their cabin enjoying a hot toddy, when one speaks up and says, "Remember the story father used to tell about that nice Mountie we had here who cracked up? What was it, somethin' to do with the hair wasn't it? Wonder whatever happened to him. It's a hard life see b'y!"

Yes, Father unknowingly was a 'punk rock Mountie', and never ever knew until years later. By then he just laughed, true to his quiet nature. He is eighty-two now, and still sleeps through the news at times. But we have decided to ban the elastics. That was far too close a call!

I CAN'T LET YOU GO ALONE

It was my first job as a new Registered Nurse, working at Grand Bank Cottage Hospital in Grand Bank, a little place on the South Coast of Newfoundland, Canada. A classmate of mine, Shirley Best, was also working there with me although we saw very little of each other due to our shift rotations. But we made time once in awhile to have tea and compare experiences, challenges and catch up on our personal lives. She liked it at the little hospital as I did. It was a small hospital, not much more than a 'nursing station', the facilities that dotted our Newfoundland and Labrador coastlines. But that small hospital was practically the heart of the community, and Dr.Wrixon and Dr.Oliver, along with seasoned and experienced nurses did some wonderful work at that hospital with its' limited supply of equipment, space and general supplies.

I lived in the Nurses Residence attached to the hospital itself and Shirley lived in the town. One of the first things I learned at that little hospital was how resourceful and practical all the nurses were, how they could think so fast on their feet, and how pleased they were to have extra pairs of hands to help them. They were excellent teachers and we soon learned the most efficient way to run a clinic, do quick assessments of trauma patients, and how to keep a good level head in the midst of chaos. Those nurses were good, and that was the way we wanted to be, efficient and skilled, and able to handle whatever was thrown our way.

When we applied for positions as graduation from the Grace Hospital School of Nursing approached we were amazed at how many choices we had. They needed nurses all along the coasts of Newfoundland, and we chose Grand Bank, and we were never sorry for that choice. The hands on experiences, the good teaching, the adventure, and the resourcefulness we learned have stayed with me always, and hopefully I passed it onto others.

The two doctors stand out vividly in my mind, Dr.Oliver with his old world genteel attitude and Dr.Wrixon with his boisterous ' run down the corridor, pole vault over the nurses' desk' And then laugh at the havoc he had created The same Dr.Wrixon went on to become a well-known Obstetrician in Halifax, Nova Scotia. He was smart, young, and full of mischief. Dr.Oliver would give him a glance over his glasses from time to time, taming him for an hour or so. It was fun, there was so much to learn from these men.

The nurses were served afternoon tea in the old English Tradition, a leftover from Newfoundlands' colonial days no doubt. Meals were cooked on night shifts for the workers, and for us children of the baby boom, the sixties were good. Our way of dress raised eyebrows from time to time, but as long as our work was good we were fine. Those were the days when nurses did not even pay the unemployment insurance premiums, the reasoning being that there would always be jobs for nurses, something that changed radically in the years to come.

However a rude awakening was in the wings for me, and it came, as most do, when I least expected it. I was doing laundry in the basement of the hospital on a cold snowy evening when there was little else to take my attention, when I heard the running of footsteps and my last name being called. That also was a tradition, the use of our last names instead of our Christian names.

A senior nurse appeared and explained the situation. They had a very sick baby suffering convulsions and he needed to go to the Janeway Childrens' Hospital in St.John's, four or five hours away, by ambulance, and he had to go right away.I was there and available and commissioned to go.

I ran to put a bit of order to myself and reported to Out Patients Department. Dr.Wrixon passed me a bag of medications and syringes, gave me a quick rundown, half a dozen papers, and said to medicate whenever it was necessary and to keep oxygen on the babe at all times.

We headed out the Emergency Room door to the waiting ambulance, and started to load up and hook up the oxygen. Dr. Wrixon was doing his last check when I heard a voice calling my name. I turned to see my classmate, Shirley, running through the snow. "I can't let you go alone on that road, I'm coming too!"

She made room for herself in spite of my protests, and off we went. The highway was icy, the visibility very poor, and the baby convulsed frequently I cannot express how glad I was, and relieved to have another nurse with me We kept our stethescopes on that little chest, our hands pushed through the hole of the isolette, changing places from time to time when we became cramped. We laughed at one point when Larry, our driver said we should be just two feet tall and we wouldn't have that problem!!

Then disaster, a flat tire, not another vehicle on the road, and precious time was taken up while Larry in his thin spring coat and freezing temperatures changed the tire. Grave concern set in, this was a much longer trip than usual, would we run out of Oxygen, would our gas gauge drop too low, would our power give out disabling our much needed suction device? So many things ran through our minds. We talked and shared our concerns, the baby finally fell into a medication induced sleep and the seizures became less.

After seven and a half hours we saw the lights of St. John's, and Larry speeded up the ambulance and we flew across that snow covered bit of civilization toward the Janeway Hospital where a fresh faced group of doctors and nurses, just coming on duty ran out to meet us. After a report to the doctor we crawled and dragged our cramped limbs into our ambulance and headed back to Grand Bank.

We had done it, we had accomplished a difficult mission, and as two twenty-one year old new nurses we were very proud. I was so grateful to Shirley and as we stopped for gas and loaded up on junk food we shared our unspoken concerns about our trip. But it was finished, the baby, we later discovered, did well. He is probably grown and a father of his own children now.

But I learned so much that night. First of all dress warmly, which I had not done, take food and water, which I had not done, get good doctors orders and lots of the required medication, and this I had been given. And when it is possible at all, take another nurse with you if they are willing.

I did many ambulance trips after that, in many different places. But none would equal that miserable night of the blizzard and the sick baby. The paramedics were better trained, the ambulances had more high tech equipment with heart monitors etc. The seats in the back of the vans were more comfortable, with more head room and speakers available to communicate with the driver if necessary.

Yes, everything changed for the better, and the more ambulance calls I did the better I got at that type of nursing. But no matter what, I learned the most on that snowy night in Newfoundland in 1969. A December night, with the next morning dawning still, the sunrise awesome, and the snow a carpet of marshmallow with twinkling crystals, as two young nurses, proud as peacocks, and their devoted driver drove back to a hospital in a Newfoundland outport town. Everyone waited at the doorway of the hospital to make sure we were OK, and to feed and comfort us.

Never to be forgotten, a learning experience, and an experience of the soul, as we sat our sore bodies down to eat lunch and tell Dr. Wrixon all about his patient, and in the middle of the conversation he jumped up and gave us both a huge bear hug, and we knew we were appreciated. Nothing could beat that!!

THE PERFECT CHRISTMAS TREE

*'Written in Memory
of Mr. and Mrs. W. B. Cornick'*

The magnificent special blue of the Newfoundland December Sky, the bright sun shining on the white snow, turning it into an endless carpet of tiny crystals, two young men at the Christmas tree 'For Sale' area of the parking lot surrounded by brightly clad children gave the whole scene before me a certain look and feel that reminded me of the stories and descriptions in the Charles Dickens books. One of the young men had taken a small fir tree and was trying to get it to twirl on his cold hand as he would twirl a basketball. He obviously was enjoying his audience as he joked, teased and continued his performance.

The children were laughing, the young men entertaining, and Christmas music was playing on the PA system. All those things together created a memory to savor. I slowed my pace and absorbed it all, tucking it in my memory bank.

Then suddenly I heard, from inside the circle of Christmas Trees, the voice of a young woman. She was obviously very intent on getting her very best tree ever.

"No, not that one dear, I want a perfect tree this year." Her voice was soft and kind.

Just then a large bus arrived with the hiss of brakes, and the doors opened with the clunking sound that only buses seem to have. The combination of the 'perfect tree' comment, the sounds and smells of the bus, all combined to open my box of memories and a particular memory from a very long time ago. It was not just the comment of the tree, but all the small bits of a common day came together to bring forth a long forgotten part of my life, the life of a student. And with that forgotten memory came to me the laughter of a group of student nurses getting on the Bonavista North bus during the late sixties. It was part of our lives to take the bus to Gambo, leaving our studies and the Nurses Residence behind, and going to Gander to visit my friend Jeans' parents. Jeans' Dad would pick us up in Gambo and take us the remainder of the way to Gander.

A few days after entering Nurses training in 1966 I had the life-altering experience of meeting a girl named Jean Elizabeth Cornick. We assessed each other, deemed each other worthy of attention and a lifelong journey of friendship began. We never looked back as we learned, worked, played, pulled practical jokes, backed each other up at all costs, and generally tolerated Residence life like chained cats.

With Jean as a 'best buddy', her family came into my life as well, and my family into hers. Jeans' parents were Madge and Wilson Cornick, but Wilson was known to all as Bill. When I found out his initials were 'WB', for Wilson Bramwell, I dubbed him WB. That nickname stuck and I called him that from then on. He got quite a charge out of the quirky little nickname. He was no ordinary 'Bill', so WB it was!

WB was married to the love of his life, a charming British Nurse he met while overseas during WWII. Madge had a lovely lilting British accent, and a great laugh, could cook like the best chef, baked great bread and rolls and was very kind. She would feed us the hot rolls with the melted butter dripping over the napkins, and sit back with her Corgi ready to listen to all our terrible woes and problems. It became a ceremony of sorts over the three years of nurses training, and one we were so fortunate to have.

Meanwhile WB practiced gruffness, but in spite of his big size, he generally failed gruffness and fell victim to laughter instead. He tolerated us all with great patience and always with kindness.

So on this afternoon of the Christmas tree sale, the bus and all the activity surrounding me, my memory took me back to a clear recollection of piling off the bus in Gambo where WB would be waiting with his big warm car to pick us up. He would mumble and grumble about all the luggage we had, and we would be making the run for the big car, with everybody talking at once, including WB.

And off toward Gander he would drive, taking us to Madge and the hot rolls.

One characteristic of friendship is the sharing of family stories, anecdotes, milestones, laughs, tears, and all that make up a life. Such was, and is, the way it went for Jean and me. So it was inevitable that sooner or later I would hear her Christmas Tree Story. And I did!

One day we were particularly bored, something neither of us could tolerate. So Jean started talking, with a twinkle in her eye.

"Ever tell you about Moms' perfect Christmas tree,?" Jean looked at me and asked.

"No, but you're going to tell me aren't ya?" I asked with a laugh. So she began her story.

When WB returned from overseas with his young bride and baby son, it was apparent that, like most of our fathers who served overseas during war time, he was filled with angst, bewilderment, and shocked by all they had seen and endured. He, like all the others, wanted peace, happiness, and a better world for their children. And WB was the stereotypical post war man. He was forever planning, and combining his wild sense of humor and his quick wit to execute those plans.

One Christmas time Madge stated she wanted the 'perfect tree', nothing else would do. So she sent WB off to fetch this tree. In an hour or so he returned, but the tree got the rejection sticker from Madge. So off went WB, with the tree dragging out of the back of the vehicle, promising to do better.

A few hours passed, and WB arrived back. He had the right tree 'this time' he announced, but Madge thought it too sparse. He happily stuck it back in the vehicle, and set off for once again. Twice more this happened. Madge saw it was getting late, but soon WB was back. He jumped out of the car in a flourish and announced that he had finally found the tree she wanted. He took it out, stood it up, Madge did her walk around inspection and proclaimed the tree to be 'Perfect'. She muttered something about the ridiculousness of taking all day to find a tree, but the tree was brought into the house and prepared to be decorated.

So what of it you ask? Well, Madges' question of 'why he couldn't do that the first time?', was somewhat unsettling. What she did not know, until many years later, was that it was the **VERY SAME TREE EACH TIME!** Every time she sent him for another tree, he drove down to the pub, had an ale with his friends and returned home. The answer as to why he was so congenial throughout all of this was that he had much festive 'spirit' that day!

During a phone conversation with Jean not too long ago I could hear Madges' laughter as if saying "You didn't fool me Bill!" And I pictured her with the oven door open, and could almost smell the wonderful aroma of freshly baked bread, and see her later sitting listening to our various issues and concerns.

We have lost both Madge and Bill now. They left so much of themselves, so many memories for us to cherish. Even the memory of a young man and woman decorating their 'perfect' tree until the young man falls asleep, knowing he is with somebody who loves him.

WB and Madge, Wilson and Marjorie, Mom and Dad, Nan and Pop, all those names, and all those roles, they treasured so much. The kindness they showed a group of young student nurses, will never be forgotten, nor will they be forgotten. They taught us so much, and their support and friendship was invaluable. We will forever remember all of it.

Thank you 'WB', and Thank You 'Madge', for kindnesses shown, over and over. Through you we learned to pass kindness onto others. You left quite a great legacy.

Thank you for all the special moments, the great laughs and marvelous memories. May you now always have the 'Perfect Tree'.

PART TWO

Saying Farewell to Newfoundland
April 1970

MOVING AWAY-1970

Our wedding was held in St. John's, Newfoundland on April 11th, 1970. I had left Grand Bank and was back working for a few months at the Grace General Hospital as I prepared for the wedding, and the move to Nova Scotia that would immediately follow it. My fiancé was a member of the RCMP, and in those days members of the force did not serve in their own province. So the relocation was a necessity.

We had our wedding, everything that had been packed was already shipped. Our beautiful wedding gifts and last minute details needed attention. My Nova Scotia Registered Nurses License was in place, and all the farewells concluded. A week after the wedding we headed out from St. John's to Port aux Basques. We were full of hopes and dreams, and neither the miserable snowstorm nor the long ferry ride to Nova Scotia could dampen our spirits. A new life lay ahead. We were to be posted in Dartmouth, and arrived there in late April 1970. Setting up housekeeping, finding my way around, having free time, something that was totally foreign to me, and meeting new friends filled our lives.

I missed my family in Newfoundland, but my husband had already adjusted to that as he had left four years before me. In particular I missed my baby sister. She was just three years old, and so near and dear to my heart. I cried buckets of tears as I continued to miss Kathy. I considered her to be mine I am sure. Being eighteen years old when she was born, I was old enough to be her MOM. Over time I adjusted, but it was a long time before I could talk of Kathy without tears.

I found a job, and from then on our lives became full and busy. We had a new baby boy in April 1971, making us truly a family. Then thirty-three years flew by for me as we became truly rooted in the beautiful province of Nova Scotia, with its' bounty of apples, fine friends, and Gaelic areas of interest.

Yes, we had moved on. Just as the young people are moving on today. There was no choice, and we accepted it. Leaving Newfoundland behind was bittersweet. Newly married and happy, but leaving a little sister and other siblings, parents, and friends and all that was familiar to me tore at my heartstrings. One day when I was particularly sad, missing all the boats, the berry picking, a day that felt like Newfoundland, with the lichen on the rocks, the gulls calling, and the warmth of the sun soothed you when you could find a place out of the wind. It was a real Newfoundland day, and I mentioned it to my husband.

We had a short time to sit with the baby, enjoying the springtime air. John David, the baby, was healthy and strong, and it was always 'John and Mom', I took him everywhere. As we played with John, I asked my husband a question. I have no idea what I was thinking, but it must have been a moment of nostalgia.

"Do you ever miss home?", I asked.

He turned to me, pointed at our son, then at me, then at himself, and said quite softly, "This is home. Wherever we all are together is home now."

That turned me around as I followed his example and learned that indeed he was so right. No matter where we were, what part of the world we found ourselves in, together we were 'home'. Four years later in Lunenburg, Nova Scotia, we were blessed with a baby girl named Heather Jean Elizabeth. And together the four of us made our own traditions, and lived through all the ups and downs of life.

It stayed that way for another thirty years, until the children grew, became of age, and left 'home', causing circumstances to change again.

Leaving Newfoundland was such a bittersweet time in my life, but so many challenges and experiences came my way in those thirty-two years, so many friends made, so much work done. They were years well spent indeed.

THE YELLOW STRIPES AND THE BLACK BANDS

Yes, that odd statement was making the rounds again, I couldn't really understand where it came from, who perpetuated it, what kind of mind devised it but it was annoying to those affected by it. It went like this 'if you can't get a man, get a Mountie, if you can't get a woman get a nurse'- now figure that out!

That ridiculous so-called joke made the rounds from time to time, probably still does, although now it would not really be as applicable or have the same slam to it as it did years ago. Now women are Mounties too, and men are Nurses, so that changes things considerably to those who have any cognitive reasoning. But up until the 1980s' that weird little remark caused many a female nurse to give the speaker a disdainful look, and then walk away!

There seemed to be a very large number of Mountie/Nurse marriages.

Most of the hospitals I worked in had at least one other nurse on staff who was a Mountie's wife, and at one point in Windsor, NS. there were four of us, all transferred into that area with the RCMP. So the communities involved got a two for one deal, the much needed nurses and the policemen as well. The psychologists would ponder why these marriages were so many, why nurses and Mounties attracted one another. There is no one answer. The altruistic personalities they would say, then another would say it was the shift work, meeting over trauma cases in the middle of the night, but nobody has come up with a clear answer as to why these people attract each other. Everyone seems to have their own opinion, and the annoying little remark gets brought up, tossed about by the older group and then it dies away for a while.

For the young woman who wants a 'SCARLET' wedding on a sunny summer day, the reality of shift work, a husband who just came home from a fatal accident scene, the transfer hither and yon, soon takes the red out of the Scarlet, beautiful though it may be. A nurse understands the angst of her husband, and he understands hers. But sometimes the stress is overwhelming and the marriage cannot survive. It is sad, but it is a fact. The divorce rates are high, and the work takes its' toll. Some of these young women barely out of teen years, had a hard time adjusting to the style of life the force required. I was fortunate enough to have a father in the RCMP so I well knew what to expect, what I was walking into and knew the language, understood to a degree what life was all about under that big umbrella we called the 'FORCE'. For others it was incredibly difficult, they were away from home and family, had to spend a lot of lonely hours and generally it was up to the older wives to reach out and lend a hand of friendship. But that would not be so easy for a working mother, whose world was full of work, childrens' appointments, shift work and all the rest that goes with running a home and caring for a family.

And as for the silly statement it was basically like a putdown, and those young women knew it and felt it and it hurt!

It had a hurtful effect because the Mounties were men, and the Nurses were women, and they did their jobs with pride, many times sacrificing their home life, or succumbing to post traumatic stress which wasn't recognized years ago.

And the children of these marriages were caught in between their nurse mom and their Mountie dad, and it was sad!

One day a few years ago, just after my husband retired from the Force, a big adjustment for me who had never lived on 'civie street', I was in the bank doing my usual payday banking when a young woman approached me. She was beautiful with large dark eyes that looked sad that day, and a wide smile that filled a room. She knew my husband had gone to work in another government department and was not in the force, having served twenty-five years. She was a Mountie's wife, and she asked if she could talk to me for a minute. Sure, especially since I knew she was a girl from Newfoundland and her and I had talked many times before. On that day she wanted to ask about my husband, how he was doing in civilian life, how was it going and so on.

Then, with tears in her eyes, she touched my arm. She was at least twenty years my junior, and needed some reassurances. I was overwhelmed at the moment because I had always seen her smiling, never knew she was distressed. She told me her concerns, and then asked me straight up "It has been really bad, does it ever get any better?"

Yes, I told her, it will get better, this will pass and you will go on. And then another hurdle will come and you will jump that one too, and as you live and learn and go on, you will become stronger.

It will get better, because you are a Nurse, he is a Mountie and you are giving the best you have to everyone around you and saving none of yourselves for each other. Learn to do that, to take time for yourself and time for your family. Leave the work at work, it's difficult at first but you will learn how to do it. You have to or your life will be chaotic. How do I know? I know because I have been through it, and I really had to learn the word "NO"-and save time for me, for my family. Slips backwards were frequent but if you are intent on saving a private life that is happy you will soon realize that there is no other option. Every hurdle will make you stronger, and through it all the stronger you get, the easier the next hurdle will be. She smiled, she had too many irons in the fire she thought, they both needed to make adjustments she said. But her one great wish was that things would improve.

We walked out into the sunshine together and went our separate ways. I often wonder how she is doing, and I can only pray that all is well for them.

They deserve it. They are living the life of the 'yellow stripes and the black band', and they give their best.

And may the Force be with them!

MY FATHERS' EYES

The work day was over and I jumped into my car ready to run all the necessary errands on my list. Immediately I was struck by the smell of leather. The leather seats, after sitting for a day in the sun filled, car had given the car a nostalgic and wonderful scent. It gave me the memory of a car my father had and with great tolerance, hands grasping the dashboard, had taught each one of us five offspring to drive. I looked up to adjust the rearview mirror and to my surprise I found myself looking directly into my fathers' eyes! It took a moment to absorb the jolt, my heart doing a complete flip-flop as I sat there and couldn't seem to stop staring into the small rectangular mirror. The smell of leather, the same movement of the hand to the mirror, the blue eyes, they were all the same, exactly like my fathers' traits, and I wondered how I could not have noticed this before now?

Another long look and yes, I did have the same eyes as dad. Those blue eyes that we had all learned to read so well, as I am sure my family could read mine. Sadness, joy, discomfort, lost in thought, tired, all the emotions a husband and father, and in fact, most of us experience on this lifes' journey, are reflected in our eyes. But my fathers' eyes seemed to show it more than most. We always knew if we had disappointed him, always knew if he was pleased and proud, and we did not need to hear it said, we could read it in the expression of those eyes.

It was then I remembered a phone conversation I had with my son a short time before that day. I had sent him photos from our home in Nova Scotia.

He called later to ask when his aunt, my younger sister had been to visit us. I had not mentioned it to him he said. But in fact she had not been to visit, he was looking at a photograph of me looking over someones' shoulder, hamming it up for the camera, and the eyes, when I checked the photo, were in fact so similar it was easy to understand his being mistaken.

Never being one to let a subject drop before it was explored beyond all reason, I started to do a mental inventory of the blue eyes, the expressive eyes, all so alike and so familiar looking. I did a step by step check in my mind, yes, we all had the same trait, and it was so obvious in my brother, he had shown much sadness in his blue eyes lately. He looked so much like father.

A friend had told me I was very fortunate because she had lost her father when she was very young and had never had an opportunity to know him, therefore can only see him in old photographs. She longs for something that cannot be. She tells me how I should count my blessings. And I tell her I do, every day.

My mother often remarked that when she met father shortly after World War 11 he had a wild look in his eyes, his mind full of horrific sights and his eyes reflecting his emotions and pain of all he had witnessed, mans' inhumanity to man so much to deal with in those hell-filled war years. It took some time for him to get some stability back and to show joy again. She tells of his nightmares and his quiet withdrawn times, obviously a result of all the traumatic stress of the times.

But then there are the good times to remember also. The sparkle that filled those blue eyes when a new baby joined our family, when one of us achieved a goal, even something like riding a bicycle. Then there were the sad times such as when his mother passed away, his eyes blank and dull then. A graduation, a wedding, an award, always something to make the expression of happiness come back. And the fender benders we would have, the falling over the wharf into cold icy water when we had been warned by him to stay away, then the eyes would be full of fire. Not a big fire, just enough to let us know he was disappointed for a time.

When father became ill the light left his eyes, but he rallied and returned to his old self, never being one to give up easily, he struggled back to health. He sits and surveys the world with interest, making us wonder always " just what is he thinking?".

In some parts of the world, in some cultures it is said that the 'eyes are the windows to the soul' and for that reason it is not acceptable to look directly into the eyes of another. How so very grateful I am that such is not the case for us, it is not our way, because I would miss so much.

Taking another glance now and then, reminding myself who I am, who the blue eyes came from, and being thankful is one way of staying grounded, and certainly connected to this father of mine. This father who at the age of eighty-two years still has that sparkle, a sparkle of blue that makes the world a much nicer place. Blue eyes, much loved, and loved much in return. That's 'MY FATHERS' EYES'!

IT'S THE LITTLE THINGS

The cold winds blew down from the Cape Breton Highlands, causing everyone to comment on the chill outside. The little town of Sydney Mines, Nova Scotia, had just had a small dusting of snow and the wind caused the snow to swirl around the parking lot of the small hospital where my first child, a little boy, had just been born. It was April 28, 1971, I was twenty-two years old. My husband and I had held him, examined him, found all eight pounds of healthy baby, and nothing else mattered, not the cold wind, the news or any other happening on our planet. John David was here and we were thrilled.

With all that had happened in our country in the past year and was still ongoing, I had grave concerns of what lay ahead for my baby. A primitive protective instinct had settled itself in me and I knew now how mothers' felt, what they tried so hard to describe. This was a mysterious feeling of change, of being very vulnerable and always on watch, on guard for your child. That primitive feeling that tells you to make a phone call, even well after they leave home, just in case all was not well. Yes, I had become a mother.

Our son is thirty-one years old now, six feet four inches tall, a kind and caring person, an experienced electrician, single, owns a Harley-Davidson, with another updated model ordered, loves to pitch softball games, is loyal and kind to his only sibling, his sister Heather, and is infatuated with his little two year old niece. He is, as the saying goes, a gentle giant, with many good friends. Over time he has learned to control his bad temper of childhood years, and has become a man who can stand on his own two feet. He is too far away, in Fort MacMurray, but that is unavoidable in our world today. He still comes home, does his great impersonations of his parents which are hilarious, strums his guitar when he is stressed, but he is too far away to give those wonderful bear hugs everyday. He has been living out west for ten years now, a good citizen, son, grandson, brother and uncle.

Our country experienced so many awful happenings in the nine months before he was born. My husband, a policeman, was away with his work from time to time, Prime Minister Trudeau was having problems with the FLQ crisis, the War Measures Act had been imposed, demonstrations were being held everywhere opposing the action, and it seemed our comfortable Canadian world was becoming Strangely uncertain.

Somewhere in all of this the Prime Minister married Margaret Sinclair, I recall my husband coming home in the early morning hours, waking me to tell me, knowing my love for the news. Then Cape Breton had a major oil spill in Chedabucto Bay causing tremendous threats to sea life and environment, and it seemed the news was never good. I have a vivid recollection of being ready for a Halloween party and my husband being called away to do Security Detail on a Cabinet Minister who was visiting our area, and he was gone for days and days. In the midst of all of this a murder took place in Wentworth Park in Sydney, NS, that eventually led to the arrest of Donald Marshall, who was sentenced to jail and served eleven years before the case was reopened and he was pronounced innocent. This was followed by The Marshall Inquiry, and I go back to that night as soon as the name Marshall is mentioned. I wondered if bringing a baby into this world was sensible, then my doctor reminded me that I was born just as the world was emerging from a devastating World War, in 1948, so think about it!!And I did, and John was born in spite of the state of world affairs, politics and so on, and he thrived and grew, giving us great joy.

We knew very few people in the little town, being recently posted there, but we had made some friends, and they have actually become lifelong friends. Alyson and Sheldon Jenkins remain close to our hearts to this very day. I was so very fortunate to have them because the road was rough after the babies' birth.

I was constantly tired, had no interest outside my apartment, anemia had zapped my body, and besides that I seemed to be adrift, having trouble adjusting ,but trying desperately to stay afloat, struggling to stay the course.

To this day I sincerely believe, other than time, that two things salvaged me from this foggy world I had fallen into. They may seem insignificant but they turned me around. For those that saw the real 'me' return, laughing, telling stories, jokes, reading book after book, wanting to go back to work, just watching the downhill trend reverse itself they tell me was 'a miracle'!

I'll tell you the two things of which I speak, and I knew I would remember all the rest of my life and write about some day.

First of all, leaving my husband to care for John, I managed to go shopping, a short lived excursion because I had no energy or interest, and I returned home. On the coffee table, with a shaft of sunlight shining behind it was a magnificent shiny Heinz pickle jar filled to overflowing with huge lilac blossoms. My husband knew how much I loved the lilacs and had prepared a bouquet, and that bouquet stuck a chord, a twinge of wanting to be better, to live fully again. To this day, every time a lilac blooms, I put a huge bouquet in a pickle jar and just have it for the memory, the warm memory of a special bouquet in Nova Scotia in 1971.

But the hills were still there to be climbed, some days they were steeper than others, but always a climb. When June came Sheldon and Alyson suggested we have a good 'Cape Breton feed of lobster'-and I was game for that, lobster being one of my favorite foods. The men fetched the lobster, we made the salads, and we got together with cold beer, newspaper tablecloths, and we ate our fill. Then we divided the remaining lobster, my friend gave me a loaf of her moms' home made bread and we called it a night. It was wonderful!

The next morning, with the church bells ringing in the background, I bathed and fed my baby, and went outside to sit in the sun with him. My husband said he would prepare lunch, and I stayed with the baby. Soon he arrived with the biggest lobster sandwich I had ever seen. Huge healthy chunks of lobster between slices of fluffy home made bread! And a little pickle topped it off, and it was indeed a work of art! He brought his lunch out and we ate in the sun, with the baby settled in his stroller. And that, my friends, was thing number two. One bite of that sandwich and a feeling washed over me as if to say "You will be OK," and we sat and enjoyed our lunch, and I hoped and prayed that the worst of the fog was gone, and it was!

So, just little things, but done with such care and devotion, that the love shone through and touched my heart and healed it. A strange story maybe, but on that Fathers' Day I found out that I was loved, a young father had done his best, and had given the best gift of all-LOVE! I was home, the three of us, church bells, sunshine, lilacs, lobster and love.

So in remembering I have decided every day should be Fathers' Day for fathers everywhere, every day, who do their best, no more can be asked, and the best is sometimes just 'the little things'.

THE TIMES YOU ASK 'WHY, WHY, WHY!

From the time you become a student nurse to the day you finish your nursing career, and indeed even after that, there are so many times that make us call to the heavens and ask 'WHY?' The individual living their life without involving themselves in the medical field in any way finds so many tragedies, so many accidents, fatal diseases and crimes enough to make them shake their fist at the sky and scream 'WHY'.

For the nurses and doctors on the front lines every day the occasions and incidents that cause them to question the Universe, and ask that big question of 'WHY' occurs so much more frequently. They struggle to maintain their equilibrium on a daily basis, put on the best front possible and continue on as they deal with the sadness of the human condition. And often when you least expect it, the big slam comes, and you wobble for a time, and in that time it is always questionable whether this is the one thing that will bring you crashing down. Most of us recover and go on, others take another road, but whatever the course taken, the scars and memories remain.

Such was the case for me one morning in mid-January, in the late eighties, as I worked my day in the Recovery Room, a little soft music playing, my patient still sleeping. Then the PA System blasted 'CODE BLUE, OUTPATIENTS, CODE BLUE OUTPATIENTS' and I knew we had trouble, big trouble. Our only anesthetist was in the OR with a general anesthetic in his hands, the roads were icy so it was unlikely we could ship the patient out, and on and on my mind went frame by frame through the possible scenarios.

One of the older nurses came in and told me to go 'to the

Code', so off I ran. There is no time to question, no time to hesitate under those conditions.

The Resuscitation Room in OPD was like a war zone. The floor covered with debris of every kind, and two or three doctors were working on a little blond haired girl, four years' old. The nurses were all occupied and I was quickly dispatched to another department for a piece of equipment they needed and did not have. I ran, faster than I ever had in my life, and got what they wanted. When I got back, I was pleased to see our anesthetist was out of the OR and doing his best to place a breathing tube in the tiny angel-like mouth of the little girl. I asked above the heads of others, by eye contact only, to my friend Carol, what in the world had happened. How did this terrible scene begin?

Carol came over beside me and whispered that the little child was not in her own seat, her mother was holding her inside the seat belt with her. The car hit an icy patch, the father couldn't control it and it went over an embankment. The parents had minor lacerations but Megan, strapped inside the seat belt, had the belt tighten and crush her larynx. She was unable to breathe. It did not look good. But finally a tube was in place, and the Childrens' Hospital contacted for further advice and arrangement of a transfer of Megan to them for Intensive Care. Lots of work needed to be done, the blood work, Chest X-ray, tubes, and more tubes, but no response from Megan. Her oxygen deprivation was severe.

The Childrens' Hospital in Halifax had a team that would come and travel back with the patient, and that is what happened. Four people, angels to us that day, arrived to take over. Two doctors and two nurses, with their pediatric expertise prepared to leave with our little blond Megan. There were tears all around, the parents distraught beyond imagination and full of self-blame, the doctors and nurses sweating, despairing and feeling all was not well for our tiny charge.

And the day continued on. The shift ended, reports given, no word from the Childrens' about our patient. We went home hoping and praying for the best. At home you're supposed to put that aside and deal with your own life, but at times it is almost too much to ask. We just try. That night I awoke from a nightmare that was to be a recurring nightmare for months to come, a frightening enough situation to send me to seek talk therapy. I would see the pink sweater and blond hair of Megan floating above my face. For you see, Megan was no longer with us, she passed away the next morning at the Childrens' Hospital. They called to notify us and to say we had done all the right things but the trauma was too great to her chest, and they had to let her go.

And we all asked 'WHY. WHY??' and floundered around, talked to each other, preached about children and seat belts, cried and suffered our bad dreams. It was very tragic, and very close to the heart. Most of us in that room that day had a child of Megans' age. And we were so, so sorry.

It took a long time for me to even begin to stop the dreams, to ease up on the seat belt speech every time my little girl went somewhere with another adult, to stop seeing Megan in every little blond at the playground. But I eventually, with Divine Intervention, I am sure, gradually let her go. I had to in order to go on.

Still it makes me ask the 'WHY', and over the years there were other Megans, and other tragedies and still we all asked 'WHY?' Maybe someday we will know why, but I sure don't know yet, don't understand it, and can't forget it!

That is life on the front line, and yes Nurses, it is OK to CRY!

DOLORES

The Out Patient Department in our hospital is where Dolores had worked for many years. She trained as a Registered Nurse at Payzant Memorial Hospital in Windsor, NS. The school of Nursing is now closed in Windsor and a new Hants Community Hospital has been built. Dolores had worked at the Payzant Memorial and was working at Hants Community Hospital when we met. She had grown up in Hants County, NS, married her highschool sweetheart, and raised two children while practicing her career. And, no doubt about it, Dolores is a dynamo.

She is short of stature but big in heart. Dolores has sarcasm honed to a verbal work of art and at times she was incredibly funny. We became good friends, thought a lot like each other, and our husbands knew each other. Therefore it just became a friendship of four people, a friendship strong and long lasting.

Dolores and her husband Frank had a cottage on a lake. It was a cottage that everyone liked to visit so consequently we had countless parties, games, conversations, and special meals and events at this special little cottage. It was at this small cottage on Lake Mockingee that most of the children learned to water-ski as Frank had the patience to drive the boat all afternoon for them. The fathers took turns being spotters and ensuring the children were safe as they learned the technique of water skiing.

We enjoyed trips to Tancook Island in Mahone Bay, taking the ferry in the morning and returning at night. We shared countless shopping trips, and outings to various places. And also we shared our joys and sorrows. I well remember the morning that she worked through the tears, knowing that her father was dying upstairs on our Medical Unit. It must have been horrible for her, but she did it. There was nobody to replace her it was said. So she put up her shield and got through the day.

It was Dolores and Frank we would call in times of trouble, and they would be there as soon as possible, where ever that might be. Frank and I did a Mr. And Mrs. Santa at Christmas time for years. Dolores and I would get together at one of our homes and bake dozens and dozens of shortbread cookies. It was just understood that we would do it, and we did. Mrs Santa had to have cookies! My kids would love to watch and gobble up any cookie or cookie bits that we cast aside.

We always had a project to set to work on, or plans made for a trip and that's the way our weeks and months passed. The on-call beeper for our Operating Room call was a part of our lives when we found ourselves working side by side in the Operating Room. It went with the job, and we accepted it, fitting good events in on our days off.

There were two RNs' on call-back for emergencies at all times, and getting called back to work was part of the job. Dropping everything and heading to the hospital in all kinds of weather, and in all seasons became a way of life. That way of life became very draining after awhile. One night in particular we were called back and spent from midnight to six o'clock in the morning in surgery. At that point there was no sense in going home as our workday started at seven o'clock in the morning. We went out back to the little lawn area of the hospital and sat at the picnic table and watched the sunrise. A beautiful, still morning with a hint of how lovely the day would become was balm to the soul after the harrowing night we had experienced.

Out of nowhere trotted two handsome ring-necked pheasants. We sat together and silently observed them and lost ourselves in thought. Nothing needed to be said, we just sat quietly together and the sight of those beautiful creatures somehow gave us a second wind and the ability to face the day ahead.

Yes, we are friends, having had a long and very established relationship which continues even though I now live back home in Newfoundland. She has been here for a short visit, and I hope the next visit is longer. I have so much I want to show her, so many things to share with her. I certainly owe her a 'guide' experience because she is the person that called to tell me the Lady Slipper flowers were blooming and then crawled around in the brush and black flies until I got the correct camera exposure and the photo I wanted. Only Dolores would do that, so I really do owe her one, one of many such kindnesses.

One New Years' Eve we happened to be 'on call' together. That would not, and did not bother us, as that celebration is not one either of us especially enjoyed. So we bought a little bottle of champagne, and sat together with our husbands watching the flames dance in the fireplace of her home as the New Year arrived.

And that was, to this day, the best New Years' Eve I ever had!

That is called enjoying a true and strong friendship. I hope it never changes.

OF NURSES AND COMETS

Very few professions create the kind of relationships with other people like the Nursing Profession. As a nurse you are the patient's advocate, and more often than not, the nurse becomes the confidante and trusted person in the life that has been struck by illness, especially chronic illness. Also the nurse develops working relationships with peers that become very close, and friendships develop that stand the test of time. In one week the nurse may spend more time with her patients and coworkers than with her/his family. The emotional roller coaster of sadness, pain and sorrow, the triumphs over illness, and the sharing of the personal side of ones' life do indeed create a firm bond, and most often this bond lasts a lifetime.

Such was the case for me during my nursing career. Special moments, personal and professional, stand out in my mind, never to be forgotten, rather I feel blessed to have had those experiences.

One of the most special was the experience of working with Joy. Joy is tall, slim and willowy, with blond hair down to her waist, usually worn in a long braid. The patients always have a habit of asking who is working on a specific day and if it happened to be Joy and myself I would tell them "Comfort and Joy."Joy and I were team mates on the same rotation of twelve hour days and nights and worked closely together for five years. Of course, the question after I told somebody who was working would be "Who did you say was working?"

I would repeat, "Comfort and Joy, you know Joy, and I'm Comfort." This retort always brought a smile or a laugh to the patient which was nice to witness. Over time it got to be a saying on our unit, everybody referring to us as Comfort and Joy.

And when we worked we usually had two terrific LPNs helping us along.

Both Joy and I had families, mine older than hers, but we shared all of our households' hassles, all the laughs, the plans, and the tears. We worked well together with never a cross word between us, knew each others' work habits, and developed a strong trusting relationship and one heck of an efficient system of working together.

But we both really minded the long twelve hour night shifts. Those hours between 7pm and 7am can seem twice as long sometimes. We did, though, have a maintenance man who would, from time to time, make his rounds on a bicycle, sending us all into gales of laughter. One night Stewart came by on his bike and mentioned that a comet was really visible tonight because the sky was so clear. Well, we looked at him in amazement! How had we missed this news? We immediately decided that later on we would go outside and look for the comet in the clear night sky. Work first, organize the shift, then check the comet, that was our plan.

Around 3am Joy came walking smartly toward me with her cup of tea and said "C'mon, lets' go gaze at the heavens!" The LPNs were there, the patients all asleep, the time was right. We did a thorough check of the cardiac monitors, taking one last glance and finding all was well, we headed toward the patio, not too far from our desk.

Our hospital was built with a center courtyard surrounded by glass. A set of patio doors opened into the courtyard, from where we could look up at the night sky. The night was late August cool, especially so at 3am, and the sky was a panorama of twinkling stars, every star looked like a special diamond against a velvet background, a perfect backdrop for the full Harvest Moon. It was very still out there, no beepers, phones, buzzers or alarms to distract us from our quest into astrology. We stood quietly, gazing upward, remarking on this and that, and then Joy pointed upward and said "Make a wish Bon." I looked in the direction of her hand where she was pointing to a shooting star, several of them actually.

In a very short time we found the comet, bright and beautiful, with its' tail a streak of white sparkling light, looking like something in a movie. We were in awe, silent, engrossed in our own thoughts as we lingered and with a sense of wonderment, took it all in. What a marvelous moment to share, an experience too magical to describe. Two nurses, two friends, who had laughed and cried together, cared for each other when we were ill, two women sharing a journey of raising a family, working hard at our careers, telling each other of our worries, failures and successes, standing together gazing toward a clear and magnificent sky in the middle of the night-yes it was spiritual, powerful, transcending time and place, as we stood in the little courtyard that night.

We both felt it and we were subdued. We knew how sick some of the people in our care were that night, and we knew that some of them may not make it to morning. We needed that celestial renewal, that moment of taking stock, it would help us cope with whatever the rest of the night would bring.

As we slowly made our way back to our nurses' station, Joy looked at me and said, "How could someone see something like we just saw and not believe there is a Power greater than us?" I just nodded. She was so very right!

Yes, a powerful experience with the comet, we watched it the next night too, and we will remember it forever. We told our patients about it at dawn when they wakened, and they just smiled, pleased that their nurses were happy.

But they will never know how powerful that Comet was to two nurses dealing with life and death, two nurses named 'Comfort and Joy!'

JAKE

'Finally, we find the answer to his noncompliance'

The favorite burger restaurant beckoned us from the highway, and the children were so determined that this would be where we ate lunch, that their father just quietly turned the car into the parking lot, and they were out of their seatbelts and into the eatery in no time. I saw that the three of them were settled and because my husband is not fond of eating establishments where you have to 'look up at the menu' as he says, I headed to the counter to purchase the lunch the kids wanted so badly.

As I waited in line I was approached by a large, very large man, who sported a wide toothless grin and was built like a weight lifter. My kids stared wide-eyed as the man and I carried on a conversation, and I knew their minds were racing and anxious to ask me about the 'don't talk to strangers' rule. Who was the man? How did mom know him? Dad, who is he?

Their father told them not to worry, that I in fact knew the man, and so did he. His name was Jake and he was no stranger to me at all. He was very well known to me as he had experienced periodic bouts of chest pain and had been in our hospital numerous times.

"Well, "Jake said proudly, "Mrs. Lowe, tis not me heart!"

"Oh, really, what is it then?", I asked casually as I juggled a tray of food, and tried to disengage somehow, because I knew this could be a long conversation.

"It's all in me a-sausages!", Jake announced. And he was so elated. His pain was a gastrointestinal problem and not Cardiac.

I passed a few more words and got back to my family. And

the questions came fast and furious from two pre-teenage children, I explained he was a man who had been sick but he was OK and was telling me so. That seemed to satisfy them and that was that. But in my mind I was silently chuckling over the 'a-sausages' comment and couldn't wait to tell my co-workers. Jake always had a new twist on an old theme and he just would not say 'esophagus', and we did not know why. That was just how it was.

Jake was around fifty-five or so at that time. I was considerably younger than he, and had a keen interest in getting him to at least try to comply with a health care plan. He was absolutely and totally noncompliant when it came to his diabetes, and consequently, other problems. He worked around town doing small errands and jobs for the merchants, and lately had managed to get a part time job as a delivery van driver for the flower shop. A job he loved and did with care.

This big, easy-going man did not have an untroubled life though. Poor, and a member of a large family, he picked apples, picked up garbage, delivered newspapers and did any job that nobody else would do really. But every job he had he took great care in performing the tasks well, and one of his favorite things to do was to stand with the Salvation Army Kettle at Christmas time. Heaven help anyone who tried to steal that from Jake, wrath would pour over him tenfold.

As the years went by, and Jake aged, his health problems increased. His wife had left him and he had developed a cardiac problem, a result of the diabetes and the improper life style he had led he said. The diabetic clinic nurse could not get him to comply with the diet sheet, he got his medications mixed up, he forgot or lost appointment cards and was a real management problem as time went on. But he continued with his flower deliveries and told me it was wonderful to be able to give some lady flowers and see her smile, the best and most cherished part of his job. The owner of the flower shop kept a good eye on him, helped him remember appointments and generally showed she cared about him, And that was indeed what he needed.

Not once did any of us ever hear him use bad language, not once did he ever complain about nurses or doctors, not once did he put himself first, with Jake the other person came first and he was very admired for his outlook on life. Appearances were certainly deceiving in Jakes' case. If approached by such a huge, unkempt, character and not knowing him would cause people to withdraw, but they soon would find out there was no need. Jake was just a quiet, unassuming character who liked to be friendly.

Then disaster hit with the force of a thunderbolt. Jake had a myocardial infarction, a heart attack, and a major one at that. He was treated in our Emergency and then brought to our Medical unit. He did as we asked, and he had many tests to undergo in the weeks ahead. Preparations were underway to transfer him to the major hospital in our region and he was prepared to go. He had procedures explained to him and we gave him a load of material to read and study, and pamphlets that explained and walked a patient through the procedure, he could be seen with his head into the books and material every time we walked by his door.

We were so very proud of how well our noncompliant Jake was coming along, that is until the lady from the flower shop called to inquire about him. I told her he was doing well, she was his only contact in the outside world by then, and seemed to be the only one who cared, so we told her the details of what was going to be happening to her favorite delivery van driver. Then I happened to mention how he was really reading and studying all the books and material he had been given, and I thought his questions were being answered. And then the shock came.

"No, he isn't reading anything." The lady said, "He cannot read or write at all. He has his drivers license through a special program I arranged and he learned how to sign his name years ago, and that is all he can do. He is fooling you because he is so ashamed!"

We were totally ashamed of ourselves then. How could this have happened? How did we let this slip through our fingers during all those admissions that Jake had to our hospital? Why did we not notice something awry?

But nobody did, because he was so skilled at covering for his illiteracy, you would be hard pressed to find out unless told. How he must have suffered, struggled through these pieces of paper given to him, trying so hard to please us, and scared to admit his failure? He knew the town so well he did not need road signs, he went by land marks and managed everything in his comfort zone the same way. He was ashamed, and we were also. Obviously his memory was his secret weapon. He remembered all his numbers, addresses, medications, but could not read or write.

So we went about teaching him with those wonderful audiovisual aids, we gently let him know that we knew his secret, and he was so relieved. The stress of keeping the secret was over. He went for his surgery, recovered well, and went back to delivering his beautiful bouquets.

Through Jake our Nursing team learned the lesson of listening more acutely, asking more casual questions to ascertain the facts regarding the patient's ability to understand and communicate, and through him we learned to be better nurses, better people, and not to take it for granted that everyone is at the same level. Because Jake proved to us that we are not. And we stopped expecting the impossible from our patients and those under our care, making life and illness somewhat easier for them to bear.

The memory of Jake, sitting on his bed, with his head in a cardiac teaching manual will stay with me always. How we take so much for granted, how fortunate we are to have the ability to read, write and express ourselves in so many ways!

Well-done Jake, you taught us so much and made us better listeners. A bouquet to you for that, and I would love to be the one to deliver it!

MY APRIL LOBSTER

Two or three years ago, while still actively nursing on a Medical Unit in a Nova Scotia rural hospital I knew I had to really work at the April Fools' joke for this particular year. It seems I somehow knew my time there was going to be shorter than they knew, and this group of nurses and staff were perfect and easy prey for a prank. I had pulled so many on them over the years that I had to dig deep to come up with a good, imaginative trick, and quite by accident I did. My husband and I had cooked lobsters one weekend. The kids were in Western Canada so usually there was food left after a meal because neither of us had learned, at that point anyway, to cook for just two people. Only I still have difficulty with it, he seems to have it under control.

On Monday when I went to work I, in a casual conversation, mentioned our lobster feast on the weekend. And while talking about the lobster I had what one could call a 'lightbulb' moment. I don't know where it came from but I found myself telling the team members about my pet lobster "Leo". I mentioned it in passing, and over the course of the next few days, I would be approached by one person, then another, asking how 'Leo' was doing. It got to the point that Leo took on a personality all his own, and every shift I worked I updated them on Leos' activities, his likes and dislikes, his antics, how I had to get a bigger tank etc. So by the end of March everyone on the unit was aware of my pet lobster and one staff member quipped that it was better, she supposed, than those Guinea pigs I had named 'Seemore' and 'Seeless' that constantly reproduced. I agreed whole heartedly, and stated that Leo was one great pet, not a word of complaint, no trouble at all. He just looked at me, waved his claw and went back to sleep.

By now, near the end of March, with miserable weather and being so busy at work, I was running out of things to tell them about Leo. It would soon be time to pounce! Questions were popping up as to when they could visit Leo, could they bring their children to see him, and so on. This whole Lobster thing was gaining momentum, and news traveled around the hospital about the nurse from Newfoundland who worked upstairs and of all things 'had a pet lobster'. And I was having a bit of a problem fending people off. Leo was becoming one important crustacean! I had a photo of him taken while he was 'sunbathing on the picnic table', I reported I would bring the photo to work one day.

On the morning of April lst I was working day shift and arrived armed with the photo, in a lovely frame. I waited until Leos' name came up, as it always did lately, and then went into action. Making sure I had a good escape route I presented the photo of Leo, sunbathing, with his Walkman on, his snack of chicken nuggets, his book and glasses beside him on his favorite picnic table.

Every jaw fell open. They all stared at the photo and then a few of the nurses managed to sputter, "But, but, but, you said he was alive!"

But you see, I never ever had said he was alive, not once. That was an assumption on the part of all concerned. I just said he was a pet. And when I launched into the story that he was red because he forgot his sun screen, I had to make a getaway because pencils, papers, paper clips, pens, coffee cups and any weapon not nailed down came flying my way. One nurse got up on a chair and started to crawl across the conference room table with every intention of choking the life out of me!! I made the escape by way of the route I had planned and never had a mark on me. Yes, that was a close call!

I think it took two weeks for forgiveness to come my way. And as for forgetting it, they never will. Nor will I!

After a decent length of time had passed, like two months or so, and summer approached, we could all sit and laugh at their folly, and my foolishness, and the fact that they would believe me after some of the other stunts I had pulled over the years.

June arrived and with it I announced that I was leaving and returning to Newfoundland. Nobody would believe me, not much wonder I thought!! But leave I did, and came back to Newfoundland and Labrador, leaving the photo of 'Leo' in the conference room where, they tell me, the story gets told, again and again, about the crazy 'Leo the Lobster' prank, and the nurse who got them good. This is followed by howls of laughter, and more stories come to the surface beginning with "Remember the time . . . .?"

I am so pleased that I left them with a story that makes them laugh, because they are wonderful nurses, and doctors, and good people. Now when should I get in touch to tell them about my pet 'Snoop the Snail'?

Very soon I think!

CHERYL P., AND HER RECYCLING PROGRAM

In everyones' life from time to time an interesting character appears, and you are left wondering what you ever did before you knew the person. In my case it was a Licensed Practical Nurse, named Cheryl P. She was called that because on our unit we had three or four Cheryls and in order to differentiate as to who was whom we used the first letter of their last name. And it stayed that way, Cheryl P was and is unique, warm, kind, works hard, causes many a good laugh with her outspoken attitude and love of life and she is adored by her circle of family and friends. There will never be a dull second if Cheryl is in the area. She lives in a big farm house outside of Windsor, NS, runs the household, the orchard, the cattle, a dog she loves dearly and a pussy cat that loves her dearly. Since her father died she has worked long hours to keep the farm and apple orchards going, and the cattle fed. She held a full time job as a LPN, nursed her father at home when he was dying, and in the middle of that mind-boggling state of affairs she was fighting a life threatening illness herself with a brave front always. She never missed a beat, and never complained.

But Cheryl P. is known most of all for her very resourceful ways and her ability to save a penny. Money will never be wasted with Cheryl around. She has been known to move every stick of furniture in the staff lounge to recover a penny. She buys good things, gives great gifts, but you may be assured that she will find a bargain, get the best buy and put her money to the most efficient use. Some of her escapades to save money have caused uproars, but it doesn't bother Cheryl P.-she knows she has won and will win again.

Now, Cheryl has the most beautiful and elegant fur jacket

you ever saw. One of her gifts to herself, probably when she was so ill. I don't know why she chose to buy a fur, but it is a divine piece of clothing. When she goes somewhere special in wintertime, she wears her fur and she looks like perfection personified when she arrives at her evening social gathering, wherever or whatever it may be.

A few years ago Cheryl decided to start into the recycling, a program that was gathering considerable momentum in Nova Scotia. She had assessed the situation and realized that there was money practically being thrown in the garbage. Well, sir, she put a stop to that. We had containers for bottles, for cans, for newspapers and all sorts of recyclables. Cheryl decided the staff fund could use a boosting and this money would do it. She started collecting newspapers, day after day, patients' newspapers, staff members' papers, anything that fit the recyclers guidelines, she collected. It was hard work, dragging all this paper around. The reader would hardly be finished the paper when Cheryl would appear out of nowhere and remind the person to save the paper. Everyone obliged because we didn't want the bother of it, and the misery of dragging all this paper around, but Cheryl was undaunted and she collected until the trunk of her big car could not hold one more sheet of paper.

Well, the day finally came to turn in the paper. The trip to the depot was to be on her day off. It turned out to be a cold, raw , winter day, and Cheryl was anticipating the mitt full of money with great glee. She dressed in her best clothes for the luncheon she was attending, complete with her fur coat, and would stop at the recyclers on the way to the luncheon.

The man at the depot helped her unload the newspapers, then proceeded to weigh them. Cheryl stood with him as they weighed all the bundles of papers, right to the last few little bundles. Then the man turned to her and said, "Yeah, very good load.135 pounds' ya got there!" And of course by now Cheryl was beaming. But the beam abruptly ended when the same man, cigarette hanging off his lip said "Yep, I owe you one dollar and thirty-five cents!"

The hands went on the hips and Cheryl took the warrior's

stance.""Well," she said loudly, "I dragged all this in here for a measly one dollar and thirty-five cents, You must be kidding!"

"Nope," he says squinting through his cigarette smoke and proceeding to roll another one, "we pay one cent a pound for this stuff. That's it!"

"Tell me this is a joke," Cheryl said, very abrasive by this time, especially as she was trying to get out of the way of his smoke cloud.

"Nope," He said, "that's it ma'am!"

Then he proceeded to look at Cheryl, appraised her fully, squinted again over his smoke and his tilted cap, and said, "Well, you have some nerve to come in here and argue with me over a few lousy cents when you can afford to wear a coat like that. I don't believe you lady!"

The gloves were off by now. That did it. "Sir, yes, I will argue with you and anybody else I want to. And it is because I argue over the 'few cents' as you say, that I can afford to wear a coat like this!" Cheryl bristled with indignance!

She wrapped her lovely fur coat around her against the cold wind, and marched swiftly to her late model car. Her head held high and her one dollar and thirty-five cents clutched in her hand, leaving in her wake a very perplexed recycling depot employee scratching his head and wondering what just happened to him as he stood beside one hundred and thirty-five pounds of newsprint. He was totally confused!

But the problem was, you see, he did not know the tenacity of our Cheryl P., but he does now!

And Cheryl P. still collects the papers, bottles, and cans, and still wears her fur coat! And all because she watches her pennies she says!

Now, isn't that an interesting character and wonderful friend to have in your life, I sure think so!And by the way,save me your newspaper,I hear there is a fur coat sale on in St.John's!!

NURSE KAREN, 2032***

You know you're getting older when—? Well, I'll tell you when I knew, other than the fact that my hair was a different color, my desire to stay up half the night disappeared, I started worrying about cholesterol and Hormone Replacement Therapy. I really came to know the day the readouts of our pension contributions, retirement date, early retirement dates, optimum retirement dates came with our biweekly pay stubs in the spring of 2000! I always felt this piece of paper offered to us was a reminder that we weren't getting any younger. However, I know that's the negative approach, but it was the only one I could take. It was annoying! Basically for a nurse it tells you on that little readout that you had better get working on RRSPs because you 'ain't gonna survive on this'!

For us of the 'baby boomer' generation and older, we had no choice but to have broken service because maternity leave was unheard of, and if you decided to have a family it was a known and accepted fact that you would work part, or casual time. So none of us, even those who had been working for twenty-five years or more, would get much of a pension, unless they worked until they were ninety. It was something we learned to laugh about, mostly because of the images it conjured up in our minds.

Well, Karen was a young nurse who worked with us, most of the time quiet, but not about to be pushed around either, she did her thing, had two children, had lots of family support and planned to work and have a long and full nursing career. Now Karen and I worked quite a bit together and she did crafts, which she knew drove me berserk, but it was funny! That Styrofoam squeaking in the middle of the night would drive me right around the bend, and she would just laugh, as would I! Karen never got rattled too easily and was just one of those Type B personalities that enjoyed her life, took things in stride and here she was stuck with me, the one who was the same age or older than her mother, hated crafts, and on a night shift was struggling with fatigue.

But she tolerated me, tormented me, teased me, and we generally did quite well together in the end.

Then the day of the pension printouts came. I didn't pay too much attention to mine, having collected so many over the years, but Nurse Karen took hers, grabbed the calculator, and sat down to see exactly how the financial situation in her life was shaping up. Later on, after watching this for some time, off and on throughout the day, someone finally asked her what in the world she was trying to do.

"Well, it's like this" she said thoughtfully, "it looks like my retirement date is 2032! That can't be right!"

Then everybody got in on the mathematics of it all! Yep, 2032 was it. And I nearly had an apocalyptic fit! In 2032 I would be, if I lived that is, eighty-four years' old! So I had to get my nose into it then, and that was indeed what it said. I told her she would be probably working when Haleys' Comet made its' next run, she would be wearing orthopedic shoes and knitting sweaters for her grandchildren while working night shifts. All in all we had quite a jolly old time teasing 'Miss 2032' as she came to be known. And at that point I started plotting my escape from that institution. Joy had a dream about getting her pink slip, only she dreamed about a closet full of pink slippers, and Karen started going through flyers, collecting coupons, and planning all sorts of innovative ways to save a cent.

So that is what pension readouts do to nurses! Never mind Karen, it's 2004 now, only twenty-eight more years. You'll be fine!

THE QUIET COURAGE OF A NURSE NAMED SARA

Ruby was in a cardiac room. That was not where she wished to be, as a matter of fact she didn't know where she wished to be, but she certainly knew it wasn't in that room, with wires, tubes, and all sorts of blinking lights and beeping machines! No, she was leaving and that was that!

This elderly woman was a lovely lady, very active in her church and community, had raised her family well and could not understand how all of this was happening to her, and she planned and schemed to escape, sometimes nearly succeeding.

Ruby had suffered a heart attack, but with the early Alzheimer disease that also had invaded her she could not put things together and know why she needed medication and medical care. For an hour or two she would be quiet, then the big eruption would take place and Ruby would be settled down, reassured and all would be quiet until the next onslaught! She decided we were jailors, molesters, monsters, and generally came to the conclusion that none of the nursing staff could be trusted, and would refuse to talk. One day her daughter came by, as she did three or four times a day, only to be met dead on with a shoe in the side of the head. Oh, yes, Ruby was a good pitcher!

The strange thing about the insidious Alzheimer disease is that it sometimes changes a person into somebody other than whom they have always been. Ruby had been a woman who never said a sworn word in her life, but now she could roll the curses off her lips, words that would make a prison inmate blush. She also had always been fastidious in her dress, makeup, hair color, and was in fact very much a lady-she had lost all of that and it was sad to see, but some days it was funny, dark, black humor, and we would have to smile at this little woman who was firing off the curse words, unhooking her monitor wires, throwing everything around her room and just absolutely destroyed her toiletries.

And it was not going to be any better, ever, that was the sad part. But one evening, just after supper, we were readying to tie up the loose ends of our work and be off duty on time when Ruby ended that plan! We heard the loud shout from around the corner, and here was Ruby, she had turned the power off on her monitor, and was standing in a hospital shirt with wires dangling, her Intravenous site bleeding and she was throwing the uppercuts like a professional boxer. It was terrible to see, so my team mate and I picked her up, body and bones, wires and curses and took her back to her room and closed the door. The goings on inside that room that night make me almost laugh in retrospect. My co-worker and I decided on sedation and I went to get it. When I got back, Ruby was finally lying down, with the other nurse straddling her on the bed. We put the pill under her tongue, she spit it out with great force, I found it in my hair in the shower later.

The battle waged on, so what to do? We made the decision to go with the injection medication, knowing we would need lots of extra bodies to help us. But Ruby was such a Rude Ruby we didn't want Sara to go into her room. Sara was a quiet, well-spoken Jamaican Nurse, and we just knew that Ruby would call her awful names, as that is what she had been doing to every minority who crossed her path in the past few weeks. Injection ready I gathered the crew, and we walked in Rubys' room, and she was wild. Sara couldn't stand all of this commotion, so she walked in too. Ruby was in a chair by then, wrapped in a roll of toilet tissue, eating cold macaroni with her nurse perched up on the windowsill-a scene right out of a 'Carry on Nurse' movie. Sara walked slowly over to Ruby, we all held our breath, scared to death that this nurse was going to be bombarded with every filthy name ever used on dark-skinned people. Sara said she could handle it, she had been called names before. We just stood back and waited for the eruption, the eruption that did not happen!

Sara reached out her hand to Ruby, who looked up at her, saw her beautiful trademark smile, with her ever present colorful hair band, and then reached out her hand to Sara. The soft tone of Saras' Jamaican voice could be heard asking "What's the trouble, Ruby? Why are you so upset?"Her voice was so gentle.

Ruby leaned over and took two of Saras' hands in hers, and by then the injection was given, as she was distracted. Then Ruby spoke. "Aren't you beautiful? So beautiful!" she said to Sara.

So Sara stayed, we all left, Sara put Ruby to bed, tucked her in, hooked up her monitor, and came out of the room an hour later grinning like a Cheshire Cat! And we applauded her. It was astounding, Ruby was like an angel to Sara, a girl she didn't know, was of a different race, and spoke so kindly-but Ruby loved her. We were pleased, but we could never figure it out and we never will!

However after that evening Sara was always called on when people would not comply. Saras' quiet courage and dignity was the turning point for Ruby, she needed very little in the way of sedation after seeing Sara, and looked for her every time the shift changed. Sara and her smile, and her kindness, what better medication for someone hurting so much. A good nurse, a brave woman, with a big kind heart, and a wonderful healing voice.

THAT'S FUNNY. HOME WE CALLS 'UM FLOWERS!

Spring had come once again to the little 'mainland' town where my lifes' journey had taken me. It had been three or four years since I graduated from 'Nurse School' as my children would call it when they were younger. Since then, life had been full. Since graduation my days were filled with wedding plans, marriage, moving away with my husband as his work took him to many different places and setting up housekeeping, making a home for ourselves took much time and we enjoyed it to the fullest. Working, budgeting expenses, making new friends, keeping in touch at all costs with those loved ones and friends left in Newfoundland made for a full life indeed. People were friendly and we never lacked for companionship or new places to go, as a couple and then as a family.

Of course as two Newfoundlanders we took our fair share of ribbing, and we took it with the Newfoundlanders' ability to laugh at ourselves. One of the things that I would express that caused a great deal of teasing, and was a source of great amusement to others in our neighborhood or at work was my genuine amazement in the spring time as my neighbors spotted the first little dandelion sprout its' little spot of yellow. Out would come the onslaught of weed killers, weed pickers, and lawnmowers. It was almost like a war zone at times. Then the moaning and the groaning would start about this terrible dandelion weed, and how would they be able to have good lawns if something wasn't done about this situation of the awfully destructive dandelion? It was so frustrating for some people that I am sure they spent countless hours planning ways to conquer this seemingly life-altering weed. In the middle of a group of friends one day, when the moaning was at its' peak, I happened to comment that I didn't know what all the fuss was about really because, and I used an exaggerated Newfoundland accent, I said 'back 'ome we calls 'um flowers'. Well, the reaction of all present would never be the same in the telling! But I can assure you I was the brunt of much teasing for long after that comment. Needless to say I had to get on with a rant and expound on my observation I had made and tell the story of why I called them flowers.

To this day I am sure it did not make too much sense to those who had to listen but I felt compelled to explain why I could not have the hatred of the dandelion that they seemed to agonize over so much. I explained it this way.

I was born on the barren, but beautiful, Labrador Coast. As an infant I was brought to Twillingate, then later my family moved to Burgeo, and then Port Saunders. My fathers' work required so many transfers but those three places in particular shaped my life the most, and was where I fell in love with the lowly dandelion. That long ago, isolated and rocky, fishing in its' heyday, a lawn was the last thing the rural Newfoundland people worried about. But as children we knew the secrets of the little yellow flower. After a long winter, with snow and ice, wind and freezing rain, the springtime sun would melt the snowy ground cover slowly but surely, and we would wait patiently for the first patches of grass and lichen to appear, and it always did. Then more grass, longer, warmer days, and then sure as shootin' there it would be- the one lone little yellow flower that would start all sorts of activities again.

Summer was coming, every day more yellow flowers, more action on the town wharf and the stage heads, then after awhile the whole community would be abuzz with everyone outside, clothes on the lines, dogs barking, bicycles everywhere, and gradually we would have thousands of yellow dandelions waving their heads in the wind. Then would come the buttercups. We had it made then, school would soon be out, picnics would start, boats launched, boilups of mussels on the beach would be a daily event, and it all would start with the pop-up of the one little yellow flower.

Every child would pick various bouquets for their mothers or grandmothers, and I wonder how many mothers' hearts were warmed by the sight of the little children with their big smiles, running toward them in their Koolaid or Freshie stained shirts, scraped knees, and chubby little hands reaching up with the precious handpicked gift of carefully chosen treasures? How many mothers put the tiny buttercup blooms under little chins and asked "Do you like butter? Oh, yes you do, I see the yellow on your chin!" And of course everyone had the reflection on their chin so the children would run off to try the trick on their fathers or grandfathers, because they were the most challenging for the buttercup trick, especially if they had a beard.

The dandelion blooms would get bigger and bigger, the bumblebees would start their work, then it was time to have a little jar with a hole poked in the lid to maintain an oxygen supply we believed, and we would spend hours trying to capture a bumblebee, only to release it in an hour or so. Just curious as to what they looked like. This activity was a rite of passage and probably continues to this day. All of a sudden one day the dandelion blooms would start turning into big fluffy seed filled balls. This caused another activity, chasing each other and blowing the fluff into each others hair.

Such carefree days, such innocent fun, such clean enjoyment, and all because of the dandelion. It brought me so much pleasure that I cannot develop any animosity toward the little weed that we always called 'flowers'.

I don't know if the point ever reached my audience really. The teasing continued, and it was always a laugh, and of course the word was passed around that Bonnie actually liked those awful weeds. And my mainland life continued on.

Then the neighborhood started to grow. More houses were built, new people moved in, families grew, swing sets gave way to having the occasional pool installed, and the children enjoyed their bicycles, but only in driveways never on the precious lawns, which by now were luscious and weed free. Then of course came the time that something had to be done to protect all those lovely lawns so the weed man was hired by everyone, and it had to be everyone because it one person did not treat their lawn, they would grow weeds, which in turn would go to seed and attack the other lawns. So, I too, had the weed man.

There were two years of weed spraying before the neighborhood was given notice to keep pets and children off all sprayed areas of grass for twenty-four hours after the application of the spray. In the 85*-90* still summer afternoons the truck would arrive and the men would jump out and apply face masks, and spray some awful smelling chemical on every blade of grass to be seen. People got sick, developed rashes and headaches, nausea and vomiting. Everyone would suffer in some way. Pets who were unfortunate enough to get outside would be very sick, some more than others. I know of one little much loved cat that convulsed, was rushed to the animal hospital, but died, leaving a young girl in tears for a week. On one occasion I, thinking after two days it would be safe, put my lovely big Peruvian Guinea Pig out on the grass for a sense of freedom from his cage. When I went to check him , he had died, his freshly shampooed fur blowing softly in the light summer breeze. I was heartbroken, and I knew the grass he had eaten had poisoned him. I quit getting the weed man that day. I felt the guilt of being so vain, being so foolhardy to bend to the pressure of exposing my family and pets to the noxious spray.

Gradually, one by one, the neighbors began to realize too that something was not right. They got together and requested the new environmentally friendly weed killer. And the lawns were all beautiful, no weeds, and only the occasional pet to be seen. Slowly the kids started off to college and couples started to say, no more spraying, its' too darned expensive.

And so it went. I still remember that chemical smell, the headaches, and I clearly remember my lost pet. After deciding to retire and return to Newfoundland, the land of the dandelion bouquets and strong family ties, we found ourselves living on the land where my husband grew up.

I mow the large lawn on the homestead property here, and a

few days ago I saw the first little yellow flower, the dandelion. There will be no spraying here, not in this little nook in Trinity Bay. My cat can fun freely, the dandelions can grow and so can the buttercups because we are home now and 'back here we still calls 'um flowers!"

OOOOOHO BABY

It was a quiet uneventful Friday afternoon at our hospital. Two of us, being Operating Room nurses, were on call for the weekend.

We had checked with all the units before we left the building and all was under control so it was a good time to take advantage of and buy groceries, or run errands, because the weekend could have us in the Operating Room for hours. Busy working mothers have to take advantage of any and all time available to them.

My team mate headed to buy bedding plants and I headed to the grocery store. We had our beepers but didn't really think we had cause to be on high alert having just left the hospital.

Half an hour later, with a cart full of groceries, my beeper started that annoying high-pitched beep that those old beepers had. The message just said "Call supervisor immediately-Emergency!" Thank heavens I knew the store well, and knew exactly where the office and phone were. I called the supervisor who was in a state of high anxiety, I could tell by her voice that we had trouble, big trouble!

"Just get here," she said, "we have an emergency, a Caesarean Section. Hurry!"

This was crazy, bizarre, as our obstetrical department had closed a year ago, and there was nothing going on an hour ago, so what was the story here? I pushed my grocery cart at the young man working at the store and jumped into my car, four way flashers on, and headed for the hospital, my head filled with scenarios, my mind going through the instrumentation for the C-section, as it was my turn to be the scrub nurse, the nurse who handles the sterile instruments and assists the surgeon and his assistant.

My partner arrived the same time as I, and we immediately went into work mode, hardly taking time to speak. The supervisor called to see if we were ready. It was then she told us the drama that had been unfolding from the time we left the hospital until now.

We worked at a hospital in Windsor, Nova Scotia, known as the 'gateway to the valley'. And that Valley was the Annapolis Valley with all its' apples and beautiful gardens. But today was not a good day for the Valley, or for the mother-to-be that had a baby in obvious distress, and was being transferred by ambulance to the Grace Hospital in Halifax.

She had started out in Middleton in an ambulance accompanied by a doctor, nurse and two paramedics. No surgeon was available in Middleton so another town named Berwick was contacted. Their surgeon was in the middle of an emergency case, so the decision was made to rapidly get the patient to the Grace Hospital in Halifax.

As the ambulance with its' worried medical team and patient approached Kentville, the babies' heartbeat was dangerously low. Kentville's hospital was contacted, but no, they could be of no assistance as their surgeon had just cut himself badly with a lawnmower. No other surgeon was available because the surgeon who had cut himself was the only one on call, and the only one in town on this beautiful summer day. Nothing was going right at his point.

So they proceeded on and contacted Windsors' Hants Community Hospital, our hospital, and yes we did have a surgeon who was available and skilled in the C-SECTION area, having done so many throughout his career. The decision was made to bring the mother-to- be to our hospital as the ambulance doctor radioed that it was now an extreme emergency. He was of the opinion that they would not be able to make it to Halifax. So on Highway 101, five minutes from Windsor, they let us know they would be there in a few minutes and the patient needed to go straight to the Operating Room.

The Nursing Supervisor had contacted the surgeon, alerted the OR nurses, the doctor to care for the baby as soon as he or she was delivered, the anesthetist, and the Emergency room staff to help admit the patient when the ambulance arrived.

And we were ready! The doctor with the patient, and the nurse came to the OR with her, feeling the necessity to stick with a patient they had been with through such a nerve-wracking experience. Not wanting anything to interfere with their relationship with their mother-to-be, which is how one gets to think about a patient that you have bonded with, they felt they wanted to see her through to the birth of her baby.

In five short but anxious minutes after coming to our Operating Room a healthy baby boy was born. Both mother and baby did well, and the mother went to the Recovery Room with one of us, while the other did the pick-up and restocking of the Operating Suite itself. The baby was transported by a special cart, one that had its' own Oxygen supply and all that was necessary for care of the newborn, to the Nursery.

There was no time for delay, no time to know the patients' name, just time to do what had to be done, and we did it!

Later on we received a warm and beautifully worded letter of appreciation from the patients' doctor, a young man who was so determined that his patient would have a healthy baby and was willing to go the last mile with her. We loved the letter. I wonder about that baby sometimes. He would be twelve years old now, and probably has been told the details of his fast ride through the Valley every year on his birthday. But what he doesn't know is how proud we were to have a healthy baby born that day, how relieved, and how teamwork, a strong bond between his nurses, and his doctors, helped get him into this world.

And one thing for sure, he doesn't know that we think of him, and the awful predicament his mother and her doctor and teams were in that day, and how gratifying it was to know that we, with our acquired skills, and good old 'Nurses Know How', combined with his team of doctors' knowledge and skills, and the facilities of a little rural hospital could play such a great role to help him enter this world, all ten pounds of him. Yes, we think of you, wherever you are! And we wish you a happy and contented life after your rough arrival! Godspeed little boy!

ONE SIZE DOES NOT FIT ALL!

There is, as the well worn phrase goes, 'a fine line between sanity and insanity'. And I know that shopping for clothes inches me ever so close to tipping over into the insanity pool. As a matter of fact I wonder if that tipping has already happened, and I just haven't recognized the fact.

At the age of sixteen, with an androgynous figure, shopping was a breeze. But now, thirty-seven years later, two children, added pounds and the force of gravity, all add up to making the shopping ordeal just that-a big ordeal! No two companies make their garments in the same size range-a size 12 may be a size 10 in one line of shirts, and that same size 12 may be size 16 in another line. It is just as well you buy a pair of drapes, sheets, or a large bath towel and head for home accepting the defeat. At least you will have something to cover you so you won't be charged with public mischief or creating a disturbance.

Little tops that bare the navel, the size large that looks like something only a seven year old could wear, neon colors, stripes that go around the body instead of running up and down-which everyone knows the size 12 and up needs to wear, skirts that bare it all, are not for the 50-plus baby boomers. Most of us are new grandmothers now . The time has come in our lives to give up the fashion trends of the day, and accept who we are, what are bodies require, and most of us do.

However the clothing companies are slow to catch up to those of us who need more than those tiny tops that allow the ring in the navel to be shown to the world. Our navels are our own business, and they are not for show, even if we could all find them! We need the one good outfit, with style and comfort being the goal, and then we need to choose the accessories that will dress up that one outfit, or dress it down, depending on the occasion. Now if such an occasion does arise, we will have to forego our comfy cotton pants and t-shirts that we wear for gardening, fishing, reading, doing housework, running errands and in fact, just plain live in, and wear that special outfit.

After a particularly long day of shopping for that 'special outfit', plowing through little clothing stores jammed tight with all sorts of garments, hangers scraping the rods they hung on, dressing rooms with florescent light that make you look like a bleached whale whose lipstick turned purple, I found the perfect solution to calm the spirit and soothe the soul. The famous Erma Bombeck whose writing I dearly love, said in one of her works that the only time she ever fainted was when she tried on a bathing suit in a small dressing room under the ever present florescent light, while wearing a pair of knee-high hose. She looked in the mirror, she reported, and fainted dead away! And I believe that can happen, and that is when you tip into that pool of insane, driven women, who have 'shopped 'til they dropped'.

My solution came quite by accident about six years ago. My daughter and I were shopping, and we had been to every store in Halifax, and I had no luck. The one outfit that would be perfect was brown, and I would rather wear a mascot chicken suit than anything brown, so consequently I had found nothing, and had a daughter who was becoming a bit out of sorts with me. Then the enlightening moment happened. I wandered into a store that catered to large, tall men and women. I spied an outfit in a cranberry color, exactly the style I wanted and I was elated. Thank heavens, some success at last. So I sought the clerk, and proceeded to ask her about the outfit. She told me all the particulars, price, types of material, and what was best to wear with it. Things were looking up.

"What size do you need dear?" she asked gingerly, all the while studying me over her glasses as if mentally measuring.

"Fourteen, depends on the style, might go to a twelve, might go to a sixteen, you can't go by sizes so I just need to try it on, so I'll start with the fourteen." I rambled on under her gaze.

At that, she took off her half-glasses and stuck one of the ear pieces in between her teeth.

"Oh, dear," she said, "I am so sorry, but we do not carry anything in a size that small!"

Well, that was a defining moment! I thanked her and left. I never asked about the sixteen, I never said a word, I couldn't speak. I was so ecstatic I was floating.

I told my daughter what had happened when she caught up to me, because by then I was heading to the other store that catered to larger sizes. 'NOTHING THAT SMALL' –well, I was thrilled, and I am sure temporarily insane. My daughter was disgusted, so without purchasing a thing, we left for home.

That was ten years ago, and since that day, whenever I am feeling disgusted and frustrated on a shopping trip I look for the stores that carry the large sizes. And guaranteed they will say at some point that they do not have anything small enough for me! And I am walking on air for weeks. It is the perfect solution, makes me feel fantastic, and doesn't cost a cent.

And that is my quiet way of dealing with the frustration of shopping for clothes. It doesn't mean I won any great war, but I surely win the battle to preserve my sanity for one day longer.

Too bad my dear daughter can't come along because she lives far away. But she says she wouldn't join me anyway. She maintains I have a somewhat odd way of achieving self-satisfaction!

I say it keeps me out of that 'insanity pool' and live to shop another day!!

ROOTS AND WINGS

On a pleasant September afternoon in 1976 I sat in the sunlight finishing a costume for my little five-year-old son to wear in the children s' parade at a local exhibition. My baby girl was asleep, and my husband at work, and it was so quiet. Music drifted from the stereo, but my mind was not as settled as it may have been on any other given day.

This was my little boys' first day at school. I had walked him to the bus stop in the morning, and coming back home I could not stop the tears, nor the fears, that this milestone was causing. I wondered how he would manage on his first school day, and how I would get through a long day without him. But I was busy with a toddler, and time passed fairly quickly. I seemed to be coping fairly well until my husband arrived home. He stood leaning on the door, watching me work on the costume. And then he spoke the words that brought all the tears to the surface.

"You miss him don't you?", he asked quietly.

The next hour was a blur as I looked at the world through tears. My husband consoled me, then we worked together for a few minutes putting the finishing touches on our sons' bicycle. Completing the decorating was much more difficult with blurred vision. However I found myself laughing through the tears, my husband left to go back to work, the baby awoke, and in a short time Johns' school bus was back.

We had all survived that first break, that first letting go, that first day apart. It was always John, Heather and Mom, together every day, while Dad went to work. I had taken a break in my career to be home with the children and I have never regretted doing so. I am grateful that I could be with them. As I look at them now at the ages of thirty-two and twenty-eight, I realize that the time with them then was worth its' seconds in diamonds.

This week the children are all decked out in new jeans, sneakers, beautifully colored backpacks and lunch kits, fresh hair cuts and wide smiles. For the occasional little children there are tears as they face their first days at school. A whole new world opens for them, new friends to be made, new places to see, and new rules to follow. Some children are more stressed than others, but they go and soon they are coming home with stories of their teacher, schoolmates, and grand chronicles of what someone did or didn't do.

Life as a student has started for each child, and for each child going to school for the first time, there is a mother with a lump in her throat and an ache in her heart. Until now the children have been totally 'Moms' charges. But not anymore. The time has come to share them with the world, to encourage them to have wings, preparing them for flight eventually. But for these first few days the mother's heart is aching. Something has come between her and the child whose life she holds dear, the child, that once born, made her for ever more vulnerable, protective, and acutely aware of potential dangers everywhere.

However to hold them back, to not encourage their growth and development, does them no favor. It is our duty to give them a stable home life, good food, care for their health and keep them safe. We create their roots by surrounding them with family, friends, books, music, and pets. We introduce them to the wonders of our world, and at the same time teach them safety rules and coping mechanisms to prepare them for life away from the cocoon of 'home'.

My son was joined in school by his sister a few years later. He was 'a big brother', keeping a keen eye on his sister that he has always adored. And since that first day of school for my son many tears have been shed, many hilarious bouts of laughter have taken place, hundreds of good-byes have been muttered into coat collars, thousands of waves of hello and good-bye as they moved up through school, left for a center of higher education, finally flying away to another province. Countless phone calls, sleepless nights, and reunions have occurred for us since the first day apart.

It has been twenty-seven years since John took that first school bus ride from the end of a lane in a little place outside Lunenburg, Nova Scotia. He paved the way for his sister who couldn't wait to join him wherever he happened to be. Yes, many years since that question by my husband and their father caused the tears to flow. He probably had tears too.

"You miss him don't you?"

Yes, I certainly do miss him, and I miss her too. My son and my daughter are part of me, as is my tiny grand daughter. But 'Roots and Wings' are what we as parents are obligated to give them.

The 'Roots' were easy at times, difficult at other times. Developing traditions as a family, growing and learning, riding out the rough spots, and helping each other, created a strong bond and a close unit, giving them the tools that prepared them to leave the nest.

But the 'Wings'- letting them go, taking flight with the very wings we gave them is by far the most difficult challenge. However, it has to be if they are to establish their own lives. Gradually we adjust, but we still long for the door to open and the lunch kits to come flying in, followed by the laughter and crazy jokes they brought home with them.

So, your child left for school, university, or a new job did they?

You will miss them, won't you? But it will be OK. You have given them their 'Wings'. It is how it is meant to be.

THE HOSPITAL ROOM

BEDSIDE TABLE-COURSE–101

As a nurse of lots of years of experience I can say, without a doubt, that there should be, ought to be, needs to be, and maybe sometime will be, a COURSE 101 ON BEDSIDE TABLES! I may have to be the one who constructs such an odd sort of learning tool. However, I have been known to do odd things before and it bothers me not, so I most likely will do the scattered odd thing again! Writing this narrative may be one of the odd 'things' for which I will become known! What odds, as they say in Newfoundland-No fools, No fun!

Let's start with this little piece of furniture that is called the 'bedside table'. Obviously this, to be in a hospital room, has a reason to be there, a functional reason, and is to be used for that purpose. This little table, usually with a small drawer, and a door opening underneath the drawer, is designed to hold the tools and supplies that the patient needs for daily care, products for good hygiene, and good oral care. On the top of the table sits the ubiquitous box of Kleenex, and sometimes a telephone. The only time, and this is true, the very only time you will find this table filled with just the right materials, and topped with the aforesaid items is in an empty room. It is just as it should be at that time, then, and only then.

A nurse should approach any and all bedside tables with a suspicious attitude, and with the light on. It can be hazardous to the nurses' mental and physical health to open that drawer to find something in the dark, and this should be applied to opening the bottom door of the table as well. And the longer the patients stay, the more careful one should become.

I have seen things in drawers of bedside tables that would make Stephen King run, seen items in the locker that would make the most stiff upper lips quiver. It is a danger zone!

Remove all needless foodstuffs at the first opportunity, such things as moldy grapes, half oranges, and apples. The fruit flies will lead you to the bananas stored behind the urinal, destroy those as well. Keep only items that are wrapped commercially and sealed until use. This may take a certain degree of decorum and diplomacy on the nurses' part as the patient may be annoyed, or worse, angry. Make sure the water you throw out is not the Holy Water Father Murphy left yesterday, but any glass with a scum on top needs to be tossed.

Cautiously approach any and all materials, Kleenex or clothing, until you have ascertained if they are one day or one month old, clean or dirty, wet or dry. Old hospital meal menus can go, as can the tape and cotton swab from sixty blood collection days. When all is done, the patient will be grateful that you found the time to help clean the mess or be hanging off the side of the bed reaching for the garbage can you have just placed in the hallway.

Yes, those little tables have sent many a nurse into a rant! And I am one of them! I have found everything under the sun stored in those little compartments, bottles of rum, old liniment that burned my eyes, black bean soup with mold, and on one occasion never to be forgotten a big beach bag full of live 'Welsh terrier," to this day we don't know how long that patient had that little dog in her room!! But it was cute, both the dog and the hat it was wearing!

Puzzle books, notes, cards, are all acceptable, even the little plants, but not the bottle of fireflies, the dog, or the hamster.

Experienced nurses learned all of this the hard way, so new nurses, take heed, those innocent tables are sitting in wait, ready to rid you of any stability you have remaining.

So goes the first draft of 'BEDSIDE TABLES 101', may you find them all clean and tidy during your career, and may that hospital you work in get patients someday, because the empty room bedside table is the only SAFE storage area!

THINGS YOU CAN BE SURE OF

1. Your first shift on a new unit will be the busiest day they have ever had.
2. The nurse assigned to orientate you will be one who does not like to teach.
3. The doctors will ignore you until they check you out with the senior nurses.
4. The bell that rings at three o'clock in the morning will be at the end of the hall.
5. The drug count will be incorrect the day you're in a hurry to get to a social do.
6. The patient you least expect will be the one to complain about the nurses.
7. The patient who lives on Kraft dinner will complain about the food.
8. Put everything possible on your med cart but the one thing they want you will not have.
9. The man who told you he quit drinking will finally admit that he only did so the day before admission, and he admits that only when the DTs' start.
10. The nurse you first saw and thought quite grumpy will turn out to be a wonderful mentor and friend, given the chance.
11. If that bra strap is going to break it will do so while you are doing CPR.
12. The day you arrive dressed as a nun for Halloween will be the day the new handsome single doctor arrives to make rounds.
13. You will eat enough cold meals that when a hot supper is served you are scared to death of the steam rising from it.
14. If your heart aches and you think you have hidden it, one of

the older patients will pick up on it and you will talk to her/him as you would a therapist. It is human nature.
15. Nursing care plans are tedious, but photocopying can be fun!
16. Styrofoam used in crafts makes a lot of noise in the middle of the night, especially when you not the craft maker.
17. Everybody is important to the running of a good unit, housekeeping, maintenance, ward clerks and volunteers all make it happen!
18. Instruments are not all in multiples of five as you have been told, as there are six of some things, eleven of others, and eighteen of even more.
19. The sick patient picks up on everything the nurse does, says, moves, repositions or touches. It is their small world in that room, try to bring something positive into it.
20. Nurses will most likely be the worst patients, best friends, trusted confidantes, amazing practical jokesters, and you yourself will be all of these and more.
21. In a room of five hundred people the three or four nurses will find each other although they have never met.
22. Nursing will bring you down, help you recover, and then lift you back up.
23. Whatever you teach a young nurse for the first time she will associate you with for the rest of her career.
24. The family of a dying patient needs you to lean on, talk to, and cry in front of, and it is OK for you to cry too.
25. Nursing is a gift, a talent, an acquired skill, a vocation, and most of all you can count on it being ever changing but yet in some ways staying the same. You are a Nurse!!

IT'S JUST A BAG OF BIRD FOOD!

The time of year had come again when the pheasants hunted and scratched around my back yard in search of some tidy morsel of food. They were the male pheasants and were spectacular in color, and so interesting to watch. The kind of interesting that makes your supper burn on the pan while you stand at the open window with the zoom lens aimed at the magnificent birds, just wanting that special shot! They are amazing, with their white ring around their necks and their plumage a mix of earth colors.

At work we discussed all sorts of things, ranging from travel, kids, recipes, how to set up for a surgical case, who likes what suture and if Marilyn was working you could be sure the conversation would take the wildest of turns.

Marilyn was my on-call buddy in the Operating Room. I considered her my mentor and friend, and still do. She was a virtual cornucopia of knowledge, being widely read and having so many diverse interests. She also knew how to console, how to make us laugh, and told us often how 'not to sweat the small stuff'. You just never knew when Marilyn would pounce, bringing up some subject that she knew would cause the conversation to become very animated, and sometimes very controversial.

I used to call my mentor a 'lady of means', because she had so many means and ways to do duties that entertained as well as annoyed, depending on how well you knew her. Marilyn didn't care, she had worked for 'one hundred years and seen it all' she would say.

So enter the pheasants as I sought advice from our 'lady of means' on how to go about getting some feed for them. She gave me the history of the pheasant, why the males had he bright colors, how long their gestational period was, how many there were in our area, how they had different calls for different reasons, and finally we got to my question, "Just what do I buy to feed the pheasants?"

"Oh," she says, "just buy a bag of cracked corn. Stop by the farm Store on the way home. Tell the cashier you want a bag of cracked corn and she'll give you a slip to take around back and the men will put it in the trunk for you. It's only seven or eight dollars." OK. Now, after all that I knew they ate cracked corn.

When I stopped at the farm store, I considered my situation. A busy working on-call mom, and ten or so pheasants, so I may as well get two bags while I'm on the cracked corn quest, and I'll have enough to do me for a while, depending on how fast they ate. I paid for two bags, stopped at the warehouse, the men put it into my trunk and I headed home. Well, that was easy I thought! Thank Heavens for Marilyn!

But I had a severe shock awaiting me! After arriving home and taking my packages into the house, I went to collect the birds' feed from my trunk. Imagine my reaction when I opened that trunk to find it absolutely full of cracked corn, each bag weighing EIGHTY-EIGHT pounds, a little fact that my dear Marilyn had forgotten to mention. I couldn't pick it up, it seemed to flow away from me, it was becoming quite clear to me that I was in a bit of a pickle, the birds would have to be fed from the car. How was I to explain this? I couldn't believe I had ONE HUNDRED AND SEVENTY-SIX POUNDS of bird food!

My son arrived home, took a look and howled, but did regroup enough to carry the bags to the shed, mainly because he possessed brute strength, but his laughing made his chore difficult!

I called Marilyn to tell her my shock, and ask her why she didn't tell me how big the bags were?

"Well, now you'll have enough" she said.

"What do you mean enough, I have too much, I'll never use it all?!" by now I'm in meltdown mode.

"You have approximately ten pheasants, and one pheasant will eat so many ounces a day, and maybe he'll visit twice a day and so if you ....!"

I interrupted her mathematical data study. I had to try not to laugh too much. She had it all figured out. But after all I thought "It's only bird food!", and well-fed pheasants they were that winter! And there was still enough cracked corn for the mothers and baby pheasants in the spring.

The only difficulty was in listening to the song, wherever I went after my foray into the world of pheasants, "Jimmy cracked corn, and I don't care!" over and over.

It was only a bit of bird food after all.

MICHAEL AND VALERIE-A LOVE STORY

I found a photograph today. I was not looking for it, so maybe it found me. I was riveted where I sat, staring into the photograph and emotions too strong to ignore came rising to the surface. This small piece of paper had a grip on me and I had a grip on it. The photograph was taken at my daughters' wedding reception in 1998. The faces of two good friends, with big wide smiles were in the little photo. They looked happy, so much in love, content to be together, and enjoying each other and the wedding. The photograph showed me the faces of Michael and Valerie, a couple with plans and hopes and dreams, and they were my friends. Michael was the local funeral director, Valerie was a nursing team mate of mine, and they both worked hard, gave a lot, and were steadfast in their love for each other and their families and friends.

They had only been married eight years, but both were in their forties. Mike as he was known, was in his second marriage, he had married for the first time at the age of seventeen, his wife even younger. Over the years they raised three lovely children and as happens when people marry so young, the time came when the kids were older and the couple realized they had indeed outgrown each other, growing up with their children. And both decided to move on. Then Valerie came into his life.

Val, as she was known, was a single parent, her son in his late teens when she met Mike. So together they had four grown children. When the photo was taken, they were already grandparents and loved it. Val with her gift for embroidery and quilting, a wonderful nurse with a special touch and quiet manner, Mike with his gift for singing, music, and entertaining, all accompanied by a boisterous laugh led the couple to have a busy lifestyle and they treasured the moments they had together.

I let myself float in the sea of memories of them as a couple. Their love was limitless, boundless and secure. I attended their wedding in 1990, a wedding that had Vals' touch, simple yet elegant, casual but mindful of the seriousness of the commitment she had made, and she looked as radiant as any bride I had ever seen and Mike beamed. He called her his 'Doll' and after the wedding, the name 'Doll' stayed, others picked it up, even our nursing team. Mike, with his work, would have to visit our unit often, causing Val to blush and walk straight to his side, getting her kiss on the cheek, then we knew to step back, Mike and Val would do what needed to be done with the paperwork, and she would accompany him until he left the hospital. They dealt with death and dying every day of their lives, as we all did, and shed tears together, as we all did, but they carried on with life, as we all did.

Doing work so closely associated with death brings you to the reality that we never know what tomorrow may bring. The memories kept surfacing, the photo of two huge bright red strawberries on a white background of a china plate that I had enlarged and framed for their wedding gift, doing a small one for myself, the times I swore off junk food forever and would walk in our conference room to see Val munching on her bag of hickory sticks or potato chips and during listening to the taped report from the last shift she would casually push the bags' open end my way and that would be the end of that resolution. Those treats were so good, and she knew I would never refuse. We laughed many times over how Val had the ability to knock me off the latest resolution of eating no more junk food. Val loved her treats, and she shared them willingly. Both Val and I were the oldest of five siblings, and on night duty we would talk, share our stories, and we were a team, Joy and Cheryl were our other team mates usually and we had one strong bond, and a system of working that was efficient and good, and we knew it. We worked, laughed, played, teased, comforted, arranged, and ran our own lives and those of our patients on a regular basis. 'Strong women who work too hard' I used to say, and they would listen to my rant, have their say and on we would go. Going to work, knowing this team was there, made life so much easier. Mike was well known and loved by everyone. I never ever knew anyone that did not adore Mike. He had been that way since childhood, his big easy smile and laughter that glided on the wind, his love of his children and his 'Doll' and his precious dog, a German Shepherd named Farrah, his grandchildren, his work, caring for the home they bought, keeping the lawn and flowers cared for, made for one heck of a content man. I pulled into their driveway one day in June, 2000. We were moving back to Newfoundland and I had told Val she could have my bulletin board for their computer station. Mike was on the lawn playing with his dog, laughing, jumping, and it made a sensational picture that has stayed with me to this day.

"Hi, Bon, Doll is not here dear." He said as he approached my car.

"That's OK, I came to see you anyway, we never have any time alone!" I told him. And the laughter started, the dog jumped and squealed and I got out to give him the bulletin board, and we both leaned on the car and talked about 'life', and that day was the last day I would ever see Mike. It is unbelievable to me that the world does not have him in it that Val lost him so quickly, that the dreams turned to dust, the plans went awry, and Val crawled into herself with grief, bitterness and anger. And a young man of forty-nine was snatched in the blink of an eye.

We left Nova Scotia at the end of June 2000 and returned to our Island of Newfoundland. Not being able to cut the ties quickly, nor do I ever want to cut them, those three women, Joy, Cheryl and Valerie stayed in my heart, and we corresponded regularly. I was retiring and it was hard to let go.

Fall came to Newfoundland, the colors of the leaves, the splendor of the sunsets and being back home was a wonderful feeling. And then I heard the crushing news. Mike was sick. He had seen a doctor. He, a nonsmoker, needed a lung biopsy. He had the biopsy and did not do well. He was very sick and Val was scared. She had unfaltering support from family and friends, but it was Mike she wanted. She wanted him to get well, they had so much they wanted to do, so much love to share for years to come. This was like a nightmare to her. She is quiet and she kept her own counsel but everyone worried. Life was good for them, Val had started working part-time so they could be together more, grandchildren were coming, yes it was a sweet, lovely time in their lives.

One morning in early November of that year my daughter called from Calgary to tell me we had lost Mike. I had a pain in my chest, I felt myself spinning, feeling faint, and I wondered if it was true, how did she know that in Calgary already? I had not heard. But in a small town like Windsor, Nova Scotia, word travels fast and a friend had called her. I was dazed by it all, by the loss, worried about Val, and concerned for her.

It happened so quickly. He had not been well after his procedure but came home. He was told he needed treatment for the lung tumor. And the two of them leaned on each other, and prayed. Then one morning Val awoke to hear strange sounds coming from the kitchen, running to find Mike in obvious distress and unable to stand. She lay him down, called 911, Farrah barking in the background, and told them to get there quick, this was serious. Mike could not breathe, and she stayed beside him giving constant reassurance.

But she tells me now that at one point he looked at her with those blue eyes looked straight into hers and she knew he was saying "Good-bye–it is over-I love you," and he was right. He died at the hospital shortly after nine o'clock that morning, a blood clot had developed in his lung. He was gone. Every one of our team mates was called and they arrived at our hospital in various states of emotion, dress, and undress. Val needed them. And it was pandemonium. But it was over. Our Mike with the big laugh, the sweet kisses for his 'doll', his laughter, his music, his love of life, was gone. And nothing could be done but deal with the grief.

It is 2004 now, and the three of them came to visit Newfoundland, came to visit my husband and I last summer. They arrived in Cheryls' van, tired from the trip, each wearing a crazy white straw hat with the price tags hanging off, and the reunion was glorious. It was the first time I had seen Val since Mike died so for me I had all the extra hugs to give her that I wanted to for so long. They had a great visit, saw the puffins in Bonavista, fished a cod, had a trip on our bigger boat and enjoyed a fish chowder my husband had made on the boat. The day we fished in the small boat was freezing, with wind and rain, but they never complained. They wanted to take it all in, and I tried my best to see that they did.

We had an iceberg in Trinity Bay last summer. Our excursion one day was to go in the bigger boat, the 'Ocean Joy' and see the iceberg. This was something none of my friends had experienced before. They took shots of the 'bergy bits' not realizing the immensity and drama of the bigger berg. We rounded the headland, the sea was calm, the skies bright blue, and there sat this huge, beautiful iceberg, tinged with a pastel turquoise color at the base. I will never forget that moment. Cheryl squealed in delight, Joy cried and Val had tears on her face as she said to me quietly, "I wish Mike could see this." And I assured her that I was positively sure he was seeing it, as sure as I am that a love so strong keeps him watching over her.

Yes, Mike was snatched from us, but Val loves him still, concentrates on the grandchildren, and gradually she moves through the stages of grief. Her bitterness is easing somewhat, I see that by the lovely e-mail cards she sends me, the way she speaks of the airplane ride a friend gave us, the moose we saw, her story of the quilt she is going to do, and she tries hard to go on alone. There is one assurance that I give Valerie, and that is the absolute certainty that she and Mike shared more love in those ten years together than some people do in a lifetime. And she agrees. She remembers her friends, plans outings with her children and grandchildren, and a piece of her heart is missing. We all know that, and we are powerless to replace it. But she knows we care, that she is loved and appreciated, and her sorrow is our sorrow too.

I placed the photograph back into the slot labeled 'people', then I took it back out .It is going in a frame, and will sit on my desk as a reminder that life is a gift, a gift we are given but can be taken away, and to make the best of each day. We, Vals' friends have not walked that road, but we know someday we may. As nurses, we see the fragility of this gift of life. I love my friend, and I loved her husband for the man he was. He left his mark on my heart too. Now he is a beautiful picture, in a beautiful silver frame.

And as for Valerie, she will carry Michael in her heart forever. She is good and sweet, and I am sure the evenings' twilight will find her gentle still.

LISTEN TO YOUR NURSE!

The small rural hospital in Windsor, Nova Scotia, had the distinction of being situated close to the highway. The nurses who worked in the Emergency Department had seen more than their fair share of odd characters. One day in particular a very strange and obviously chemically fogged young man wandered in with a badly fractured arm. He was loud, verbally abusive, obnoxious, and in tremendous pain, which did not help his temperament. He wouldn't give too many details about himself or the fractured arm, saying that someone had dropped him off on the highway and he walked to our hospital. He produced a health card from another province, said that he was whoever the name on the card said he was, and it had to be left at that for now. He was prepared for the Operating Room and brought to us in the OR in a fairly sedated condition. His arm was realigned by the surgeon, a cast applied and he was taken to the Recovery Room. We all waited for him to wake, wondering what his reaction would be after an anesthetic.

And wake he did, yelling, banging, screaming, punching and none of us could calm him even with the Morphine that was administered. It was utter chaos in that room, and thank heavens he was in there alone. I thought at the time that I was fairly fit and strong, but I was no match for this difficult out of control man. And being struck in the head by a plaster of Paris cast didn't help!

Finally my friend and coworker, Dolores walked in, and walked up to the aggressive man, with us warning her to watch the flying fists and pillows.

"Oh, yeah, we'll see about that!" she said over her shoulder. All those years in Emergency Room Nursing before coming to the Operating Room had taught her how to deal with the combatant patient.

She looked down at the wild unmanageable young man and said loudly "Lie down, be quiet, and stop being so mean to those nurses. Do you hear me?"

Everybody held their breath.

"Why should I listen to you?" the patient asked, his cast punching at her while she stood just far enough out of reach to really anger him. "You're not God are ya?" he went on to say.

With that 'Dolores the Daring' put her hands on her hips, ready for battle, and pulled herself up to her full five feet two inch height.

"No, I am not God! However I am one of his angels and you are going to lie down and be quiet this minute! Do you understand me?" she bellowed.

The angry young man looked her up and down, flopped back on the pillow and never uttered another swear word, or threw another punch. After that moment everything changed. He turned completely around, used please and thank you when appropriate, even at one point saying 'Thank you, I really appreciate it!"

Dolores kept dropping in to assess him from time to time, he even went so far as to smile at her.

We were speechless with astonishment! And we all watched her as she went on to her other work.

"Ya just gotta know their language and give it back to 'em!" she told us as we stood with our mouths open.

And certainly nobody was going to argue that point after witnessing this interaction. Thereafter she was given the nickname "ANGEL", a name she certainly earned and deserved. Unconventional approach maybe - but effective. And Dolores entered our memories never to be forgotten!! She said all it came down to was the fact that these rude people needed to be told they were rude, and it was totally unacceptable .And that was that!!

She was so right!!

WHEN THE LIGHT OF THE NURSE FLICKERS AND DIES

She is a nurse, a woman, a daughter, a mother, a wife, she is the organizer and chief controller of dental appointment, doctors' appointments, she has to be at the soccer and baseball games, get the kids to music lessons, arranging her schedule to accommodate everyone, and she is tired, tired all the time! She feels guilty if she takes a day off sick, she runs to the grocery store late at night, and tries to look reasonably normal to everyone, family, friends, patients and most of all herself. But she is far from being normal, and as each day passes, as each shift at work becomes more chaotic and hectic, as each thing she forgets becomes more of a major issue, she begins to realize that she is sick. She is sick and tired of it all, all the time, she is not sleeping, she eats junk food as a pick-me-up as she is running on the human version of a 'hamster wheel', and after a few months of this she will crash. She will not be able to find the effort to take a shower, to buy the groceries or cook a meal, and she certainly cannot care for the sick. She has become BURNED OUT! And everyone who knows her will wonder 'why' or 'how come' or the news around town will be that she has had a breakdown for any number of gossipy reasons. Really what has happened is she has used her last dribble of energy, and the time has come to reassess and nobody is more surprised than she! Spending days feeling guilty, hours feeling hopeless, considering her future and feeling like a failure, she will cry tears of utter desperation. She is a NURSE, and now she is a shell, because she is human and her resources are all used up. She needs time off duty, time to rest and treat herself well, and it is the hardest thing she has ever done.

Most nurses, if they have a fairly lengthy career, sooner or later will succumb to this sinister, all pervasive and creeping infection of the soul that is called BURNOUT. The nature of our work is itself draining, and the systems in a state of disorder and relentless frustration, the lack of extra hands to help, all add up to a massive split in our hearts. And there is no choice but to step back and let time heal you, because now you are the patient.

During shift change report one night I noticed my team mates face. Tears were running down her cheeks, and she couldn't continue. I turned the recorder off and we talked. I knew how she felt, I had been there, twice in fact, and I made the joke that I was now 'toast'! This had not happened to Lisa before, but everyone who had been there saw it coming. She had not been sleeping for months, not a good sleep, she was experiencing nightmares, she was more short tempered than anybody had ever seen her before, she was losing interest in life, and she could not leave the hospital behind when she went home, calling in numerous times on her days off for various things. Her social life had dwindled to nothing, and she didn't even show an interest in skiing anymore. Her whole life was work, work, and more work. The only place she felt fulfilled was at work she said. Yes, I knew about that. I remembered leaving a lawn chair and a book and driving to the hospital to check on something on my day off, ridiculous in retrospect, but I did it!

Lisa gathered herself together and we did our twelve-hour night. Her face sad, the tears coming from time to time, and she wondered what she would do. She knew her health was affected, she knew her kids had said she wasn't herself, and she knew her turn had come. But she didn't want to step out of the ring, like a boxer who just can't throw in the towel, she, like me, railed against the fates that did this to her, that robbed her of her life, because she, also like me, was doing the work she loved, work that was fulfilling and wonderful. However we were like many other nurses, we had kept going until there was just an empty hole with nothing left in it for others. And you cannot be a nurse when you feel that way.

The next week Lisa took time off, reconsidering her husbands' suggestion of a vacation, saw a doctor, had a complete checkup and obtained something to help her sleep for ten nights. Then she was on her own to do her own reassessment, her own soul searching, and she did it. The guilty feelings were there but gradually after a month or so she smiled again, and after three months she felt well enough to come back to work. She is only in her forties, she doesn't want it to happen again, although she knows it probably will if she is not on guard at all times. What a miserable creeping germ of the soul and body this burnout, attacking those who give so much, and want to give more.

Our candles do go out, we do cry, we hurt, we try to fill all the roles required of us, but often a big hole devours us and we are never the same. After two bouts of agonizing burnout I had to reassess my life, my needs, my wants, and make sure I was heading in the right direction. I wasn't! That was abundantly and definitely clears, so I had to make the decision to work at 80% of a full time nurse, then I went to 60%, but the guilt was incredible. And the overtime hours always added up to the equivalent of working full time. Terrified of that big hole of BURNOUT, I kept myself ever mindful of what I was doing, and when the time came, I retired at age 51. Nobody could believe it, least of all ME! Sometimes it is still hard to take it all in!

Lisa is watching herself closely, as are others who have been there. For me the right choice was made, on my time, by me, so I could leave with my head up, still active, and return to my beloved Newfoundland and start a new life.

I am and always will be a NURSE. I loved my career, loved every minute with the patients, but the system wears you down. No person working Palliative Care and watching friends and acquaintances die at the age of 40 or 50 years, and younger, cannot but stand back and reassess where they are going. And that is what I had to do. Difficult, oh yes, necessary, oh definitely!

I passed my candle to Lisa, I hope it adds light to hers, and protects her a little bit more from the slings and arrows. She is a terrific nurse, and mother.

The road is difficult at times for nurses who give so much of themselves, but it is a road that I am glad I traveled, and I would do it all again, next time I would make sure my candle was just a little more protected.

Godspeed and God bless nurses everywhere and may your light burn brightly as you walk your path.

THE TALE OF THE NIGHT OF THE WINE!

Miss Sigsworth was a retired school teacher, a very fine lady with fine taste in food, clothes and wine. She was a refined professional who had lived a full and active 84 years, and she was now our patient. Even though age, illness and infirmity had enveloped her, she maintained her standards and ate her meals from her hospital tray as if she were dining at the most elegant of eateries! And she had her wine, three times a day with meals, and another toddy at bedtime. It was a cream sherry, and she loved it! As nurses, we dispensed the wine as a medication, although she bought it herself, it had to be kept in our medication cupboard and locked up. Miss Sigsworth understood, and just as long as we brought it on time, she had no problems with our system and rules.

From time to time she would laughingly tell us that we should have a party after she died and drink whatever wine was left in the cupboard, and speak of her and remember her. Such was the kind of lady she was. We promised her we would do that and it became a standing joke, and we never dreamed of such a thing taking place because we always thought she would get well enough to return to her own home with her home care supports. But that was not to be. One morning when our team reported for duty, we were told that Miss Sigsworth had passed away. And we were shocked! But we remembered our promise to her, and with great spirits we planned the reunion with the one bottle of cream sherry that remained.

The night of the gathering arrived. It was to be held at my

house, and I had the wine chilled, the munchies out, and the group of six or so nurses on the team dribbled in one by one.

With lots of laughs, memories of the dainty lady who wanted us to do this, and the carefree attitude of the young, we opened the bottle. With the first little wine glass poured, one of the nurses tasted it, and almost succumbed to the awful smell and taste of this supposedly lovely wine.

"We can't drink this!" she croaked, her eyes watering. "It is absolutely gross!"

We all took a tiny sip. She was right. It was more like a putrid engine oil than fine wine. What did little Miss Sigsworth see in such an awful wine, a wine she claimed kept her going? So another bottle of my own wine was brought forth, enjoyed by all, and by midnight we decided to say our goodnights and get home. But I was home, and I was not staying in the house with that wine bottle staring at me. I sneaked out and put it in one of the nurses' cars, they found it, took it out and put it on the lawn! What to do now was the next question!

I could not give it away, I could not keep it, I would not pour it out in case Miss Sigsworth was watching-I was in one heck of a muddle! So I went out again and begged two of the higher spirited nurses to take it off my hands, please! They said they would.

And off they went with the wine.

The next week I discovered that they all stopped on the small bridge connecting our towns and poured the wine into the river, throwing the bottle and cap in after it! Laughing their hearts out, they headed for home and that was that. Everybody had a grand tale to tell about 'THE NIGHT OF THE WINE'. And the routine of work continued on and the wine was all but forgotten!

Until the day we decided to clean out the medication room. During the cleanup THREE BOTTLES OF CREAM SHERRY were found! We all knew they were not there before, we don't know where they came from, we knew what the wine was like, we couldn't drink it, couldn't have another wine night or it would be the end of us, so we deliberated for weeks over this strange phenomenon! Where did it come from anyway?

Finally the same group that disposed of the first bottle chose a moonlit night, met on the bridge and had the 'Ceremony of the Wine'!

Then drove out of there like mad!

No more cream sherry ever appeared, actually nobody looked in that cupboard again that I know of, too scared of what would be there.

The moral of the story "Don't ever promise dainty little ladies that you will drink upon their demise. You may be demised yourself!"

And that is the true tale of Miss Sigsworth and her delightful wine.

JENNYS' SONG

One bright cold winter evening I had to visit the corner store for some last-minute necessities. It was a quiet evening with a hint of snow in the air. I glanced at the clock and saw it was soon ten p.m., when all of a sudden the door flew open and in rushed two handsome, healthy looking young men, picking up food items for a night at the cabin they said, and they proceeded to fill their shopping cart with food and another cart full of beer to complete the list.

They obviously knew the cashier, as she was scolding them for leaving for a cabin so far away on such a cold night.

There were five of them they said and they would be OK. In the days ahead, I fretted about those young people as if they were my own ,but no news is good news and in our small community news travels fast , so I knew that they must have been OK.But I was constantly reminded of another time when the ingredients did lead to one horrific catastrophe, and incredible grief and pain.

Four young people, two boys and their girlfriends, were in a fun-time mode on an autumn night with the harvest moon lighting everything with an aura of bluish light. Their vehicle left the road, and was airborne for a second or so, then slammed into a one hundred-year-old oak tree.

The car impaled itself on the big tree, and the passengers thrown like garbage around the farmers' field. Shards of broken beer bottles, food containers and clothing scattered about the area as if it had fallen from an airplane.It was close to Halloween, and the first Mountie on the scene said it was the most macabre sight he had ever seen so far in his career, and he would never like Halloween again. There was nothing to be done really, except pick up the pieces, notify the next of kin and carry on.

On our Nursing Unit, this was close to the heart. The cars' driver was known to us. He was the only child of our housekeeping support staff member, Jenny. Jenny shared her love of Mike with us every day; she had for years. Her husband was important, but Mike was loved and adored by his mother. And now he was gone, his life wasted, leaving a trail of pain for four families. Jenny had sent Mike to Driver Education, bought him the best she could afford from the money she earned cleaning at the hospital, meticously keeping our workplace spotless, making sure everything was in order, every day. She knew we appreciated her. She sang as she worked-old hymns from her childhood, country and western music ballads, you name it, she sang it. And sometimes we would join in at the end of the workday, a crazy bunch of nurses playing the broomstick guitar and getting our photos taken for memories sake.

How would this woman ever cope with this loss? How would she manage to go on? The center of her life was dead, and with that being bad enough, he took three others with him. She would never survive it and we feared for her.

As experienced as we were with life and death, none of us nurses could go alone to the funeral home. We, in the days ahead, chose a place and time to meet, and we would all go together to see Jenny and her family, and pay our respects. How could WE deal with this?

At the funeral home, we looked up and down the street at all the Halloween decorations, which now seemed ghoulish, the Jack o'Lanterns frivolous considering the situation we knew we would be faced with when we opened those large doors into the funeral chapel.

But open the doors we did. Only three of the four victims of the accident were being waked there, the fourth was in a nearby town. The sorrow in the whole area was palpable. The three young people lay like beautiful, lifeless dolls in display cases. It was the worse I had ever had to deal within all my 45 years of living.

Jenny was numb, her heart destroyed. Her husband did not want to talk about it at all, and he never ever did.It made the burden hers along to carry. The faces of the families involved looked like masks of pain and sorrow.But the faces of the young friends who dropped by were white, drained of any color by the emotions they were experiencing.

So many of the young people asked "Why?" So many said, "I told him not to go!" But it was too late now.

We had our visit, said what words we could get out to Jenny, our tears mingling with hers. I never want to see a sight like that again-if I am to be spared anything, spare me that, I prayed.

After all the funerals, all the paperwork, all the quiet she could bear, Jenny, much to our surprise, elected to return to work. She wanted to be with people. She said she could not bear to go into Mikes' room, her husband withdrew into a world of pain and she needed to be with us, she said.

Subdued and serious, and not singing, she took her place with her mop and worked away day in and day out. Gradually she opened up and talked, little by little.Over the months, she began to accept what had happened. What else can I do she asked? Autumn turned to winter, and winter gave way to spring. Lambs were born, Easter came, then the hotter days of summer with the warm breezes and the smell of apple blossoms surrounded us. Little ponies and calves frolicked in the fields, soccer games were being played outside again, yes, summer was here now.

And then it happened.A group of us was standing together when someone said "Listen. It's Jenny!" And it was! She was singing, quietly at first, and then louder, her beautiful voice skipped down the hospital corridor toward us. We all walked toward her. She couldn't see us until she turned around. Someone said through their tears "Jen, you're back, you're singing again!"

Her eyes filled with tears, as did all of ours.Jenny was back-always a piece of her heart missing, but she was back.

In the few days after seeing the young men at the grocery store with all the beer, so much machine to handle, so healthy and strong, I worried about them as if they were my own son and daughter. The trail of pain, the waste of talent and skills, the stolen futures are all there with the mix of drinking and driving. Yet it happens repeatedly. Would it help to take those young people, as one high school did, to a morgue, to a prison, a courtroom, a funeral? If it would help, we would do it I am sure.I have seen so much carnage, so many broken young bodies, victims of their own or someone elses' drunken driving, of trucks, snowmobiles, four wheelers, and sea doos. It is the worst waste of humanity to lose those fine young people, whether they were the drivers or not.

The impaired driver, be it through drugs or alcohol, is out there, lurking, and they come in all ages, from all walks of life, both genders, all socioeconomic groups. Why, why?? Why do they do it?

Every time I hear of a fatality in which alcohol is involved I cannot help but go back to Jenny, seeing her pain, hearing her ask "Why" over and over. And she wept and could not sing.

Then there is the memory that is good and sweet-"the day Jenny sang again", as it came to be known on our unit.

And also there was the wish that she would see Mike graduate from University, that nothing had happened to make the singing stop, and those lifeless dolls I saw would have all been just a bad dream.But it Wasn't, sad to say, It wasn't.

JOEY AND THE CHRISTMAS SMILE

Christmas Eve had arrived once again, how quickly the years go by we remarked to each other! Once again Christmas Eve found Mr.and Mrs. Santa Claus making their special visits, saying a goodnight to the children of friends and neighbors. Frank and Dolores were good friends of my husband and me, and we had weathered many a storm together, as well as enjoyed many interesting excursions. The Christmas Eve visiting of Mr.& Mrs. Claus was expected by many of our neighbors and various friends around town. Frank, with his blue eyes and gold framed glasses made a divine Santa, and Dolores had made a skirt for a Mrs. Santa Claus and I had the most lovely red wool hat, trimmed with white fur that blew in the wind and gathered sparkly snow crystals, dangling Christmas earrings and rosy red cheeks, with a red ankle high boots and black leotards, and we put it all together, and there I was, Mrs.Claus! And Mr.& Mrs. Claus liked children, theirs were grown up by now, and Dolores and my husband drove the sleigh for the visiting. We did this for years, Dolores taking my OR call while I was dressed, and we frolicked about in Franks' big car, spreading our cheer, Frank ringing his bells and doing his 'HOHOHO', it was fun but it was also a very gratifying mission especially to one household, the one Santa really loved to visit and he usually saved until last so he could spend more time.

Yes, it was a special household, and a special family, a family that had more than its' share of heartache but kept going, holding each other together tightly through the sad illness of their son.

Joey was a patient at our hospital. I met him when I started work there, first when he had been diagnosed with a degenerative brain disease that slowly and destructively invaded his body. The picture on his little bedside table was of a smiling blond haired tyke, holding a wedding ring cushion, the photo having been taken shortly before his first seizure, the first shocking sign to his family that something was dreadfully wrong.

All the investigations were done, he seizured frequently but his Mom took time off work and cared for him at home. He had an older brother and an older sister who cherished him. But no amount of love, hugs, or kisses could make Joey better. His health gradually declined, his mother and father exhausted, and he was brought to the hospital. From time to time at the beginning his family would take him home but as his illness progressed the home visits became less and less, and the pattern reversed, his family let him be hospitalized, but they were there, night and day sometimes. His father, an engineer was always trying new things, some way for Joey to have his tube feeding more efficiently. His Mom was a smart, bright a petite woman with tremendous spirit and energy, and faith. The years passed, Joey slid away from the real world surely and slowly, unresponsive most of the time.

I have a memory of helping Joeys' nurse one evening, and of his Dad sitting there talking to us as we worked around his son, and when I looked at him more closely I noticed he was making little nurses caps out of Styrofoam drinking glasses and drawing black bands on them with a marker. Yellow bands for the LPNs' were there too. And he was putting names on the little caps and decorating Joeys' room which was as much like a room at home as it could be after seven years in the hospital. The image of that father making those little caps, sitting in the big chair with an air of resignation, was an image I have never forgotten.

By now, after all those years, his Mom had returned to work, but came to visit every lunch hour, his father came in the evening, his sister was at University but she brought her big smile into his room when she came home on break, his brother visited but not as often, he was too heartbroken to watch this happen to his younger brother. And the years just passed for Joey as he fell deeper and deeper into the coma.

The nurses loved him. He was special. Our hospital staff from the cook in our kitchen to the Administrator would drop in and say hello. He had music playing most of the time, his parents had found he was less agitated if he had certain types of music. He was a baby again, and he received the Tender Loving Care babies deserve. But he was a very sick boy.

Joeys' parents were friends of Frank and Dolores, and Joeys' brother was a friend of their son. So Santa knew Joey too, and so did Mrs.Claus.And every Christmas Eve, regardless of weather, regardless of commitments to any other event, Joeys' parents took him home. Feeding pumps, a suction machine, medications, everything making the corner next to the Christmas tree a mini-hospital. His family was sure he knew he was home, that he knew Christmas, and remembered, and maybe he did. They took turns, all the family members of staying awake all night to care for him, and thethey loved having him home.

So Christmas Eve became a special time for a very sick and very special boy and his family, because not only was Joey home, but Mr.& Mrs. Claus always dropped by. They did it every year, even after Joeys' sister married and was home for Christmas with her husband, the tradition carried on.

We would turn the car-sleigh into the long driveway, bounce out of the car into the frosty air, and run toward the house that was so beautifully decked out for the season. And we go right in and right to Joeys' bedside, Santa would talk a little while, then he would ring his bells, and it never failed, JOEY WOULD SMILE! He knew the sound of the bells, he knew Santas' voice, a memory somewhere deep inside from long ago still remained and he would smile. That made Christmas perfect for everybody, that smile was magic! And as the years passed and the Christmas seasons came and went Joey deteriorated, but he still smiled at the Christmas bells. It was truly amazing, and truly a gift to everyone who loved him.

At age eighteen, after all those years of illness, Joey passed away. His Mom and Dad were grief stricken, now, but he was really gone forever. But time healed, and his mother smiled again, his father carried on with his work, and they remembered the long years of illness, never bitter, but longed for things to have not been that way. They were parents who went above and beyond the call of duty for their sick son. They had no regrets.

And Santa and Mrs. Claus had no regrets either. I remember the tiny nurses caps strung around the hospital room, the Christmas Santa bells ringing, a very sick boy smiling, and a Mr.& Mrs. Santa standing beside a mother and father watching the smile, and tears running down their faces.

It was indeed Christmas then, you could feel it in the air, with the Christmas music playing softly, and Joeys' sister standing next to her brother holding her own baby boy. Joey had a life of eighteen years, even though he was ill, he had a life. And he had a smile that enriched others' lives, and made others appreciate the things we take so for granted I think Joey has Christmas bells whenever he wants them now, and all his favorite nurses, and he can enjoy his gifts. But the best gift of all he left for us, the memory of that CHRISTMAS SMILE!

THIS LITTLE LAMP

Newspapers cluttered the floors, the furniture was topsy turvy, cardboard boxes were stashed, taped and shut, and in general our house was in a state of complete and utter chaos. It was moving time again, but this time the moving choice was ours, we were packing our things, and relocating to a place we both loved so much, Newfoundland. We had lived in Nova Scotia all our married lives, thirty three years and a few months, more time than we had lived in Newfoundland. Our children were born and raised there and it was and is a beautiful province, with a wonderful people, great climate and we had made many friends over the years. But the time had reached the hour, it was time to come home. Never ever had we planned it, never discussed it at any length, although we visited every year, sometimes twice a year. But our lives had changed. The 'children' were grown, educated, and gone to Alberta to find their own place, work, and build new lives of their own.

Through all of the years in various towns in Nova Scotia we worked, contributed to the community, had nice homes and good lives. But now the treadmill was a little too fast, we seemed to be on a fast train to nowhere. We had too much house, too much work, had watched friends in their late forties and early fifties die, and I had to make a change or I felt I would wither and die without ever getting in a boat, going out on the bay, catching a fish or having the experience of living near my sisters. So we made plans to retire, my nursing was so precious to me that the decision was so very difficult. My husband led the way, steered the course, taught me to move on, not to look back with regret. And I learned that what he said was true, move on, move back, get another lifestyle and do it now, while we were reasonably young enough to be adventuresome.

So we placed our house on the market, thinking that in a few months or so it would sell. It was June so we would have the summer to make all sorts of preparations, but no, the house sold the same day the sign went on it, probably before that. So the rush was on. And what a rush it was. The farewells, the summers heat, finding us running out of time, selling off things that were now just burdensome, all very physically taxing and bittersweet. My brother called to say how glad my family would be to have me on the Island after all those years, and tears flowed and flowed.

But in the middle of the upheaval one day, even though pushed for time, I took a precious possession off the shelf and sat on a crowded sofa with it in my hands. The tears rolled down my face as I carefully held and brushed the dust off the dear old lamp, a kerosene oil lamp that had been mine for years and years. It was in a metal stand, or hanger, with a hole in the back for hanging on a wall. It stood sixteen inches high, with a fragile glass chimney that was fourteen inches around the widest part. A decorative pattern in white ran around that widest part of the chimney and a shiny reflector was mounted on the metal holder, when lit the light would reflect beautifully, doubling the effect of the lamp.

This was no ordinary lamp. When I was a student at the Grace General Hospital School of Nursing from 1966 to 1969, I, of course, had to do a stint in the well baby nursery as part of our Obstetrics, and I loved it. I was eighteen years old in 1967 and Mrs.Smallwood was the head nurse in the Nursery on Second Floor.One day she was going through a closet and all those lamps were sitting in a row on a shelf. I asked her about them, seeing as how I had been commissioned to be the one assigned to help clean out this old closet. She told me story after story of being a student herself, of those lamps hanging on the walls, of nurses feeding the babies in the middle of the night by the lamplight, and of the beautiful picture it brought to her mind. I picked a lamp of the shelf and asked her what they would do with them now, "Oh, I suppose they'll go to the dump, nobody cares about them now!" she replied.

"Well, I do," I remarked.

"Well Jarvis, if you want one take it, it's yours! But promise to take care of it!"

And I promised, and walked away that day with my little lamp. Little did I know that my lamp would follow me to Grand Bank, St.John's. ,various places in Nova Scotia, and always would occupy a special spot in my home wherever I was. So many people asked about it, so many people admired it, and the most amazing thing of all is that through all the moves, packing and tossing around it suffered, it never ever got broken, other things did, but not my lamp. It sits here on my desk as I write today, back in Newfoundland, me and my lamp, still together.

It was used once or twice during power failures when winter storms hit, it was knocked off the shelf by someone looking behind it for a book, it was in a box that a moving van lost, but eventually found and brought back, and still it stayed intact.

Yes, a precious possession.I sat in the chaotic household that day and held my lamp. To me it signified my life, my career and my own resilience that at times I thought was gone. I carefully, very carefully packed it for the journey back to Newfoundland, a place we both needed to be. And if it could speak, what marvelous stories it could tell! So instead I will have to do the story telling, I will trim the wick again, and maybe some cold winter evening I will light my little lamp and let it shine its' golden glow again. The image of nurses in starchy white uniforms feeding the babies under that golden glow makes me feel warm and content. The lamp has lasted and stood the test of time, it is my light, my lamp, now it is up to me to care for it and see if I can stand the test of time too.

A nursery lamp, with me for thirty-five years of living. There were times when I would look to that lamp and wonder if my tired legs could go on, times when it comforted me beyond all else.

So, Mrs.Smallwood, I kept my promise. I cared for the lamp you gave me and I am grateful for it. This little lamp of mine,may it always be able to shine!

KEEPING THE WATCH ON CHRISTMAS DAY

'A special elderly patients touches hearts in a strong way on Christmas Day'

Nurses usually alternate taking Christmas and New Years' holidays off, and it usually gets worked out to some degree of satisfaction for everyone.

Working Christmas Day after the children were grown and had left home altogether was easier to handle and could, many times, be quite rewarding. Any nurse who has worked a Christmas Day will certainly have a story of her experiences at Christmas time, usually a story they will never forget.

As I prepared for work on Christmas Day in 1998, little did I know that this would be my memorable Christmas, and all because of an elderly gentleman on our palliative care unit named Norman.

Norman was a proud man. He had been a farmer all his life, raising five sons and four daughters. He was a Veteran of the Second World War, and was a widower, but he had most of his family living, if not in the immediate area then certainly within driving distance. This gentleman was an elective admission-he could no longer care for himself and could not keep his pain medication straight. This was going to be his last Christmas and he knew it, as did his family.

After our morning report from the previous shift, all of us nurses made our rounds, dispensed medication, soaked up the compliments from our patients as they remarked on our casual festive dressed up clothes, had pictures taken with them, admired their gifts, determined who was going out for the day with family and generally overdosed on all the goodies and chocolates our patients insisted we try.

They were a wonderful group. They had so much spirit, so much faith. We prepared the medications for each one of them leaving on a pass, so they could take them on time, and we prepared Normans' as well. He said his family was coming, so his care givers got him dressed in his Legion blazer and grey flannel dress pants, with his beret nicely perched on his shock of white hair. Such a quiet man, shy in a way, but so loving and caring, courteous and kind to all who knew him.

One by one the families came by the desk to sign the "Out on pass" slip; one by one the patients left, warmly dressed and bundled up against the chill of the day. They would be back by 8 p.m.., they assured us.

Those who were too sick to go received all kinds of special attention from visiting family and nurses. A young man, who walked with his IV pole, was fighting for his life against the disease that had ravaged him, had half a dozen young women in attendance. They were all healthy looking friends who came to help their classmate get through a rough day.

As I settled down to do the mundane paperwork for the day, I noticed one of my senior team members coming toward me, flustered and near tears.

"Nobody has come for Norman," she said. "Where are they all?"

I assured her that surely someone would be along. Not to worry. She went on to tell me he was parked in his wheelchair in his special place, a strategic spot from where he could see the elevator doors and the stairway entrance. He wouldn't leave his parking spot. But nobody came.

By 11am. , it was time for Plan B. We manned the phones and tried to locate somebody for Norman. Nobody answered the calls. Norman refused to eat. He was having dinner at home he said. But nobody came.

Time wore on. We jokingly asked him to come and dine with

a bevy of beautiful nurses. He smiled and said, "No, they'll be here." But they weren't.

Norman took his pain medication, allowed himself to be wheeled around to visit a few patients he knew, watched the Queens' Christmas message on television and returned to his parking spot. Still, nobody came. All our hearts were breaking for this dear old man. This was to be his last Christmas and he was spending it without one family member. He was alone.

By mid-afternoon, Normans' head was drooping. We knew he had to be hungry. What could we do? So the phone calls started again. Still, nobody answered.

The young man, with his friends in tow, went to Norman and gave him several little wrapped Christmas gifts, bought him a cold drink, and made conversation with him. He would not break his vigil, though. He would wait. Even the young man and his friends were upset by now.

Norman was no fool-he knew the roads were clear, he knew the usual time his family had Christmas dinner, he knew something was not right, but he would not give up. Still, nobody came.

Soon the twilight of the winter evening descended on our little hospital, making the Christmas lights twinkle and reflect off the snow on the window sills and patio. Cars began to return with our patients. Norman watched it all with keen interest, but he knew there was nobody coming. The air was quiet as people were medicated and put to bed, telling us stories of their wonderful day. Then the time came when, as team leader, and much to my dismay, I had to go talk to Norman. He must get out of that chair. He was exhausted.

With a crew of supportive nurses around me I knelt down and coaxed him to come to his room and open his gifts that had piled up on his bed during the day. He reluctantly let us take him back to his room. We had punch and cake, and encouraged him to open his gifts. We brought other patients in to enjoy it all with him. We took his picture.

This man was tired and heartbroken. Half of us were in tears, and when he started to cry, we were all in tears.It was time to settle him for the night. One of our younger nurses elected to stay with him as we finished our days' work. Before I left the hospital that evening, I went to say good night to Norman. During our talk I asked him what his job was when he was in the service during the Second World War.

"I was a gunner, and a lookout, mostly," he said, his eyes brimming with tears. "But you know nurse, this was the longest watch I ever did." I stood there as he fell into a medication induced sleep. I was riveted by the heartache of this man who had served his country, but his family did not serve him. And it was even more upsetting because of the season of the birth of Gods' gift to man, when families try to be together to celebrate that gift, and the joy of having one another.

Yes, my dear old man, I believe you. Nine children and not one 'random act of kindness or senseless act of beauty' for their father on his last Christmas Day. It was a very long shift of keeping watch indeed, and for nothing.

Norman passed away four days after Christmas, quietly, and in the middle of the night. When his nurse checked him and discovered he had passed away, alone, she was devastated. Then she noticed that in his hand was one of the little gift boxes the young man had given to him on Christmas Day. It obviously was something he treasured because it was given to him when his heart was broken, and his spirit destroyed.

So, the next Christmas, Norman did not have to keep the long vigil-his watch was over. He left for a better place.

THE MATRONS' EXPERIMENT

1. (Assume the crash position)

After marrying and leaving Newfoundland for the 'Mainland' in 1970, I found myself living in a little town in Cape Breton. My husband had been transferred there from Dartmouth, and we found a little apartment in an older house just meters away from the hospital. The rent was one hundred and ten dollars a month, in our price range, and again we set up housekeeping. I had decided to take the summer off and get to know Cape Breton Island, its' unique history and culture, and return to work, hopefully, at the hospital just next door at summers' end.

However, it did not quite work out that way. My husband was away for long stretches of time, my only company a little dog that I had acquired and given the name 'Noodles'. Noodles was good entertainment, a great traveling companion, but he did not replace human contact. I knew absolutely no other human in town and time was beginning to drag. I took Noodles for a walk one day, and as I walked by the hospital with its' weathered wooden steps, the pull to connect with nurses and patients and get to know people was too great to ignore. So, after tying my dog to the worn railing of the steps, I ran up toward the large wooden door and into a different world.

The lady at the reception desk was friendly and told me that in order to inquire about anything in the area of 'Nursing' I would have to speak to "Matron". And I wanted a job, I had enough of this hanging about, so I let the nice lady take me to Matron. I was ready, willing and able to work, and work I would.

We walked down a hallway with glistening hardwood floors, past a ward containing twelve beds, a small out patient department, and doors with glass doorknobs and brass name plates, all brilliant and lovingly cared for it seemed. The little outpatients' department was full of men receiving aerosol therapy, and made me so aware that this was a coal mining area and these people were miners, all suffering from 'Miners Lung', something I would come to know quite well in my time there. But these aerosol machines for respiratory therapy were ancient, I had only seen them in a discard room at the Grace Hospital in St .John's during my student days. I never had seen such antique equipment, long dark hallways and heavy solid wooden doors, and I came to the realization that this was a whole new world for me. What was I getting myself into I wondered?

Then we arrived at a large, wide heavy door. On the door was a shining brass plate with the words 'MISS E. RIGGS, RN. MATRON'. By then my reserve was faltering but it was too late to turn back as the lady accompanying me had knocked lightly on the door and suddenly it flung open. And there she was, the Matron. Her white cap and black band, long sleeved stark white uniform with shiny gold RN cufflinks, and high heeled white shoes spoke what everyone seemed to know, 'Matron was power', and don't ever doubt it! Although short in stature, she was quite an imposing sight with her lovely white hair speaking of experience, her stiff attitude telling me to 'behave or behaved out'. Miss Riggs looked at me over her gold framed half glasses and barked "And just who are you?"

I proceeded to tell her, and after a moment or two, she waved her hand as if to say "Enough!" No nonsense for this lady.

"Can you work hard?", and I told her I could. This was followed by the same style question and answer interview, short questions, short answers. She got up from her desk at one point and walked a complete circle around me, as she still had me standing in front of her for all this time. And to my horror I remembered I was wearing a hair band and did not look like a Nurse should look for an interview.

"Well, I suppose you'll do. Bring me all your identification when you come to work tomorrow. And I expect they are all in order, and I expect hard work. Go away now. I'm busy."

I was out of that place in fifteen seconds at the most! Little did I know then that I would make friends and enjoy working at that little hospital for two years. Experiences that I would never forget, friends I would grow to love, and then have my first child, a little boy born there. But that day I doubted myself and what I had gotten myself into.

I worked with wonderful nurses and doctors, cleaning staff, and dietary staff over the next two years, under the watchful eye of a very strict Matron. And I learned more about the Matron, and her desire to save time, to run an efficient institution, spend money wisely and most of all she loved dallying in the pharmacy trying to develop methods to save nurses time at the bedside with the dispensing of medications. My fellow nurses told me that Matron was, they thought, planning an invasion of some country, although they did not know which one. They would tell me hair-raising tales such as the fact that Miss Riggs lived alone with her poodle and her poodle 'Fufu' was giving her strange ideas. And we would laugh our days away, trying not to get caught but enjoying the fun of it all. Word would get passed on if Matron was at some bizarre experiment again, and it wasn't too long before someone came up to me and said "Run for cover, Miss Riggs is in the pharmacy fooling around." And everyone would scatter less they be conscripted by Miss Riggs to aid her in her experiment of the moment.

I wasn't quick enough that day. Miss Riggs dragged me off to the one room, no window pharmacy with her. She, it seems, had decided that mixing the famous black and white liquids that make up a purgative could be mixed in the large brown bottles in the pharmacy and the nurse at the bedside would have it all ready and would not have to open two bottles to mix it, and time would be saved. And that is exactly what she and I did. I had no choice in the matter. A gallon of white, a gallon of black, all mixed and ready, pharmacy cleaned up, and having sworn me to secrecy she dismissed me.

But obviously the fact that this mixture was a good purgative was because it 'worked' inside the body, stimulating the purge, and causing the urge to get to the bathroom, quickly! It had not occurred to me until a few hours later because I was frozen with fear and took time to thaw. But I was sworn not to tell, and I didn't!

A week went by, night duty time rolled around. And on my second night shift the big bang happened, shook the first floor of the hospital, scared everyone out of their wits and the fire department was called. The noise came from pharmacy the nurses reported, so Miss Riggs was called. And she appeared, complete with hair rollers, fluffy slippers and Fufu under her arm. She unlocked the pharmacy door to what could only be described as a gooey, brown, glass-filled cubicle. I said nothing. The fire department left, housekeeping would clean in the morning. And the big bang would become part of the stories of Miss Riggs and her experiments.

The mess took housekeepers the whole day to clean, Miss Riggs arrived for work before I left in the morning, and sought me on my unit. She need not have worried. I was too speechless to tell the tale. However she saw fit to remind me of my promise to say nothing, and I nodded an affirmation to that. And off she went.

And every time for the next twenty-eight years that I mixed that purgative I thought of Miss Riggs and Fufu. And I wondered who had the idea first, Fufu or Matron.

The staff held a farewell party when I left Cape Breton. The matron was not a party goer, but she sent her best wishes. The next morning, just as the moving truck arrived, I noticed something sticking out of our mailbox. In it was a package with a little note wishing me all the best in my career, and thanking me for my contribution to the hospital in the past two and one half years. I opened the package. It was a bottle of white purgative, and a bottle of black. Written on the labels was "Mix in equal parts, AT THE BEDSIDE!"The note was signed 'Best Wishes, Matron.'

A wonderful experience, a somewhat crazy memory, but I would not trade it for anything. The lesson learned "Keep things in perspective, mix in equal parts!"

A MAD COW IN STITCHES

It was time to leave for home. The surgical suite was polished to perfection, our work was done, and the hot August day beckoned. Just as my partner and I started for the changing room the phone rang. She passed it to me.

The voice on the phone was out of breath and upset, "Bonnie, can you come to the farm, Bob needs you?", my friend Sandy yelled.

"What for, what's wrong?" was all I could manage with my mind racing through various scenarios? She explained that Bobs' prize cow, Wickie, had a large slash cut in her back. He was upset. The cow was crazy, and the two veterinarians on call were out on other emergencies. And this could not wait. Wickie was a show cow, the best of his Holstein herd. I had heard about Wickie and her personality disorder, and I knew this would be a challenge, and I also realized that this was too much temptation to resist. I agreed to go to the farm.

Bob and Sandy had a dairy farm in Castle Frederick, just outside of Windsor, Nova Scotia. The farm land itself was massive, with corn fields, apple orchards, prize milk producing Holsteins, and all in all it was a massive enterprise run by the family. Bob had done a magnificent job of building it up after the death of his dad at the age of fifty-two, when Bob himself was just fourteen years old. He finished his schooling while managing the family farm. His young age was not a deterrent. Eventually Bob married and started a family. He has two lovely daughters and a handsome son. Bob is fifty-two now. His daughter has studied agriculture and is to be the farm manager someday.

His mother lived in the big farmhouse, Bob, Sandy and the three children lived in the smaller farmhouse next door. Bob worked eighteen hour days, calves were born, cows got sick and at all hours of the day or night Bob did his farming with the help of a sister, a brother-in-law and the rest of the family. And he built Bovidae Farm into one of the finest dairy operations in Nova Scotia.

We socialized when Bob had time, he never forgave me for taking him and Sandy to see the movie 'Cujo', which left him with nightmares, and I never forgave him for the answer he gave me when I asked how he prepared a cow for artificial insemination, or 'AI' as they referred to it. I thought it was a sensible question, but Bob looked at me, grinned and said "Just a little lipstick!" I was annoyed, even I was not that stupid! I knew about fishing, not farming. But it was all a laugh, and Bob has a joyful laugh that is contagious. He is a big man, with a big heart, full of life and spirit. One year he was 'Canadas' Best Young Farmer', quite an honor for one so young.

No bulls roamed around his cows, they were all entered by number into a computer and when the time came to have them bred he had the artificial inseminators breed them with the best genetic bull stock, and he built one fine prize herd of Holsteins. Modern farming with a good old fashioned hands on work, that was Bovidae Farm. He explains that his farm is called 'Bovidae' because it is Latin for 'cattle'. His choice cows have a special magnet neck ring that opens the feed trough by pulling the metal key with the use of the magnet and they get extra feed. So what in the world would they need me for on a Sunday morning? Sandy told me that Wickie, named because she was so darn 'wicked', got away and got caught under the silo and slit her back badly. She needed sutures. Bob had all the equipment but nobody could stitch, so they thought "Ah, ah, Bonnie, the Operating Room guru–we'll call her!"

I arrived to see Bob, Sandy, and a young man holding Wickie in a stall. She was bleeding but oblivious to pain. She was concerned with inflicting pain on humans, and intense pain at that! Manure was splattered all over the stall, Bob had a face full of it, Sandy was almost unrecognizable, and the young man was red from pulling on this wicked Wickie who had become an ox all of a sudden. She was one mad, mad, cow that day!

Bob yanked out a stool, got me up on it, and handed me the sutures, while the other two held the cow, I stitched and Bob cut the sutures and poured penicillin into the wound. Wickie spit, kicked, bit, threw herself at us, stopped to get a breath and started all over again. We were exhausted, and it was a long slash to stitch. Then more fresh manure, kicked around a bit, then more spittle, but gradually the stitches got finished. We all held onto this large mad cow, Bob patted her, she bit him, he gave her water, she spit at him, Sandy was gathering up the suture kit, the young man was up in the hayloft, and we were all covered from head to toe in sweat, silage and manure. When it looked as though she would settle Bob backed us all out of the stall, and closed the gate. Then Wickie turned around, faced us all and spat full force in our faces!

"There, take that!" she was saying. This was no manner of etiquette for a trophy bovine! But you didn't mess with this debutante cow; that was what started the whole thing! Bob brought her out to groom her for a show and she wasn't in the mood. And she was not going to be either. She was mad, and planned on staying that way! In a week Wickie allowed Bob to remove the stitches. Wickie continued on in her aristocratic manner, and lived a grand life. She refused to go to prize shows. She still had her neck magnet, she allowed herself to be milked, and was still a valuable resource for the farm.

But now when any of us hear about 'Mad Cow Disease' our minds go back to the ten showers and baths it took to remove signs and smells of our 'mad cow. and we still have to admire the tenacity of a Royal cow named befittingly-'WICKIE', who is still strutting around Bovidae Farm , daring anyone to put her into stitches again.

THE SKUNKS OF SUMMER

It was definitely on of the 'dog days of summer' in the Nova Scotia Valley of the Apples. It was already 28* at 8:00am, the air so still and thick that I was hard pressed to distinguish between real pets and lawn adornments. Every living creature was slowed down to a stop it seemed. Driving the big old pickup truck with the special payload in the back was certainly one of those times when I would say to myself "How the heck did I get into this pickle?"

The winding old highway with its' hairpin turns, hidden driveways and blind crests took careful meandering, luckily for me, because as I came around one of the worse turns I could see a police road check. Now, considering the smell surrounding and in the truck I was driving I reckoned this was going to be very interesting indeed! The young policeman waved me toward him, checked for seatbelt usage, and all was Ok. Then he asked for my Drivers License, causing me to turn to my backpack and root around for it. Then I felt a tap on my shoulder, and I turned to see what had been a young mans' pleasant face turning into a grotesque and distorted mask! His eyes were full of water, and I am sure his bottom lip was up over his nose. Obviously he had been struck with the full force of the penetrating odor surrounding me and my truck, an aroma that was even worse in the hot weather.

"What is that smell?" he managed to croak.

"Oh, that, don't worry, it's just a skunk in the box in back. It's a skunk trap and we are trying to relocate a family of skunks that have settled under our shed. We trap them at night, with peanut butter on a stick in the box, then in the morning we bring them out to the pond and let them go!" I explained.

I kept trying to be casual about this whole daunting escapade. In the few seconds it took me to bounce out of the truck and walk to the tail gate asking "Do you want to see this one?", there were three suffering policemen gathered, but standing back a fair distance from the vehicle. I opened one end of the trap and sure enough there was 'Pepe la Peu', stinking to high heaven! The men all backed away and indicated I could, should, please 'take it out of here'. I dillydallied, knowing the smell would not get any worse than it was right now. A skunk cannot spray unless it can raise its' tail and the trap would not allow him to do that. I had learned this from a crash course in 'skunk trapping' a farmer friend of mine had given me. The trap was built, and we started catching skunks like crazy.

After working all night, and the heat suffocating me, I would not rest knowing that little animal was being asphyxiated and could die if left all day in that box. I had no choice but to set it free. I would take him to the pond where we took the others, tilt the trap, and open the end door, and he would run off toward the water, obviously following the scent of where the others had gone. I did this many times that summer, never ever got sprayed, liberated the skunks, drove home, got a shower and that was that.

Now back living in Newfoundland for almost three years, those days of skunks, raccoons, porcupines and snakes, not to mention the big ugly 'June bugs' seem so far away. None of those creatures are part of our ecosystem here. I didn't mind the animals but the skunks could destroy a lawn in a day, digging for bugs, raccoons would ruin a cornfield, snakes were seemingly harmless, porcupines quiet and unobtrusive , but the June bugs terrified me. The big fat old raccoon that slept draped over the high branches of the willow tree didn't bother anyone, he left during the dark hours, but the skunks could be downright confrontational. If a skunk sprayed, its' manner of protection, then it would be costly and time consuming to clean up a pet, furniture may as well be destroyed and for the human it would be two days in a shower! So the family of skunks we had definitely could not stay under the shed. My husband put the lawn mower in the shed, left it on, and hoped to gas them out, but all that did was bring neighbors over to ask him if he knew 'your mower is on in the shed?'- causing many laughs. Of course he knew, but the skunks didn't care. So that is when the trapping went into high gear.

However, all the land we were living on was orchard land, land that had become occupied by humans. So indeed we were in their space, not them in ours. But nobody wanted to hear that rant, and I kept on truckin' skunks, and kind of got to like the little things. I was tempted to drop one off at a place where people would be quite perturbed but did not give into the temptation.

Summer went on, lots of skunks were relocated by one of our household members, or by me, and the little creatures were not harmed, I never got stopped by the police again. I did go into the parking lot of the local bank and came out of the building after about ten minutes to find a crowd gathered around the old truck. That was an experience. Little children were brought to our place to see the baby skunks, lots of peanut butter globs were made up for bait, and lots of conversation revolved around the skunk project.

So it's a memory now, and the Nova Scotian saying of "You got skunked!", meaning you lost out, is still used by us after so many years in that beautiful province, and we get odd glances when that is said, but that's just fine. I liked my skunk summer, and I was always sure the police would not stop me again, and I had seen the transformation of a young mans' face into a rubber mask–not too many people get to see that sort of thing!

Ah, yes, the skunks of summer–what an odoriferous memory!

BECKY

*'A backward glance
at a precious and loving friend'*

I was driving through Cape Breton, planning to catch the ferry to Newfoundland that night. I picked up the cell phone with great hesitation, saw the look on my husbands' face, because he too knew what I would hear. I was going to retrieve the messages from my home voice mail, from our home in Falmouth, NS, having made arrangements with a co-worker to leave any and all messages concerning Becky on my machine and I would check regularly. The call confirmed what I already knew. Becky was gone, approximately one hour before my call. My friend Valerie, one of the nurses had left the message as we had planned.

I had said my goodbyes the evening before, knowing that she would not be there when I returned from Newfoundland. I hoped she knew I was there, I think she did. Nothing more could be done for Becky, just pain control and keeping the vigil so she would not ever be alone.

So, that was that! I would never see her again. It was so difficult to believe, so hard to understand. She was just 47 years old, same age as I was also. My mind wandered back to the first time we had met. It had been at the little Elementary school in Falmouth where the girls, in grade one or two, were involved in a school band concert. The second time we met at a Brownie pack outing, then a Mother and daughter Brownie dinner, and by then we were buddies. Her daughter, Michelle, known as Squiggy to her friends, and for reasons adults could not understand, but Squiqqy was part of our lives for years, and still is. She and my daughter Heather were inseparable. If they could not be found at our house, they most likely would be at Beckys' house. Our paths crossed constantly, many outings with the girls were enjoyed, and before we knew it the girls were grown and off to University. Michelle, her sister Shelly, my daughter Heather and son John were all finding their own lives. It had been a long time since that first little school band concert.

Becky had suffered the loss of her husband Gary just five years before her own death. She had nursed him, cared for him, loved him, even learned how to give him his pain injections. She never wavered. When he died, she knew she had done her best, the community rallied around and she gradually found her way as a single mother, and learned to smile and laugh again. Her self-deprecating humor was back, and our talks continued on her back step.

But the biggest problem then presented itself. She had been a stay-at-home mom, one of the best around, but she had no formal training and now had to go job hunting to support the family. Education costs were expensive, as was the running of a household. But in no time Becky had a job as a clerk in a drugstore, a job she loved. She was in the work force, getting her own pay cheque, seeing people every day and touching lives in her special pleasant way. If you stopped at the drug store, Becky could always make a dull day seem brighter.

Life was just getting good for her again, the battles fought, the grief easing somewhat, the girls in University, then her eldest daughter graduated and came back to town, bought the towns' only theatre and forged ahead in the business of bringing movies to the community, something she loved, and her mother was so proud. Michelle and Heather were still in University, John had gone to Alberta, and still we had our chats and glasses of pop when I stopped by or she came to visit.

And then it happened! Becky became ill overnight, so quickly that it would take ones' breath away to watch the downhill slide. She was taken to the bigger center in Halifax, and I went to visit. I walked in the room just as she returned from having a CT scan, and she looked at me and started to cry "You know what it is don't you?" she said. I assured her I didn't know, but her tears led me to believe it was not good. She had an inoperable tumor she told me, but she would fight, and fight she did. With a chin up she went through the treatments, although she was told they were for comfort only. She continued her battle, smiled through her tears and quietly kept her own council.

This woman did not have much in the way of material goods. She asked for little in her short life. She weathered her losses and won, many time over, and she had raised her daughters well, was looking forward to being her own person for a few years anyway, forty-seven is young and she had suffered much.

Her struggle continued. All of us, her ring of friends brought her books, food, anything she wanted, asked for, wished for, we tried to do. She craved ice-cream and her freezer filled up, causing her to laugh at us all! She cried and there was always one of us to hold the hand that had held so many others.

But nothing could stop the downhill process. She was admitted to hospital and even the oxygen therapy didn't help anymore. But with good pain control she did brighten up, and it was wonderful to see her enjoy things and smile again. And then she began to slip away, as surely as summer turns to fall, Becky was leaving us. And the phone call was the confirmation of her departure, and only the tears were left.

Later on that night, just before we docked in Port aux Basques, my husband walked toward me, looking like he was hesitant to tell me something. It had not been a good day. But he finally says "Princess Diana died tonight!". I felt like I was in a vacumn, how could this all be?? I went to the Television area and sure enough every news channel was covering the tragedy.

But Beckys' death would not be covered by the media, she had no riches or fame, she did not dine at the Ritz, nor would she have wanted that kind of life. Her life was fun-filled, grief-filled, with times of pride and times of hope, with family gatherings and the company of good friends. Her struggles to make ends' meet made her appreciate every little bonus that came her way.

And she was so proud of her daughters, had close relationships with both of them.

So yes, I grieved for Princess Diana as did the rest of the world, But before that Princess died in France, a woman who was a Princess in her own way died in a little rural hospital in beautiful Nova Scotia. I missed her so, and I think of her often, more often probably than I think of Princess Diana, because the Nova Scotia Princess was closer to my heart, she was my friend, and I loved her.

I will remember her always with a smile, just as she would wish it to be.

BEVS' BATTLE

Beverly, known to all as Bev, has been my friend for many years. We met in Falmouth, Nova Scotia, during my years there. Our daughters were best friends, were the same age, and it followed that Bev and I would become friends. As the girls grew and shared their lives, we shared ours as well. My birth year is 1948, hers is 1942, so we were both babies of the forties. A friendship between Bev and me is a bond of two totally different personalities. Bev is quiet spoken, I am opinionated, Bev was a greenhouse worker, a drugstore clerk and finally a school bus driver. I know I could never grow nice flowers like she did or be trusted to drive a school bus. I am a nurse. Bev lived near all sorts of family, I was far away from mine, she was an only child, but I was the oldest of five. But we became friends and our differences balanced themselves. It was always a joy for me to spend a few minutes with Bev, she seemed to be so well grounded, so kind, and my daughter loved her dearly. And we adored her daughter, Jenny, nicknamed 'Jenny Piccolo' by my husband who obviously watched 'Happy Days' on Television. Bev had a son and two daughters and her husband was a fine finish carpenter. I had a son and a daughter and my husband was in law enforcement. Bev has a great faith, I tend to be cynical, but after a chat with Bev I always felt more assured. She was and is a wonderful person, wife, mother, grandmother, worker and friend.

 My friend grew up in the area in which we lived, and was known by all for her community work and her readiness to help in times of trouble. She worked at the fruit and vegetable stand in the summer and scooped up the greatest ice cream cones for us. Her husband was also from the area that was the gateway to the Annapolis Valley of Nova Scotia, and their family was well established in the town. They worked, raised their children, and our lives paralleled. When my daughter married, Jenny was in the bridal party. Then in the year 2000, I left Nova Scotia and returned to Newfoundland, saying a fond farewell to my old friends in that beautiful province.

In March, 2001, my daughter mailed to tell me Bev had become ill. It was a shock to everyone because it just seemed that Bev would always be busy, working two jobs at times, and appeared invincible. Now Bev was under attack, vulnerable and ill, weak and getting weaker daily.

It started with Bev stumbling several times getting on the bus, and she had noticed that she was weak and uncoordinated also. She limped and did not know why or what was happening to her. Finally she was sent by her doctor to a specialist in Halifax, returning with the diagnosis of Amyotrophic Lateral Sclerosis or 'Lou Gehrigs' Disease' in May of 2002 .Now Bev found herself floundering in a vortex of frailty, her life spiraling out of her control, having had to leave her job in January of 2002 she felt adrift and afraid. She began to study this disease that was robbing her of her independence, changing her life completely. She soon found out that ALS as it is commonly known, is a progressive disease of the nerves coming from the spinal cord responsible for supplying electrical stimulation to the muscles of our body. The body becomes very weak, and the weakness leaves the person susceptible to other ailments. ALS occurs most often in the fifth through seventh decades of life, and Bev and I were in our fifties. There is no known cause for this curse, and Bev felt her life becoming more out of control as she gradually went from a cane to a walker, and then to a wheelchair.

I was grief stricken for her, and being far away made it worse. But Bev got a computer and keeps in touch with the world that way. She loves her computer although her arms are weakening and some days it is difficult to type. I tell her not to try and answer my messages, it is not necessary, once a week or so is fine, I understand how difficult it is for her.

Now a lift is being installed to make the transfer from her bed to a chair more efficient, the community is holding fund raisers to buy her a van with a lift for her wheelchair.. Her love of children is still strong. She had her wheelchair take her to the end of the driveway to see the children as they did a fund-raising walk for her. Her downhill progress is fast, her life has changed so much, yet she can tell me in an e-mail how fortunate she is to have such friends and family. She is, and always was, a special woman. She was in her wheelchair for the ALS walk-a-thon last year and will be again this year, pushed by her daughter Jenny who has been a strength and a support to her mother, as is her sister and brother. And my daughter in Calgary will run in the fund raiser this year, wearing a picture of Bev on her shirt. She loves Bev and wants to help. Jenny is the same, a tribute to the strength and determination of two young woman that Bev and I raised to adulthood.

We never know what life holds for us, and it is best we do not. We question the fairness of situations, the tragedy that befalls a person, but we have no answers. We do not know why Bevs' husband had a major heart attack and then a few years later this very special woman is becoming incompacitated. Our hearts ache for her, we shed tears for her, we shake our fist at the universe about her, and the strange part of it all is that it is Bev herself who comforts us. She has her photo on the ALS website, she will talk to anyone newly diagnosed, she has enormously strong faith and is so grateful for lifes' little joys. Her soft quiet voice stills the broken hearts of her family, and her gratitude makes us all want to fix it for her. But we cannot.

She is still a young woman, a woman who worked very hard over her lifetime, a woman who loves being a grandmother but cannot take her grandchild for a walk, but is accepting her condition. She is a guiding light to all who know her. She is aware there is no cure, but she prays for just that, a cure for herself and others like her who are halted suddenly in the best years of their lives.

I saw a photo of Beverley recently, I saw the same kind smile, the same look of caring, and I can hear her saying "Let Heather stay Bonnie, she will be Ok with me." And I knew she would. So Heather would stay, and Bev would care for them keeping them safe from harm. Now they want to care for her. And they will.

As for me, I try to stay in touch. Bev touched my heart a long time ago. She has been a friend, a patient of mine, a great listener and I have never seen her faith waver. I admire her, I love her, and I worry about her. She tells me her arms are weaker and I feel tears, she tells me how grateful she is for all of us in her life and my breath catches in my chest, she says she has to accept what she cannot change and I agree, because it is so.

Yes, we are different in personalities, but we are women, mothers and grandmothers in our fifties, and we are now far apart in miles. But Beverly is not far away from my heart, as I think of her daily and send her photos and quotes and things I know she enjoys. She is a lesson to us all. She still our Bev, and although she is ill, she is a shining light to all who know her.

I can close my eyes and remember driving home from work and meeting the school bus and the big smile of the lady driver directed my way, and I remember the wonderful ice-cream cones she made. Most of all I remember a woman who graced my life and teaches me hope as she copes with a battle that attacks her from all directions and has rearranged her life drastically. But Bevs' battle will never destroy the quiet words of comfort she gives others or change the caring person she was and will continue to be.

I pray for a good life for her while she fights her illness. She is very much loved and admired. We will support her as long as she needs us and we will always remember that big smile that lit up our lives on our rough days, the big smile that is still there for us in spite of the battle for her life she faces every day. She is a bright candle in what for her is a confusing and difficult world, and for that we adore and admire her. And we will also spread the word of ALS, and the fight those people face daily and pray that a cure will be found, for Bev and those like her who have been afflicted by this tragic disease. We care for her dearly and want her to know. This is written for her, to let her know I care for her. I see in my mind the endearing smile of a courageous woman named Beverly McCann who is fighting a battle for her life.

We love you Bev! Keep that bright light shining as you fight your daily challenges.

JANINES' JOURNEY

Amyotrophic Lateral Sclerosis was originally known as Motor Neuron Disease. It is a rapidly progressive fatal neuromuscular disease characterized by degeneration of a select group of nerve cells and pathways in the brain and spinal cord, which leads to progressive paralysis of the muscles. There is no brain impairment.. ALS, the letters for which this condition is also known 'Lou Gehrig's disease' after the famous baseball player who died at the age of 38 from this illness in 1941. . June has been named ALS month because it was in June that Lou Gehrig retired from baseball, and June is his birthday month. Between 1,500 and 2,000 Canadians currently live with ALS, and the disease is no respecter of age or gender, however the usual onset is between 55 and 65 years of age. . A beautiful young Newfoundland girl, Janine Cassandra Harris developed ALS at the age of 18, and is the youngest Canadian to date to die of it to date. This is her story.

Janine Harris was a young Newfoundland girl, who, at the age of 17 years, with thoughts of a full life ahead of her, devoted parents and friends, a love of life, music, laughter, art, and a dream of becoming a nurse, had her dreams destroyed, and her life robbed by Lou Gehrig's Disease.

Clyde and Ruth Harris lived for Janine, and Janine in turn loved them without fail. Janine was the only child of Ruth and Clyde Harris. Beneath the thin veneer of normalcy, the grief of the loss of their daughter eighteen months ago is raw and difficult to witness. The light is gone from their lives. They were in Lethbridge, Bonavista Bay to visit their daughters' grave, on what would have been her twenty-first birthday, and they visited me also. Their tears flow, and one can feel the sense of complete loss they are dealing with daily. However, they tell me it is Janines' spirit that keeps them going, and they will do what they can to raise awareness of this stealthy, deadly disease.

Janine Cassandra was a student at Bishops' College in St. John's, NL, having dealt with and fought dyslexia with a steely determination and won. At some point she had started showing an interest in photography , and life was good. In January of 2000 this healthy girl began to have trouble with her right arm. Her mother noticed that when her daughter applied lipstick, her hand trembled. Janine attributed it to carrying a heavy backpack. However it worsened, and they sought medical help .Numerous tests were done and all resulted in normal readings. But her mother is a bright quick woman, her father a strong, intuitive man, and they knew that something was terribly wrong. July 26,2000, they visited Dr. M. Stefanelli, and more examinations were done. During this time Janine had a fall, and the doctor remarked that the muscles of this young womans' legs were abnormally small. By this time Janine had learned to print with her left hand, fighting her disability every way she could. Her courage was truly shown when she continued to do volunteer work, reassure her parents and face her circumstances head on.. She received a Charles Grant Memorial Award for Perseverance and Achievement, for defying all obstacles, an award well deserved. Graduation was around the corner and she and her friends looked ahead with great anticipation.

By January 2001 she clearly was deteriorating, although she continued to drive, and declared to one and all that 'can't' was not a word she used, but soon that activity came to an end. More doctors, more tests, and a referral to a doctor in Ontario in February turned into a nightmare for her parents. The weather was bad on the day they were to fly to Ontario to keep the appointment with Dr. Strong, causing them to miss the appointment, and another was booked for April. The downhill trend by then was escalating and her mother was spoon feeding her. By the time the April appointment came to be, Janine was using a wheelchair. The letter to the Ontario doctor had frightening words on it for her parents. Those words were 'QUESTIONABLE JUVENILE ALS'. Janine was not told about this, but the doctor in Ontario confirmed the worst-it was indeed ALS. Dr. Strong is a leading authority in the field of Neurology and ALS, and the confirmation of the diagnosis by him was devastating

April turned to May, and the family home was sold. Another was bought, one more accessible for their daughters' wheelchair, the hydraulic chair and bed, and other necessary aids, because by this time Janine could not walk. She did not exhibit anger, she accepted the inevitable, and gave strength to her parents. When she no longer had use of either hand and arm, her father devised a way to let her access her Television, DVD player, and stereo. He taped the remote control to her foot and Janine learned how to change the channels with the toes on her right foot. We will never know what she was thinking during those difficult days, but she kept others going with her positive attitude.

June brought another series of painful treatments. The medical community had realized that by removing spinal fluid and replacing the same amount of fluid with Gamma Globulin gave the ALS patients some degree of mobility. She endured thirty of those painful procedures with grace. But even with her strong determination, the help of two devoted parents and a wonderful friend, Jennifer Hicks, she continued to slide downhill.. Vitamin E, physiotherapy, medication and everything that could be of any possible help was advised by Dr. Mark Stefanelli. But there were no new therapies. Janine and her friend Jennifer spent time together and this devoted friend kept Janine in touch with the teenage side of her life. Home care was accessed in July to help the family care for their daughter. Ruth had quit her job to stay home with her months before ,but the time had come to seek help. Janine was by now totally disabled. . Despite her broken heart Ruth continued to care for her daughter.

October was the point of a frightening turn of events. Janine was short of breath, and needed oxygen. She was taken back to the hospital. Her respiratory muscles obviously had become affected, and although Jennifer, Ruth and Clyde did their utmost, they could not reverse the course of this deadly ALS.

November came, and with it the cold winds, but also preparations for Christmas, a favorite time of year for Janine. She would point to ornaments and gifts in the flyer, and her father would go and buy them, bringing them home to her friend. In early November Janine suffered a seizure and thereafter was dependent on home oxygen continuously, and her parents watched helplessly as they saw a bright beautiful girl become even more incapacitated. Finally on November 6, 2000, her mother told her the worse news. And Janine was still cared for at home, where she wanted to be. Her mother says her sweet daughter really never got out of bed after that. Her friend sat with her and comforted her , although in turn Janine was comforting everyone else. She was a remarkable girl, facing death, yet choosing Christmas gifts. Her interest in hockey was still strong , and she teased her Dad about the scores of the games. Her mind was as bright as always, with a phenomenal memory and a quiet acceptance of her fate. She worried about her parents, and asked to talk to Aunt Ivy, her mothers' sister. Aunt Ivy was special to Janine and she verbalized her wishes to her. She asked Aunt Ivy to make sure that her Mom would return to work, and her other wish, because of her love of Christmas, was that her photo be placed under the Christmas tree every year.

On December 4, 2001, she suffered another seizure and was immediately taken back to the hospital. Her oxygen deprivation was severe, but her memory still quick, and she had the phenomenal wisdom to refuse life support, knowing that her parents would have to make a decision to withdraw it at some point. She told her Aunt Ivy that she did not think her parents could do it, nor did she wish to put them though that devastating process. There was no going back home this time. Janine told her aunt she wanted to be buried in Lethbridge, a place she had visited often as a child. On December 5, 2001, with her devastated mother holding her close in a narrow hospital bed, she was given Morphine for discomfort, and in her mothers' arms she quietly slipped away. The bright blue eyes of her father poured tears of grief and helplessness. Janines' journey was over. She would suffer no more, she never became the nurse she wanted to be. But I am sure that a young Newfoundland girl is in a place without pain and sickness, wearing the graduation ring of a nursing school, and an award for bravery. The incapacitation, the broken arm she suffered from a fall, the painful treatments, the oxygen tubing, the days of changing channels with her toe, were over. Her desolate parents honored her wishes, overwhelmed by her courage. Her Dr .Mark Stefanelli attended her funeral, having developed a close and caring relationship with this special girl.

May 23,2003 would have been her twenty-first birthday. Her parents came to visit her resting place, and the tears flowed ,and the memories surfaced, as they struggled to deal with the heartbreak of losing their only child. All they had endured, all they had tried, from the first symptoms Janine had, to her confirmed diagnosis, to her leaving this world behind has stunned her parents. They too are brave, and need have no regrets. Six months from a confirmed diagnosis of ALS to death has left them reeling in pain and anguish.

They are strong people, a testament as to where Janine found her strength of character. Both of them are working with the ALS society, helping to raise money for research. It is therapy and a constructive way to deal with their grief. Nature has programmed us to somehow accept the death of our parents, but nature cannot prepare a parent for the death of a child. Clyde and Ruth should be comforted by knowing they did all they could, loved her so much, but the loss will hurt until the day they die themselves.

When you see the symbolic blue Cornflower symbol, and the ALS signs set up in different places in June please remember Janine, and her parents. Janines' journey is over, but many are still struggling.

And also remember a bright and beautiful nineteen year old Newfoundland girl, the youngest to succumb to this disease in Canada, who died as she had lived, thinking of others, facing difficulties head on, reminding us just how we should live. It reminds us to give our loved ones that extra hug, just as Janines' father showed her mother and her how to hug. Her tiny mother would straddle the wheelchair, and he would hold Janines' arms up around her Moms' back, allowing her to hug her Mom, causing their tinkling laughter to ring through the house. Ruth will forever remember the warmth of those hugs. A beautiful memory in an expanse of desolation and sorrow., given by a father to the two women he loved more than life itself.

As Ruth and Clyde prepared to leave for home, she gently pulled from their van a little kitten. A soft tiny kitten, something to hold, to shower with love and care. They need this little kitten. Janine will forever be remembered ,and may Clyde and Ruth be comforted by knowing that others do care, as they work through their grief.

" Love comforteth like sunshine after the rain"–William Shakespear.

THE 1973 DODGE DART

The car that just wouldn't quit!

It was truly one of the 'dog days of summer' that August afternoon in 1991, the temperature soaring to ninety-two degrees, not a puff of wind, the grass all brown from lack of rain, and if you looked closely you could see the heat waves a few inches above the pavement. I had just returned home from a long day at work and was approaching a complete meltdown as I entered my home in Falmouth, Nova Scotia. This was one of those days when the sea breezes of Newfoundland and the coolness of the beaches, the wind on the hilltops where we would pick our Newfoundland blueberries, all added up to a memory that caused an ache in my heart. A dream of returning someday kept me going as often dreams do. Our house was cool, but many chores awaited there for a working mom. But then came a knock at the door.

    I sauntered to the doorway expecting a salesperson, a friend of my two teenagers or maybe the paperboy. What met my gaze was two men, probably in their late twenties, covered in tar and grease, sweat making little trails down their faces. In this quiet 'Gateway to the Annapolis Valley' neighbourhood they looked decidedly out of place in their heavy work clothes on such a hot day. They launched into an explanation of why they had someone drop them off at our house. We had placed a 'For Sale' sign on our wonderful old car and they had seen it and decided immediately that they had to have that car! They went on and on, explaining how they had seen it early in the morning on their way to work with the road crew, and could hardly wait to get off work to come by and purchase the car. They had seen it, and just had to have it, wanted to test drive it, and to indeed buy it, just like that! I explained that my husband would not be home for an hour or so and he was the salesperson that would have to deal with on this matter, so they said they would wait. They found a shady spot on the lawn and sat to wait for my husband, and I thought to myself "Boy, they must really want that car!" And I returned to the ever present chores that awaited me.

As I worked away, I thought of how the Dodge Dart had come into our lives. She was created in 1973, then found her way to Bridgewater, Nova Scotia, where an older gentleman and his wife had her for years, using her only for trips to the grocery store and to church. Kept out of the weather, lovingly cared for and looking like new, she came into our family s' possession in 1982. We were on the lookout for a reliable second vehicle, not too expensive, but in good shape. Then came a phone call from Bridgewater, a friend of ours had sighted this wonderful car and just knew it was the car for us. Fourteen hundred dollars, a short drive to the South Shore and she could be ours. And that is how we acquired the 1973 Dodge Dart with a Visa Card and enjoyed her for nine years.

When the Dart arrived in our driveway, I, of course, had to do the usual inspection. What a car! Military tank green, spotless interior, a smell of leather, an ashtray never used, so no tobacco smell, white walled tires, a V8 engine and only 31,000 miles driven, all of those in town miles with the lovely old man at the wheel, a back seat that looked like it had never been used at all, and a radio blasting a country music channel with a clear crisp sound. I had often been told during my formative years to 'never love something that can't love you back' well, I'm sorry, but I loved this car. She was to become my beloved transport, and my friend in the middle of the night when I was called back to work, finding her way to the hospital in all kinds of weather, and never ever failed me.

The Dart was such an appropriate color as the military green was so perfect for the armoured personnel carrier for a group of teenagers, a place for me to sleep when we were rained out at Girl Guide camp, and so many other adventures too numerous to mention, not all pleasant may I add. In the town a few miles from ours was a small town two man police department who had one car. I drove to that town about twice a year. On one of those excursions, with the radio blasting and the sun in my eyes I had the awful, embarrassing misfortune of running broadside into that darned patrol car, the Dart stuck into the fibreglass shell of the new patrol car like a forklift into a pallet. Sixteen hundred dollars damage on the police car, not a scratch on my Dart. But a million dollars' worth of embarrassment for me!!

The Dodge Dart was a delivery truck, bringing home thousands of dollars worth of groceries, carrying hundreds of Christmas packages to the Post Office to mail to Newfoundland. She was well behaved for my son as he learned to drive and got his drivers' license with her, and she waited with him as he in turn waited and mumbled when he was sent to pick up his younger sister. That car also conspired with him on the days he played hooky from school.

Never much trouble, never quit in a snow drift, never groaned when six fair sized young people weighed her down, never failed on me on our way to work. No doubt about it, she was one heck of a vehicle.

But the years brought changes, my son bought a truck, gas prices shot up and the Dart loved to drink gas, the wear and tear and depreciation of the years required she have an owner who could give her the care and attention she needed, the skills our household did not have, nor did we have the time to spend with her. So she was put out in front in the driveway with a big 'FOR SALE' sign in the window. My heart was heavy but the reality was that she had to go and that was that.

I gave the young men waiting on the lawn a cold drink, they sat and continued to wait and finally my husband arrived home. They were all set to bargain and plead but my husband said only "If you want her that bad you can have her!" They jumped for joy. The paper work was done, the keys handed over and they got in and waved as they drove away.

It was August. 1991, 100,000 miles later, memories too priceless to share ran around in my mind as I watched her drive away. I realized later that they also had my hair band, and the extra gas can for the lawn mower, two of my favorite cassette tapes, a windshield washer thing, and most of all, a huge big chunk of my heart! The car that wouldn't quit was leaving, and I am sure for years after she was still going, and one thing is sure, when I look at the huge photo I did of the car for my son, I see the kids piling into her, and hear the laughter of all the fun times in the 'car that just would not quit' and my heart hurts with the sweet memory of it all.

ONE OF LIFES' BIGGEST DECISIONS, KNOWING WHEN TO QUIT

It was one of the hottest June days ever in our little Nova Scotia town, and everything was still, the flowers all in bloom with the buzz of the bumble bees, the moan of the lawn mowers and the swish of the lawn sprinklers making it a very usual summer day. It was the year, 2000, and this was no usual day for me. As a matter of fact it was a most unusual day, and one that stays with me although with time the angst of it has lessened. That afternoon I sat and collected my thoughts, surrounded by boxes, books, and photographs in their frames lying on every bit of space the house allowed. This was the day the packing started, and tomorrow would be the day I worked my last shift at Hants Community Hospital, a hospital I had worked at for years, with nurses I had known for the same length of time as my stay.

Many of the nurses were good friends, many of my patients had become special to me, and it was so bittersweet, this leaving it all. But chores had to be done that day, so I forged on and prepared myself for the 'last day at work'.

The next morning dawned just as hot and hazy as the day before. And I took special care as I readied myself for this day. The decision to leave and return to Newfoundland had not been made lightly. As a matter of fact it had been never in our thoughts until the year 2000 came, and all of a sudden it seemed that it was imperative that I do something to change my life, a life of work, work and more work. I was 51 years old. But the decision had been made and I was more than ready to return to the land of my birth, looking forward to feeling more grounded by my Labrador coast and Fortune Bay roots, living closer to family again, and knowing I was back to stay.

My nursing career had almost killed me at times, and at other times it had saved my life. A motivational speaker I had heard many years before had told us that our job should be one third of our lives, our family another third, and the other third for ourselves, for personal development, spiritual pursuits and recreational activities. Many times I had allowed my work to become two thirds of my life, if not more, the other third or what was left was for family, but none was left for me, something I never even realized was happening. It was unhealthy, and in retrospect, so unnecessary. But the shortage of nurses and the higher demands of the job required this, or so I thought at the time.

When I would almost fall, I would pull back, regroup, and then forge ahead, gradually getting better at setting limits and priorities. I loved my work, but I seemed bound and determined to let it devour my whole life. So I had made the ultimate decision after all those years, just when I got reasonably good at priorizing, to walk away. Nobody believed I would do it, but I did, I had no choice. The time had come to change a way of life that was actually a hazard to my health.

The last day was so bittersweet, I wore my 'CAP' just for old times sake, as the cap had long been cast aside as a requirement for nurses. But we had a lot of fun that last day in spite of all the work.

One young nurse approached me and asked "How do you keep that thing on your head?" It is a special secret but that day I took my cap off and showed her how it was done, and she was amazed.

Then she asked if she could put it on, sure she could. Being the same age as my daughter, with dark brown shiny hair, she loved divine in the cap with the black band, the Grace General Hospitals' special cap with the black band that I earned in 1969. It was the same band, the same strip of velvet I had first worn when I became a Registered Nurse.

I was struck by the similarity of the color of her hair, the style so much like mine when I started out 32 years before, that an unexpected moment of teary-eyed nostalgia washed over me. I felt as if I were looking at myself so many years ago, so many shifts ago. I put the cap back in its' place, gathered up my things and said my farewells. A party was planned for later in the week, but there were patients and their families, doctors, lab staff, dietary staff and all those people who make up the system of a working hospital, that I needed to say farewell to in the proper way. So after all my farewells, I walked out the door of that hospital with no regrets, just memories, and lots of good memories.

Nursing has changed, but it needed to change. Nurses are more and more becoming a part of the team of professionals who treat the 'whole' patient. The never-ending paperwork will be there, computers or not, and nursing is moving into the twenty-first century, at times kicking and screaming, at other times quietly flowing into the changes. But Nursing will always be a caring profession, and the young men and women who carry on the work will have their own 'watershed' moments, their own stories to tell.

As for me, I am back where I need to be, in Newfoundland, enjoying the water, the boats, the boil-ups, writing, photography, reuniting with old friends, living closer to family and living in a new home, built for retirement. At times the road has been rougher than I would have wished but the ratio of the thirds is more even now. I may finally have gotten it right-I think!

I miss my Nursing career, I miss the connections with fellow nurses, but it is easily overcome because I have three sisters who are nurses in various fields, and we do ' nurse-speak' many times. Writing, having a new grand daughter who is the love of my life, and having more time to be 'ME' is not so bad after all.

As a very wise and experienced nurse told me years ago at the Grace Hospital, "The hardest thing in life is knowing when to quit." And it was.

PART THREE

'The Year 2000'
Coming Home to
Newfoundland and Labrador

'And the Remembering Begins'

A SPECIAL VISIT TO THE 'KYLE

The little rental car I was driving steered obediently as I drove the stretch of almost empty highway in the direction of a sign that read 'TCH West', the radio turned off, the cool air blowing through the air-conditioned car a contrast to the hot August atmosphere outside. This was the last leg of a very necessary and important journey for me. It was 1999, I was fifty years old, and feeling a restlessness that was all encompassing. My life for the past thirty four years had been lived in Nova Scotia, having married a member of the RCMP. But Newfoundland was forever in my heart. This feeling of uneasiness had forced me to set out once and for all, by myself, to make a big decision. I needed to know if I really could leave the province of Nova Scotia with all its beauty, farmland, a place where my children had been born and grown up. I had many friends, worked as a Registered Nurse in a hospital where everyone knew everyone else, and I was well entrenched in a way of life with my work, friends, and family.

This urge had swept over me so quickly, the longing to be back in Newfoundland, with the rocks, the sea, boats, family and a place where I grew up but had left at the age of twenty-one. I had lived in so many places in Newfoundland, having a father who was a member of 'The Force' as well. Out of nowhere came the incredibly strong desire to be back in Newfoundland, back where I had spent my childhood years. And now I had set out to make my decision in that summer of 1999, before the new century began. I had taken time off work, so tired, anxious for my life to change in some way, longing to find the answer to my restlessness.

In an off hand conversation someone had told me that the 'KYLE' was sitting in the harbor at Harbour Grace and had been repainted and looked so like she did when she ran as a coastal boat. The whole thing came as a bit of a surprise because over the years I had visited Clarkes' Beach and my good friend Jean who lived there, had seen the rusting hulk, the remains of a ship obviously but had never known that it was my 'KYLE'. And to find out it was her, and she was looking better was incentive enough to set out to see her for myself.

Growing up around the coast of Newfoundland in various communities I was certainly quite familiar with the coastal boats, the steamer reports, the term 'stormbound', and it was an accepted part of our lives in the outports. Those boats such as the Northern Ranger, the Baccelieu, the Burgeo, and the Bar Haven, to name just a few were like todays' air transports such as Labrador Airways, Provincial Airways, and Air Canada, they were necessary to carry goods and people from place to place and were an absolute necessity for the isolated outports of the Northern Peninsula and Labrador. When the steamer was due in, everyone would head to the 'government' wharf to watch the activity, the unloading of goods and passengers, and although we were warned as children not to dare go around the wharf, we still did it. We were just really inquisitive and wouldn't miss it for the world. And many a case of seasickness would be forgotten as we watched all the activity from atop a grassy hill.

So, here I was, still going to see the 'coastal boat', but in a slightly different way today. In no time I was driving Roaches Line, and then through Harbour Grace. The sun was shining, the flags fluttering in the wind, and as I rounded the final turn I saw her in all her beauty, or so it seemed to me, the painting of the hull had done wonders for the dear old ' KYLE'. She was sitting out her retirement years in Harbour Grace little viewing stand had been built, a little plane named 'The Spirit of Harbour Grace' sat nearby, and I felt my spirits soar. So many questions I had for the KYLE ,and I wished she could answer them for me, but obviously I had to find my own answers.

You see I had a connection with this dear old boat. This was the boat that came to the edge of the ice in Mary' Harbour, Labrador and took me on my first boat trip. Born in November in the Nursing Station in Mary' Harbour made it a cold and uninviting sea voyage for my mother I am sure. We were to go home to my father, a Newfoundland Ranger, at Port Hope Simpson. Probably it would have been December by the time my mother and I were taken to the KYLE, the Harbour frozen, the biting winds almost unbearable. But the boat was the only way back to my father and so the KYLE did the job, and did it well.

A few hours passed as I sat and wondered, fretted, mulled and tossed the decisions around in my mind, with my eyes fixed on the old boat sitting on bottom, the tide low, the gulls flying overhead. I wanted to know where Mother was on the boat, was she cold, was she sick, was I a good baby and didn't fuss too much? All things to find out another time. The KYLE took us to Port Hope Simpson and in a short period of time we would move to Twillingate and live there for six years.

The KYLE sat proudly, valiantly trying to hold herself upright, her colors bright under the sun, and I thought and thought, weighed the pros and cons, and looked and listened to the sounds of the day. After an hour or more, I got up to go. I had made the decision, a decision that I have never regretted, and never will regret, I was coming home to Newfoundland.

The feeling of coming full circle, of being where I belonged, and where I should be had taken hold. There was an unmistakable drive to be back on the Island where I had grown up, where my roots were, my family, and where the childhood memories kept me grounded.

Yes, coming full circle, feeling complete, and best of all feeling at peace with the world.

The KYLE is still in Harbour Grace, and I plan to visit her again soon. But this time I will be on a different journey, a journey taken from a new home in Newfoundland, with the comfort in my soul of knowing I am where I need to be. The Newfoundland Mountie and the Newfoundland Nurse have come home.

THE OLD LILAC TREE BY THE SEA————

*A flood of memories is unleashed
by the scent of a Lilac tree.*

The brilliance of the sunshine, the deep blue of sea and sky, the comforting buzz sounds of a small boat making its' way across the harbor were all a welcome set of stimulations of the senses after the last few dull, wet days. Winter supposedly had passed but a gray for boding layer of fog lingered just long enough to make outdoor activities uncomfortable, if not impossible, for the last day or two. I needed and wanted to be outside in the fresh air, working on the land, preparing for summer, and remembering other summer days spent in this little community in Trinity Bay, Newfoundland. But nothing could have prepared me for just how intense the experience of memory could be.

This was to be the first spring spent in Newfoundland for more than thirty years. We had moved back to our Island home after thirty-plus years, most of those years were spent in Nova Scotia, twenty-two of them in the marvelous Valley of the Apples, the Annapolis. I had all but forgotten the smells, the sounds, the feel of the salt air, the shore breezes of home. The soft wind to the day baffled my little Newfoundland flag back and forth, and the dazzle of the sunshine on the water was balm to the soul as I worked on the garden.

My life for so long had been guided by the ebb and flow of hospital life in my work as a nurse, the seasonal concerns of the farmers, the blossoms breaking forth on the apple trees, haying season and the talk of the cost of this years' corn or strawberries, then the fall harvest, and the abundance of produce that one could never eat the tomatoes fast enough before they spoiled. It had been a totally different view of life from the one I had now, one that I had yearned for, just to be outside and look at the ocean was a dream come true. It has been said that 'the savage craves his native shore', and that is exactly what happened so unexpectedly to me, the pull back to the Island of Newfoundland, a feeling that took me by such surprise that it was very discomforting to have a sense of not being where you felt you should be. This was not something I, nor my husband had planned for nor anticipated. It was time to come home.

So, after all those years of vacations, sometimes an extra unplanned visit for a week or so, making it four weeks some years, and five weeks other years, we planned our return home. Emotions ran high, the moving was bittersweet because we were leaving so many good friends behind, a comfortable way of life, a more moderate climate, in fact a whole different way of life. But the pull back to Newfoundland was too strong to ignore. Our house sold in one day, taking us by surprise, and from then on it was nonstop planning, saying our farewells and getting on with the relocation. After all was said and done we drove off the Argentia ferry onto the shores of Newfoundland at one o'clock in the morning on June 29, 2000. Not even the two-hour drive to my husbands' childhood home in Shoal Harbour, socked in by fog, driving separate vehicles, with an upset cat, did anything to dampen our spirits. We were back, come what may.

There was so much to do, our children had grown and flown to the Canadian West to start their own lives, so it was just the two of us again now. The old family home of my husbands stood silently waiting for us that night, or should I say early morning? We entered the house, it was cool and damp, fatigue had started to affect us and the feeling of being overwhelmed gave me goose bumps. Our new house was to be built, but we knew at least a year in the homestead lay ahead, until everything was in place, tradesmen and supplies, location chosen, and so many other things to consider.

The old house just enveloped us, no sounds, no answers to our questions of "Are we doing the right thing?", "How much had we changed over the years?", "Would our friends be the same?", "Would they find us the same?" Naturally there were a few nagging fears, but all soon put to rest in the days ahead.

After a few hours of restless sleep, a beautiful dawn through the big window beckoned us. The awareness that we had unlimited work to do became a reality. My husbands' parents, Nanny and Poppy Lowe, were gone now and we inhabited their space. The cycle had begun again.

Summer passed quickly, difficulties arose and were overcome. Winter soon came and we were blessed with a grandchild, a little girl, so we truly became Nanny and Poppy Lowe in Shoal Harbour, just as they had been here for their grandchildren, we were now here for ours. Could we do it right, would this new stage of life be all that we wanted it to be? Would we measure up to the expectations of this time in our lives?

The winter was snow filled, it was my first time on a snow machine, first time for winter boilups , renewing old friendships, enjoying the people and their unique way of looking at life, something I had missed so much, the music I loved filled the house again, the lilting accents to get accustomed to, and it was all such great medicine for the soul.

Then came spring and time to get out and work on the garden and trees again. Time to get outside and prepare the land for the new house, also time to do some outside work on the old house.

So we go back to the beginning of my story-the beautiful spring day that found me pruning the rose bushes, the black currants and blueberry bushes had survived another winter and last but not least, the dear old Lilac tree still standing the test of time, having grown so much over the years. I raised the pruning shears and snipped a few old limbs, then all of a sudden I snipped a small shoot and I caught the scent of the Lilac, and memories long locked in the chambers of my mind came tumbling forth, a rush of treasures held back by time. The scent was the key to the lock.

The memory of my first visit here to meet my future in-laws, graduating from nursing school at the Grace Hospital, planning a wedding, meeting my finances' friends from childhood days, now seemed so fresh in my mind.

Then there was the wedding, the moving away, coming back bringing a baby boy who loved to jump and sway in the Jolly Jumper, the dent of the hook still visible in the doorway that held it for him. The little boy loving his times with his grandfather who taught him about woodworking, the little boy who is now a man of thirty, stands six feet, four inches and would probably have to bend his head to walk through this same doorway. Then came the visit back with him and his baby sister, a little girl who loved the flowers, the beach, splashed glue and paint on rocks and stuck them together to make 'Pet Rock families'. Two children who grew to love the visits to swim in the Trout Hole, the days spent berry picking, the picnics, birthday parties with family and friends, and the trip to Terra Nova National Park on each vacation. And the one special trip to the park when the capelin were rolling in and they stood in the water with the little fish swirling around their legs yelling "Look at all the fish Mom!"

Then too were the little friends they made, the friends that joined us on our little forays sometimes, my sons' attraction to his Poppys' workshop, the fascination my daughter had for the paint and paint brush her Poppy gave her, her red paint dabbed here and there on the workbench and step.

The old Lilac bush caused a stir every year at blossom time when I would call my mother-in-law and let her know that my Nova Scotia Lilac was in bloom, and every year she would patiently tell me that Newfoundlands' growing season was a month behind Nova Scotia but the buds were out and she expected blossoms any day! It became a family story, the Lilac blossom competition. The sweet memory of the children picking the black currants, the sea roses, and the lilac blooms and bringing them to Nanny, with a few buttercups thrown in for good measure. And Nanny making such a big deal over finding a nice vase to display her bouquet, carefully arranging it while they watched, so proud of their offering.

Then also were the sad memories, those of coming home to

funerals, of opening Christmas gifts already arrived from Nova Scotia but Poppy would not get to open. Then coming home with just a young daughter, her brother having left the nest, then of course coming back again without her, back to being just the two of us again. Then the not coming back as there was no longer anyone left in Shoal Harbour to visit anymore.

The lilac is in bud, the smell so sweet, and now is lovingly pruned as are the roses, after five years of being forgotten. The Lilac stands alone, the trunk weathered and old but the new shoots holding the promise of blossoms once again. It faces the sea, and is a living reminder that life continues and traditions live on.

The little girl who visited here for so many years comes back to visit now, bringing her own little girl and her young husband and they visit all the old familiar places that she remembers from her childhood. So we are the Nanny and Poppy Lowe now. Now we know how they felt, why they didn't care about a splash of red paint here and there, why they didn't get upset about the bucket of carefully chosen rocks spread out on the kitchen floor, why they didn't complain about the noise of children sliding down the worn stair bannister. Now we too know why the terror of an unidentified insect brought into the house in a bottle and set free, causing Nanny to stand on a chair until the huge moth was recaptured did nothing but cause us all to laugh with her as she overreacted to the incident, purely for the children s' entertainment. Now we Know.

The house is in and of itself a box of memories, the Lilac a symbol of times past- standing in quiet company beside the house. Now it is our turn, that stage in our lives that finds us waiting anxiously for the headlights of a vehicle coming down the lane when friends or family is expected. Now we know the wait is worth it when the hugs are spread around and everyone is talking at the same time, carried away with the excitement of the reunion.

The lesson is told that life is a continuum, but we don't really know that until we experience it on a personal level. Now we know the best lesson of all, we know that we are back again in the place where we belong.

THE LITTLE BOATS OF NEWFOUNDLAND

Summer 2001

Yes, the little boats are going out to sea tonight, and tomorrow and tomorrow night and for many days and nights to come this summer. It is the first night of the 'Recreational/Food Fishery' and the little Newfoundland boats are bobbing proudly around on their moorings just waiting to be unleashed and allowed to do what they were made to do-run through the waters and stop and go at the bidding of the master at the helm. The cove is different this evening, a much different and more free feeling in the air, more activity at our small wharf, more vehicles and children waiting to see who comes in first, who fished where, who caught the biggest fish, and all of those things that accompany the fishing itself.

It is an amazingly beautiful calm evening with a spectacular sunset, almost as if the Controller of the Universe is saying "All is well." The reflection of the pink sunset on the still water of Shoal Harbour makes the whole harbour look like a gigantic sheet of pink satin, and as each small craft leaves it appears to be cutting the satin like a seamstress would cut the lovely material. The red, yellow, blue and gold of the life vests add another dimension of color to the picture and it is truly a sight to behold. The race is on, and the little boats are straining at the bit to get out to open water where they most like to be, to do what they were made to do.

Last year was our first year back in Newfoundland after many years 'up along', and the food fishery opened, and we watched the boats leaving one by one. My husband had no boat, but friends and neighbours invited us to go along, so he went with them, caught fish and enjoyed it so much. This year he has had time to shop for and buy a boat, and is happy to take whoever would like to go, repaying kindness and courtesy that was shown to him in the Newfoundland tradition. Tonight he already had planned to take a friend with him when another young man called to see if he could join them and take his young son too. Sure he could, and off they went, happy faces reflecting the general feeling that prevails over us all.

Yes, this year we have our boat. We searched every nook and corner in Trinity Bay and beyond until we found her, and as soon as we saw her we knew she had to be ours. She is brand new, built by a man and his son in St.Jones Within. She is a beauty, a strong, sturdy craft. Sixteen feet long, six feet in the beam, and we think we have the Queen Mary. The twenty-five horse power motor moves her along slick and sure. Every day that she does not leave her mooring we can still drive by the little wharf and see her patiently waiting for us. I call her the ' Kylee G'. After our little grand daughter who lives so far away. When Kylee is older, she will know that a smart, beautiful little boat was named for her, and she will know that we were thinking of her always, even though a long distance separates us.

A friend dropped by to see our boat on his way across Newfoundland and remarked "I thought you would have a bigger boat than that!". I was crushed. I thought we had the best little boat in the world, and I still think so! When we were shopping for a motor for her my husband remarked that if he didn't soon find a motor he would have to grow longer arms to be able to row his boat. The Kylee G. bobbed about as if she were laughing.

This small craft gives us the freedom to explore the bays and coves, to have boilups on different beaches with friends, to search for mussels at low tides while the eagles circle overhead. She comes obediently to us from her mooring and stays while we load her full of everything four people would need for a day out on the water. Then our friends get aboard, then us,, and we just sit there and think she is a grand ship.

The little boy who goes out fishing tonight will love her, his eyes wide with the delight of it all, especially when he is in the company of his dad and the other men. He has his new life vest, his blond hair ruffled, his toothless smile a sight for any photographers' lens.

When we were looking for the Kylee G., we saw so many boats that looked sad, so many boat owners now too old to fish anymore, so many who had moved away, the boats falling into disrepair with nobody here to care for them. To see an elderly fisherman having to sell his boat is heartbreaking. He stands beside his boat and tells stories of better days, when the fish were plentiful, days when he was young, and his boat was new. One man said he would prefer to burn his boat than sell her to someone else, all so very sad. Probably that is what led us to the Kylee G. She is new, with fresh paint and no past history, her history begins with us and it has already started.

It makes me ask "What happened?". What happened to the Newfoundland of my childhood when the first question after school was always 'Goin' out in boat?'

Our scrawny knees and attitude of 'No guts, No glory' leading us to mischief like commandeering someones' boat, rowing around for as long as we liked, then losing an oarlock or towpin, and having to scrounge one from someone else s' unsuspecting little boat to replace it. None of us could swim, we were all warned to stay away from the wharf, but the pull was too great, and we repeatedly went to the boats, went fishing, and caught the fish too! Now a little boy thinks it is a real adventure to go out on the bay for an evening. What a change there has been, but the fish went and with them went a way of life.

But for the length of time of the open fishery maybe we will see the Island of our younger days. The boats will be launched, men will be yarnin' on the wharves, women complaining about the mess of the men, and telling them to hurry up, there are things to do at home! Hopefully Newfoundlanders will see that part of our heritage of the sea come to life for this short time. More people and boats out, more friends made, more proudness in their voices if they catch a good size fish, and with it catching for a brief moment some hope for the future and for Newfoundland.

During the time of the open fishery maybe some dear old fisherman will catch his last cod, and maybe some young child will catch their first one. At least we can hang on and hope, and enjoy Newfoundland the way it used to be. It will never really be the same, as the winds of change blow over everything sooner or later. Our Island in the Sea is changing, and we need time to adjust, to let the next generation steer the course, and I am sure we will find that the universe is unfolding as it should. Meanwhile, we are going fishing. We are going to feel the salt on our lips and the wind in our faces, and we will smell the salt air and remember.

As we move out little boats into the future, the fighting Newfoundland spirit will get us through as it has before during bad times. We will get through the loss, and we will accept whatever the winds of change will bring.

I never dreamed I would have one of those little boats of Newfoundland when I played the song about them over and over while I was away from the Island, but now I do have one. And it is glorious. Those little boats of Newfoundland really do mean the world to me. So for a short time we will use our little boats, get a glimpse at the Newfoundland of bygone days, and hope for the wind to be at our backs as we move into the twenty-first century.

SO, EXACTLY WHAT IS A BOILUP?

A short time ago a few friends from "the mainland" where I had spent so many years, were visiting me in my Newfoundland home, my real home as I called it. Of course they were curious about our way of life here in Newfoundland, and wondering how we were doing after two years back on the "Big Rocky Island", a direct and funny reference to my teasing I gave any and everyone who said they were going to the "Island" for vacation. I would immediately perk up and ask, "OH, which Island, the big rocky one or the little sandy one?",knowing full well that they meant they were going to beautiful Prince Edward Island.

It got to be a standing joke and they always clarified to me which Island province they were planning to visit after being asked that same question many times over. But it always produced a good laugh, and served as a reminder to all that a Big Rocky Island did exist too, and not to forget it! Everyone took the teasing well, as did I, and the point that Newfoundland existed and was not to be overlooked was well taken, and that was that.

So they had decided to come to the 'big Rocky Island', and I had spent days making special preparations for their visit, and enjoyed every minute of it. Newfoundland would be well represented in my household, with Newfoundland Tartan being the basis of my decor. We had a wonderful reunion when they arrived and we all sized each other up and decided we had weathered lifes' storms rather well during our time apart. Then the 'catching up' stories started, some good, some bad, but always of interest to us all. They sized up the Komatik, not having seen one before, saw my sea roses that I always longed for so much, the lilac was in bloom, and they saw that Newfoundland didn't have too many people living in igloos after all-something I always told them I would do when I returned home.

Of course we did the usual things, the women wanting to visit the craft stores, shop for Newfoundland prints and souvenirs, see the quilts and knitted goods of our province, and the men went off to look at the boats and chat with other men at the wharf. Several times during our shopping time, someone would ask me if we had had a 'boilup' lately, and if not when were we going. When we returned to the car one of my friends could not stand it anymore, and finally asked me the question of the hour "So exactly what is a boilup? You say that on the phone all the time and I hear it here now I humbly ask 'what the heck is a boilup?"

I laughed at her expression. She had been too proud to ask before but finally could not stand it any longer, and succumbed to her natural curiousity. So I tried to explain that it was a picnic outdoors, same as we used to have on the mainland, just took some food, went somewhere and boiled the kettle and had an old fashioned picnic, that's all.

"Well why is it a boilup here and a picnic back home?" she persisted. I went on to explain that in Newfoundland we had our picnics in the woods, in any season, away from fancy picnic tables and awnings, and signs pointing this way and that, and everyone dressed in their sparkling white summer clothes. No our picnics were different because we always had an open fire, they were held in any season, in the winters' freezing cold we used a skidoo, in the fall we used a four-wheeler or 'bog-bike', in the summer most likely a little boat. The concept of a picnic in winter eluded her completely. She told me in no uncertain terms that anyone who would leave a perfectly warm house and drive to some unknown spot in the woods, have a fire and eat their lunch had to be crazy, and that was that! And put that way I was inclined to agree-for ten seconds or so!

Yes, a boilup to the uninitiated might seem 'crazy' but we all know it isn't, not at all. We love those times, no fancy clothes, a wide variety of foods that we all bring to share, and good old fashioned tea boiled in our little Newfoundland flat bottomed kettles. We catch up on the happenings in each others' lives since we last met, exchange stories of family ups and downs, and generally enjoy each others' company.

The men rib and tease each other about who builds the best fire, and the women sort out the food, spreading it over any level spot that is close enough, and the variety over the course of a year would boggle the mind. Usually an assortment of rabbit sausages, bologna strips, moose jerky, the sweet and sour ribs, baked beans, brown bread and too many kinds of desserts to list. The birch bark nearly got eaten one day because one resourceful friend brings the birch bark with her so she doesn't have to fetch it to help start the fire, and her bag of birch bark got laid out on the log buffet table!

Our table is always a rock or a log, our picnic basket a canvas bag of sorts, our clothes are full of flanker holes and our shelter if it snows or rains is the God-given trees, if the weather is good our ceiling is the brilliant Newfoundland sky. In fall and summer we have the magnificent mosaic of colorful leaves and berries, in winter we cut a skidoo trail through fresh white snow, bypassing a huge rock where we know an old bear is sleeping the winter away.

When the engines of the machines stop there is a complete awesome silence of the universe, broken only when someone with hesitation says,"Well, let's get started!"

In five minutes we are a veritable bee colony, everyone doing something to help get the meal ready, the men work the fire, the women chat and display the food and share laughter, agonizing over whatever they forgot and reassured that there is enough for all. All the worlds' problems fade, lunch and tea is enjoyed, and friendships flourish. At the end of the meal a few may stay around the fire, sharing a private conversation, others wander off to take pictures or just look for moose sign or rabbit trails, berries, flowers, and anything that tweaks their interest. It is a time to reflect, to enjoy the last glowing embers, and when the time comes to go there is a reluctance to leave, to head back to a world of noise, cell phones, answering machines, and the routine of daily life. For the time of the boilup we are children again, and it is an ethereal experience. To call it a picnic just doesn't do it, it is a 'BOILUP'. It is a time to enjoy a sense of comradeship, sharing, laughing, helping and a soul mending experience it is for all.

If indeed we are crazy for engaging in such activity, then crazy we will continue to be, because after every boilup we are already making plans for the next one, and the one after that. Yes, we will be crazy with our boilups, and we will look at every flanker hole with warm memories of times shared and smile at the headiness of it all! The richness of the experience is so difficult to explain, but oh, so easy and glorious to experience.

MY SEA ROSES

I stood beside the beautiful, heavily bloomed wild rose bush in the front garden last summer. The calm water of the harbor reflected everything that it contacted but it could not reflect the nostalgic joy and staggering memories that the sight and smell the 'Sea Roses' gave me. Yes, the lovely old bushes finally bloomed with many dark pink blossoms and a scent that pierced the heart, my heart, and I felt that I had come to the place where I needed to be, filled with the sights and sounds, the smells and memories that I had missed for so many years. The quest was worth every venture, every fork in the road, every tear, every disappointment and with it all, also worth the joys and achievements that had filled my life away from Newfoundland for so long a time. Like the lilac tree before it the rose bush lifted my spirits to wonderful heights.

Every woman throughout her life, hopefully, has roses from time to time. The red roses of graduation and promotions, of love and devotion, the yellow roses of promises and 'just because', the coral roses that are special and so exquisite. My share of roses has always been so appreciated and so photographed, but nothing beats the 'wild rose of the seaside' that I yearned for over the years, longing for the scent that would take me back to childhood days in so many places around Newfoundland. And now here I was, standing beside a group of rose bushes by the sea, blooming on their own I am sure, because my green thumb is nonexistent, and besides that, they bloomed for years when the old house stood here empty, sharing their scent with the blueberries and black currants, and the occasional family member who happened to drop by. But this year they shared with me, and it fulfilled and met every longing moment as if they knew this year they had someone to admire and appreciate them in such a special way. The sheer curtains would blow in the breeze, bringing the sweet aroma in the sunny bedroom, what a way to start the day!

During the summer I had occasion to be in Harbour Grace and while my husband tended to some business I happened to see an enormous rose tree, the wild sea roses making its' branches bend to meet the ground. I had the greatest urge to get out of the car and touch the blooms but on second thought it would seem strange for some lady to look out her window and see a stranger sniffing and playing with a rose bush. So I sat and admired it from afar. But lo and behold when I got home that day I discovered my rose had bloomed, my first and very own rose.

For years I would talk of those flowers, the memory of them being in my life in different little outports around Newfoundland, the summer Dad took us to Sagona Island where my aunt had a garden full of roses and gooseberry bushes. The days in Twillingate when my sister and I would walk on the beach squishing the ink out of the squid and getting filthy, then buying a soda pop for five cents, and walking home passing beautiful roses by the sea. In Port Saunders and Burgeo where it seemed the special little flowers graced everyone s' garden along with the potatoes and all sorts of hardy root vegetables. As a student in St.John's I would occasionally find a special sea rose bush on a walk from the Grace Hospital to Lems Lunch with a friend, to buy a licorice pipe for two cents. Did my friend ever know how much I loved those roses? I doubt it, I probably never mentioned it, as our heads were full of too many other things in those days.

While in Nova Scotia during an especially difficult time in my life my husband and I took a walk around a little provincial park near Chester, called "Graves Island Provincial Park' and it was located right on the sea. From this island you could see some of the many islands of Mahone Bay, especially a group called the 'Seven Sisters', as they were all lined up in a row. Campers were enjoying their weekend but my heart was heavy. Then I smelled the roses special scent, I ran ahead of my husband saying "That's the Roses," and I found them and picked a few, but when I looked back he was standing holding a little bouquet as well, his hand offering them to me. He had found a rose bush before I did and thoughtfully made a bouquet. It was a bouquet that helped heal my heart, and I saved the petals from those roses until they were in a dish of pot pourri.

A very thoughtful friend went to Maine on vacation and brought me back a candle called 'Sea Rose' and it had the identical scent to the rose I loved. I carried the candle around with me from the car, to the locker, to the desk, and finally as it started to fade I lit it, and enjoyed it fully. A very nice thing for her to do.Somone who understood my longing to be beside the sea. So now I have my very own Sea Roses. They were so beautiful last summer but now the bloom is over, the bushes lie in wait for another season, another time to bloom as the cycle continues.

Yes, I am back home, back with my much longed for land, complete with all its' beauty and its' flaws, but so very, very special. Back to where I picked my first little sea rose, thorns and all and put it in the baby carriage with my baby brother the day he first smiled, in a garden in Twillingate forty five years ago.

How could anything so special ever be forgotten? The flower itself is unique, its' petals not always uniform, but neither are we perfect and always in special order. The thing that makes it unique is the very thing that makes it special, as it is with people. It is the memory of times past, the new baby, the new boat, the passing grade, the teenage crush, the illness finally passing, the buzz of the little plane readying to land on the harbor, and the sun filled day, the calm water and the scent that is like an expensive, wonderful perfume. Every little memory accompanied by a special little flower that costs nothing but is more precious, far more precious than gold.

A VISIT TO A SPECIAL PLACE,

SHOAL HARBOUR, NL

The two large windows in the front of the little post office gave me a great view of the copper colored kelp spreading out from the little causeway into the deeper water. The postmaster remarked on how low the tide was today, and we all agreed it must be the extreme tide of the full moon. I had left my house to do a few errands and now, half an hour later, I was still only two minutes from my house, but at least I had the mail. Running into two ladies I knew, then joining a 'tailgate' conference as I call it, that one of the women s' husbands was involved in, exchanging news of the day, and of course the inevitable remarks regarding the weather were shared all around. As I gazed over at the wharf through the large window I wondered out loud if the 'Vegetable lady' was over there today. The postmaster confirmed that she was and then advising me to " be careful, Nanny Lowe!" which always brought a chuckle as I was adjusting to being a new grandmother, he bid me good day and off I went to the Vegetable truck. Not too many there now, I thought, so a good time to pick up my necessities.

As I walked up to her she asked "Where's your husband lately?" That caused me to go into explaining that the boat was docked in another place and so she didn't see him at the wharf as much now. She told me about her sore hands, I told her what cream I used, stashed my fresh produce in the car and left, an hour and a half has passed by now. But there's a reason for this you see, it is because I live in a little community tucked up in the bottom of Trinity Bay called Shoal Harbour. It joined Clarenville in 1994 but ask anyone around and if they are from Shoal Harbour, then that is what they will tell you, not Clarenville, the adjustment has not been made quite yet.

This little community has a population of approximately fifteen hundred people, (combined with the Clarenville population there are fifty three hundred people in total.Shoal Harbour has two small grocery stores, a church, post office, municipal building, two furniture stores, a gas station, an iron works company, a winery, a funeral home ,a fly-in charter service ,a locksmith shop, a garden nurserybusiness and two recreational vehicle sales businesses, plus a recreational vehicle and small engine repair shop. It also has a long history of being linked to the Newfoundland Railway, and also people worked at the Hardwoods plant in Clarenville. It has just the right mix of people to make life interesting, characters who can bring a laugh on the worst of days. It is small enough that the local people know me even if I don't know them, for you see, it is I who am the 'newcomer'.But anybody who knows the Lowe family knows me from our frequent vacations, and they know and appreciate the fact that I love this little town. Shoal Harbour has a big heart, and people with concern for others, and they show it. It is a little place but it is an anchor in the lives of its' people.

Two years ago my husband and I returned to Shoal Harbour to retire. He is a Lowe, a descendant of one of the founding families of Shoal Harbour. For thirty-five years we were away, but the pull for Shoal Harbour brought us home. Shoal Harbour has changed quite a bit since that day in 1967 when my husband first brought me to visit his parents. The fishery didn't affect this community as much as the decline of the railway, and eventually the loss of it completely. It was then that the winds of change started to blow over Shoal Harbour, and it has been evolving and changing ever since then.

Let me take you on a tour through our little town. For me the day starts with sitting and looking out the big windows of our house onto golden and orange leaves falling now, pumpkins sitting on a rock, and the birds pushing and shoving to get a good seat on the feeders that I keep filled for them. All seems well so we can start our tour. We will drive to the gas station at the top of 'Milton Hill' as it is called, because our town ends there and Milton begins. A building supply and furniture store, with an adjoining convenience store and hair dressers shop complete the picture here. Always a beehive of activity usually, and generally one meets someone they know and a yarn begins. Then we turn back, down past well kept lawns, lovely hanging baskets, and occasional yard sale signs. The sea is always visible on the left driving down through and one can see Random Island and a small boat can be seen making its' way to Smith Sound, going under the 'bar' or causeway, that connects Random Island to the mainland.

Along the route there are small businesses, then a large business with a parking lot full of trailers, snowmobiles, seadoos and all sorts of outdoor equipment.The lane to our house is just beyond that parking lot. Further along there are more carefully for properties, a little lighthouse sits on one lawn, and a windmill to swirl in the breeze for effect. A little convenience store comes into view, and just down the road is a furniture store that at one time was a school, then down from the store is a fenced in a playground with usually several brightly clad children enjoying their playground by the sea, with their caretakers watching over them. Further along are a Municipal Building, and Post Office and next to the Post Office is a beautifully kept United Church with the Graveyard on the hill beyond it. A graveyard where one can see the headstones with the familiar names of Mills, Ploughman, Clench, Lowe,Tilley,Tuck,Wiseman,Mills, and other ancestors who have walked here before us. Houses are springing up everywhere. Further in the road is the elementary school with its' recess time music of the childrens' voices. The road will take you up and around the cove, past Shoal Harbour River, always gorgeous, and up around the bend some beautiful big trees, lovely homes, and if you are still you can hear the call of the blue jay and the rushing of the river. This road will take you down to the wharf and the end of Shoal Harbour as it gives way to Clarenville, to the wharf where the lovely lady sells her produce. Otherwise you can drive straight over the causeway and come to the same place, the wharf where a small boat named 'Misty Sue' sits on her collar, with other little Newfoundland boats keeping her company.

In summer and fall, people are walking, chatting, their dogs on a leash and straining to chase the seagulls. One seagull has laid claim to a rock and at a low tide he looks like a mighty ruler, sitting on a granite throne surrounded by golden seaweed. The sandpipers dash to and fro on the shore and an occasional kingfisher dives for his prey. In the winter we have geese that stay and slip and slide around on the ice, but they stay. They leave in summer and come back in late fall. It is considered a strange phenomenon these geese, but that is what they do, and in winter one can find people feeding them from the shoreline. Shoal Harbour is in fact a Canada Goose Sanctuary, and proud of it.

Lines of freshly laundered clothes hang out to dry, a clothesline of salt fish hanging on a line in the sun looks wonderful, and the tricycles of the preschoolers can be seen here and there, and usually the children wear their helmets now. I often see things that are reminders of days gone by but at the same time it is a community where most of us have e-mail addresses, and send messages back and forth in the way of the twenty-first century. But it is still a place where a man can find, always, a few people to help haul his boat up on the point, where the minister and postmaster know your names and the names of your children, where people call my husband by his given name while I use a nickname, and it causes a chuckle many a time.

We have had our tour, come for coffee? Small community isn't it? But who left the bag of tomatoes on the doorstep, who came and plowed the snow when it was necessary, who called when they wanted a nice photo taken of their skidoo, the people who live here and share with us, that's who, a nice touch to life. We sit over coffee in my sun room and look down past the colorful trees and see an enormous barge of wood coming into Clarenville, and the binoculars come out, yes, it looks like a moving island! How do they do it? And, no, you will not hear a lawn mower start on Sunday morning until church is through, until people are out walking the trail of the old railway bed, the dogs are barking as their owners throw bright orange balls for them, and the boys have their bikes out. Shoal Harbour has changed, and is changing constantly. But the change is not all bad, because to move ahead requires change and the people know that.

My husband arrives from his foray into the woods, cutting firewood, takes a look over at the barge, asks if the Flicker woodpecker was here today, he says he saw his friend at the garage, and was told that one of the community elders was very ill. We all know the lovely man and are sad about his poor health.

Come back and visit us again. The tea and craft sales will start soon and the church ladies will be all decked out and looking wonderful, making tea, serving cookies, and admiring the crafts and preserves. The geese will be in the harbour, and people will welcome you back as will the honking geese.

Yes, you have visited Shoal Harbour, as I did for many, many years, but now I am not visiting, I am home. This little shoal water harbor, tucked up in Trinity Bay has brought me home to stay. You'll be welcome if you come back, I'll be here, and so will Shoal Harbour and if you have time I will show you the Trout Hole, a deep hole further up the river where the children always like to swim, and maybe take you to some other secret little beautiful places as well.

And if you have enough time we can share some stories of the days gone by, the antics of the now fifty-plus age groups, and the stories they remember from their younger days here. Folklore is everywhere, and is just as interesting as Shoal Harbour itself. A little community that has stood the test of time, and has a beauty that continues to overwhelm, and a character that you can feel in the air. Shoal Harbour is moving into the twenty-first century with its' head up, looking forward to the future with a genuine belief that although things change, some things can remain the same. For me it is 'Home', and to be here is a dream come true.

YOU'RE DARN RIGHT, I'M GOIN' FISHIN'!

Well, the rain stayed and stayed, it ran in little rivulets down the side of the windows, taking dust and debris as it went. When the showers stopped everything looked so very fresh, smelled so wonderful, the greens so bright, that it was difficult to stay angry at the rain. So, it was time to settle down with a good book and forget that I had fifteen fish waiting for me out there in the bay.

The supper time news was hardly over when I heard the words "GOIN' FISHIN'?". That did it, I remembered the old saying 'there's no bad weather, only bad clothes!' so up I jumped, "Yes, Yes, Yes, I'm goin' fishin, "and in five minutes or less I had on the rubber boots, bright yellow rain gear, packsack stowed in a tied up garbage bags and I was ready. Everything else was secondary, fishing time was here and that was the most important activity as far as I was concerned.

The little boat moved away from the wharf, the motor hummed and the salt water splashed in my face, mixed with the fresh water of the rain drops. It felt wonderful! In ten minutes we were in our special fishing spot and putting squid on the hooks, ready for an hour and a half of fishing. According to the tide times, the daylight left, that is all we had, an hour and a half. And we made the best of it.

In about twenty minutes the first cod came aboard, a fresh white belly, a small whisker on its' chin, and images of cod au gratin raced through my obsessed mind. So engrossed in fishing, baiting hooks, losing a big one and looking at the fish already onboard, I failed to notice that the rain had stopped, the water on the sound had become as smooth as a mirror, with the fog now caressing the tops of the hills as if saying a good-bye.

The world on the water that night became so still, evens the fish caught and landed in another boat made itself heard a long way away, flopping around trying to escape the fish box. And the excited cries of the fisher folk echoed off the water and skipped toward our little boat. Just the two of us in our boat, just quiet, taking it all in for memories sake.

I don't know when I finally realized that we were in a surreal space, maybe it was when I glanced up and noticed that shore lights were coming on and reflecting off the water. And as soon as I noticed that, I kept my head up, scanning as if on a mission. And it was a mission, a mission in search of memories to be stored away, to write about, to tell others, and to open up the memory bank on an especially bad day, to make me feel better about it all. The catching of the fish I realized, and all the rules and politics involved, was so secondary to this feeling of being one with the universe, of having the experience of being out on the water in a little boat and of smelling the salt air, and feeling the mist on my face, the whole experience was worth the dressing up for the rain, of facing the elements, of dragging gas containers and supplies with rain dripping off the beak of my cap, of slipping and falling on the wet planks of the wharf, and the messy awful feeling of the seaweed as I pulled the haul off line and brought the little boat into the dock, everything has a price, and this was a small price to pay for this fantastic feeling.

After an hour or so of moving the boat here and there, catching three nice codfish, the darkness started to overtake us and it was time to head for the wharf we had left such a short time ago. The handlines were brought in, the fish already tagged and cleaned lying in the fishbox, was a bonus to such a majestic evening.

The little boat let its' master lead it back to the wharf, leaving a lace trail, spotted with the emerald colored twinkling of the phosphorus in the water.

The lights of the town reflected in the still surface of the sea like the laser beams in a science fiction movie, yet at the same time reminding me of the Twin Towers of New York City before

September 11, 2001. The still water reflected the lights of varying colors as straight lines, giving the effect of a tall structure, rather than a deep hole. No wind, no waves, no fog, no rain, just an amazing sight to see, and a gift to be given. Another gift, one of many the sea and shores of Newfoundland had given me in the past two years. However did I stay away so long? However, did I live without this bountiful basket of sights and sounds, of salt air and sea spray? But I was back now, and those questions would never be asked again, nor would there be an answer, because lifes' journey takes us to places of the heart, and places of the mind, and it is meant to be so. And it is and was meant that the journey would bring me home.

In a very short time my flight of thought was broken as the little motor quieted and I realized we were nearing the dock, where the other little boats, safely on their moorings for the night, bobbed up and down as if they were welcoming the Kylee and her passengers home. Time to unload, time to face reality, time to make a commitment to put it on paper and have it to remember always, and to share it with others. The evening was over, darkness fell so quickly, no moon to be seen and we unloaded our precious cargo and jumped into the old pickup truck and headed for home.

For some it would be an average evening, uneventful, for me it was such an experience of heart and soul, such a realization that for so many years I had longed for this and had not even realized it. But now I did. And now I was home.

The boat, the lights, the salt water, the fish, and the magnificence of nature, all in my life again, and now I would hold tightly to the anchor of it all.

I don't ever want to lose it again. Not ever!

A LETTER TO MY BELOVED NEWFOUNDLAND AND LABRADOR

Every year nay sayers start the same old negative story. They start by saying there is no spring in Newfoundland and Labrador. Well, enough is enough I've decided, and I am writing a letter to my province to tell the province, and its' people, that it is a myth that there is no spring, and to explain my thoughts on the matter. It reads like this:

Dear Beautiful Rugged Newfoundland and Labrador:
It seems that not only are you battered by the wind and the waves, but by the negative thinking of many people, at home here with you and those away from you as well. Rumor has it that you jump from winter into summer. The time in between has become known as 'misery', and that you have no spring. I have been asked many times since I returned to your shores whatever would I do in Newfoundland where there is no Spring, the reasoning being that I like spring, my camera likes spring, and I would not have it anymore.

This is a myth. Newfoundland, you do have spring. It was always here every year before, so if it is gone, who took it? So I set out to investigate who took your spring. I asked one gentleman in particular about the issue and he said that he had seen an actor interviewed who had been on your shores for some three months and the inevitable 'they', whoever 'they' are told him there was no spring in Newfoundland. And of course these would be the same people, the 'they' who say, do, commit, disappoint and yet nobody knows who 'they' are when asked about it. It is enough to cause me to go into one of those Newfoundland rants, but I won't. I will write to you instead.

Two years ago I returned to Newfoundland and last year I watched, pursued, asked all sorts of questions, and I documented Spring with my friend the Camera. I followed a bud until it was a leaf, I watched a seed sprout, observed, and then observed more closely and in doing so I know that "Yes, my dear land, you will have spring," regardless of what 'they' say.

Spring officially starts March 20th and extends to the first day of summer, June 21st, and it will happen again this year as sure as we are surrounded by water.

Let's start with nature, Mother Nature knows all about it, having the trees start to bud, the sun warmer, the days longer, all combining to melt the snow, and if snow comes it won't stay long. The animals will start to prepare for the birth of their young, and if you walk down a road or a trail and stop and listen you will hear the little trickle of water underneath the snow, and then not too long after that the snow collapses. Stick a tap into a maple tree and the sap drips as if trying to escape its' wooden cell. The birds will stop frequenting the feeders as often, rabbit hunting season is long over and the men turn to other types of outdoor activities. The ice will start to break up into large pans, making me remember the pan-jumping days of youth that I would be scolded for, and actually the pans still look inviting! The breakup of the ice makes travel by snow machine unreliable, and the various other means of transportation starts to appear. The motorbikes, the four-wheelers and skateboards can be seen everywhere.

And then it will happen-you will see a robin, or a group of robins, running back and forth over the patches of now exposed earth looking for some morsel for their lunch, and they find the leftovers that the Grosbeaks, Chickadees and Jays left behind under the feeders. Soon, any time after that, kittens, lambs, ponies, puppies, calves, and all sorts of little babies, can be found if you know where to look. It is spring! A time for new life, rebirth and new beginnings.

Yes, Mother Nature knows, and like any Mother she will take care of her responsibilities. Soon, very shortly after the buds appear on the old maple tree, the tulips, daffodils, and crocus poke up through the ground. And after that is the noble Dandelion and Buttercup, and you know you made it and spring is really here, the winter slowly being forgotten.

People behave differently during springtime as well if you pay close attention. I don't really mean that they get a 'spring' in their step because I think that is a phenomenon that happens when you go from twenty pound boots to two pound shoes and can't stop lifting your feet too high! No, people start wearing more colorful clothes, spend more time outside, women start 'spring cleaning', men get at their boats, mothers are flustered getting their graduating daughters and son's ready for parties and ceremonies, men stand for hours leaning over the tailgate of a truck having their 'tailgate conferences' and solving all of the worlds' ills, young mothers are walking their baby strollers, and life generally shifts into an altogether different mode. And once you see the young children on their new bicycles, their laughter riding on the wind, you can sit back and say quietly to yourself as the warm sun soothes your back "Spring is here!"And the gardeners start to till their soil, winter coats are shed, and the long cold winter fades into memory. The smell of fresh earth fills the air.

So Yes, indeed my beloved Newfoundland and Labrador, let nobody tell you otherwise, you will have your spring. And you will be loved in spring as in every other season, for your splendor and beauty, unsurpassed and sometimes taken too much for granted, but not by me. My photos of you last spring took me through this winter, and now we start again, and you know you will be cared for and your flag will fly in the warm spring breeze, your people will grow their flower gardens into gorgeous patches of color and your sunrises and sunsets will be as glorious , maybe even more magnificent than ever before. If we all, every one of us Newfoundlanders, stopped, looked, and listened, we would all see spring, even on a cold April or May day, because Spring will come, as always. It is as perennial as the grass that comes with it, let nobody discourage you or tell you otherwise. And majestic mountain majesty will always be yours. We Love you Smiling Land, in spring time we see you fresh again, and we are grateful for you and for your rugged beauty! May God Guard thee Newfoundland.

BECOMING A LONG DISTANCE NANNY

The flames with their mosaic of colors could be seen leaping and hopping, dancing and flickering, as if waiting for the opportune moment to escape the through the glass window of the stove door. The wood crackled and popped, warming the house and making the blizzard and freezing temperatures outside seem worlds away. My cat, my book, and me, could be found in our favorite spot, in the big stuffed chair in the corner of the glass encased sun-nook at the front of the house. From this vantage point I could see the little birds fighting for a spot on the feeders, and I could see the bay, but yet watch the flames reflecting in the window. This was just heavenly. The phone rang, and having forgotten to take it with me to my little corner I had to leave my cozy nest to answer the call.

My daughter was calling from a place very far away, there were far too many miles between us. Like so many other young maritimers, my son and daughter had finished a good education and left to find work in their specific fields, to make their own way in the world. Both my offspring had been born and raised in Nova Scotia, but had a strong Newfoundland heritage, and much to our amusement both called Newfoundland their home. Both were working hard and making new friends. Heather, a real Nova Scotian girl, had met and married a young Newfoundland man, and they have an enchanting little girl in their lives now. Her name is Kylee Elizabeth and she is my first grand child. She is a bright, beautiful child with a mischievous smile and an independent spirit, like her mother before her.

While we talked Heather walked into Kylees' room, telling me that she had slept for too long and needed to be wakened now. But lo and behold Miss Kylee was awake, quietly playing, content to do just that for now. Her mother picked her up, tried to get her to say 'Nanny' but, as children are, she would not do anything she didn't want to do. She was sleepy still and wanted just to cuddle her mom.

I could visualize the scene so clearly. Her mother told Kylee she was so sweet when she woke, and I could imagine Kylee cuddled in her mothers' arms, and my heart ached to be there. So very clearly I could see the moist curls on the back of her neck, her cheeks rosy, eyes sparkling, her little hands holding her favorite blanket. Heather then said the magic words that made my heart ache that much more.

"Oh, you smell so sweet, I love you so much!" she said softly. And I wanted to be there, to have time with them, to hold a little child fresh from their afternoon nap, to pick up that warm little body and have those tiny, but chubby, arms wrap around my neck, put a blanket over her and sit and rock her until she was fully awake.

The time immediately following a nap was always my favorite time with babies, the after nap ritual- the cuddling, and sweet tender moments when the child is not fully awake and enjoys the closeness of an adult. Nostalgia ran through me as I remembered my own baby siblings in my childhood days and then my own two children. I was taken aback at this strange feeling that had settled in my heart.

I just didn't understand it, and I wasn't prepared for it, although we had visited Kylee shortly after she was born, and I loved her long before her birth, this emotion was strong, unfamiliar, and all encompassing. Heather is a good Mom, Lance is a good Dad, there is absolutely no doubt about that. But what of me, am I a good grandmother? I haven't walked this road before, what is expected of me, what role will be mine when I am so many miles away? I try to write Kylee a letter a month so she will have a collection of her grandmothers' letters further along in her life, words that will tell her who I am, what I do, how I love her, and how I longed to be with her.

Many of my friends and co-workers were grandmothers, and

I could see the obvious change in their demeanor when they talked of their grandchildren. They would tease me mercilessly, mainly because I said I wasn't interested in 'doing the grandmother thing' and had said so often that I did not want to be called 'Nanny'! Anything else but 'Nanny'.

"Is that right now? We will see won't we?" they would say.

Then along came Kylee and I am enraptured, I want to know what she is doing, if she is getting her bedtime story read to her nightly, getting interested in books, how is the bump on her head? I am sure her parents must be relieved at times that I am so far away I think to myself. But she is partly mine and partly Grammy Joans' too. Both of us are living in Newfoundland and trying hard to be part of Kylees' life.

I cannot teach her to sew, it's an activity I cannot abide, but I can read to her for hours, I cannot play endless board games, but I can make great 'play dough.' I was never much of a doll person but I love Teddy Bears and will fill her life with them. I cannot, and will not, ski downhill but I can take her on a skidoo or a four wheeler, or teach her to ride a bicycle. I cannot be bothered with trout fishing, but Poppy and I can take her out to see the little coves and bays around Newfoundland in our comfortable boat. I can't, or won't light a propane stove because even Nannies have fears, but I can teach her how to use a camera. I cannot come close to growing plants like her great grandmothers but I can show her where the biggest blueberries grow, and I cannot be with her every day, but I certainly can love her every day!

Yes, I am now a grandmother, became one at the age of fifty-one, and it is just glorious, even being called 'Nanny' is just fine with me.

A magical, fascinating, beautiful tiny enchantress has entered my life, and now I know of what they spoke. So to my darling Kylee, may you live a long and happy life filled with all the wonderful gifts that the Universe offers, just as you are a gift of joy the Universe has given me. I will love you until the rivers run still, and send you my love every day.

HOW SWEET IT IS, A DAY ON THE BAY

The extremely hot temperatures of the calm summer day beckoned us to the wharf and to the little sixteen-foot boat that waited patiently on her mooring to be released. The food fishery was open, summer was here and this summer in particular was to bring us many of these sun-drenched days. The call to the sea breezes became too inviting to resist, so we threw cares and caution aside, rounded up two friends and hurriedly put together the necessities for a boil-up. In an hour or so we were all aboard the little Newfoundland boat, all talking at once, wondering aloud if we had this or that, where's the bait, who needs sun screen, do we have a kettle and all the questions that got asked but nobody answered, a familiar characteristic of this group of friends. After all was deemed 'AOK' my husband flashed up the motor and we headed for my favorite place, the waters of Smith Sound.

The four of us were energized by the headiness of it all, feeling like kids playing hooky from school, full of enthusiasm and ready for adventure. Every time we had an outing, whether by snow machine, four wheeler or boat, we came back with a new lease on life, shored up for the challenges that life inevitably would bring our way sooner or later.

The mirror-like water off Grindstone Head reflected the trees and rocks of the cliffs, the sun was hot on our necks and arms, the red and yellow of our safety vests added to the party atmosphere. The sea gulls haunting cries, the grace of the large eagles, swooping and soaring, displaying their skills were all part of our afternoon. Occasionally a whale would blow and we would all turn and stare in the direction of the 'swoosh' sound. The little boat moved along obedient and sure.

The first stop was usually off Grindstone Head, and the first throw of the grapnel was always significant to me. With the casting of the little anchor into the sea we could mentally cast aside our cares and worries to the sea as well. My husband and his lifelong friend, Gene, would stop the boat many times, looking for just the right place to fish! My friend and I continued to chat, handlined for fish and generally relaxed into the day, soaking it all up for our memory banks. The conversation of our husbands, catching up on thirty years or so of stories was mixed with laughter, and ours joining theirs and the sound of the laughter skipped across the calm water. It was surreal to me, dreamlike for sure, to be back in Newfoundland, back with old friends and family, back home to stay. It was just marvelous to be back!

Soon it was supper time and the boat was hauled onto a sandy beach, the water at the rear of the little boat so clear we could look down and watch the little starfish and crabs moving about. The boilup supper, then on with the sweatshirts to protect us against the evenings' chill and we scrambled back into our little boat, loaded all the gear, and headed out for another hour of fishing. The evening was closing in, no time now to waste.

A few more fish later and we noticed twilight descending upon us, much more quickly than we expected. The sky changed to red, orange and gold, the sun a large orange ball against the pallet of colors. It looked as if the Master Artist of the Universe had painted a mural, another beautiful mural, one of many we had seen in the past weeks. The harbor lights started to twinkle, it was time to steer for home.

We were all strangely quiet, as we watched the sunset and slowly moved the boat toward the harbor, stopping to take photographs for a moment. Everyone appeared to be in awe, lost in their own private thoughts, when my friend Lorraine touched my arm, looked at me with a smile and said with a tad of lighthearted humor "How good do we have it a'tall?"

I looked back at the wake of the boat, a lacy pattern twinkling with the phosphorus as if emeralds were dancing and following us, looked at the magnificence of the sky, and looked back at

Lorraine and Gene, and said to her and to myself "Pretty darn good, my friend, pretty darn good!"

We watched the sun slide behind the mountains just as we neared the wharf. Yes, indeed, a glorious day to be given, a true gift. And I remember it today as I sit by the large window and watch the snow swirl around outside, and the wood stove glowing inside.

Yes, Pretty darn good it is, all of it, darn good.

A WILD GOOSE CHASE

Sometimes along lifes' way an event, person, place or thing causes you to detour and you find yourself in the midst of the most enlightening adventure.

My little adventure began in the still, colorful days of autumn and continues to this very day. I fell in love with the 'Shoal Harbour Geese'.

Little did I think I would have such a strange relationship with a gaggle of geese when I walked down to the old railway track one beautiful afternoon in late October with my trusty camera. For years I had been coming to Shoal Harbour for vacations, but had never spent a whole winter in Newfoundland for thirty-two years.

I knew that Shoal Harbour/Clarenville was a Canada Goose Sanctuary. In late September and early October I had noticed the geese on several occasions as I drove the causeway connecting the two towns. However, my attempts to photograph the wily birds were proving totally fruitless.

On this particular afternoon, however, it was a low tide, the geese were close to shore, it was a quiet day, and I had film, lots of film. I walked to the Shoal Harbour wharf where friendly people always met, buying vegetables from the ladies fresh vegetable stand, or attending to their boats. I thought that since there were no boats coming or going, and no shocking noises to scare the birds, today was the day I would get my photos.

Well, I am sure you have heard of the best laid plans that go astray, the geese where nowhere to be seen. There happened to be an older gentleman sitting on the wharf. I approached him and asked he if he had seen the geese today.

With a strange look, and with one quarter of a cigarette dangling precariously on his lip, he squinted at me over the smoke and asked, "What geese would that be Mrs.?" So I launched into a song and dance about these beautiful elusive birds that I wanted to photograph, and it just seemed to amuse him. Then he suggested that I could easily get a picture of a gull, just throw the feed to them.

No, I wanted geese, lots of geese.

Then the smoky gentleman posed the brutal question, "Ever eat 'em?"

By the look on my face he knew I was shocked and laughed all the way back to the angle iron and four tires he called a truck, leaving a trail of laughter and smoke. So much for that I thought.

Then the kind lady selling her vegetables approached me, and told me the geese had left a short time ago but they usually came back just before a low tide to feed. I decided to take her advice and try another day.

Now, my interest in these birds didn't happen overnight. It came just as a gradual interest stirred by an offhand remark by somebody that these geese stayed in this area as long as they had some 'open water'. To determine how long they have been coming here is difficult. When asked, everyone replies, "As long as I can remember!" Whether the person is twenty or eighty years old, that is the token response to the question.

There is some folklore about the geese, but I'll research that another day. Right then I just wanted to enjoy their beauty, and gracefulness, feed them, and take photos.

My understanding of Canada Geese is that they are programmed by nature to fly South to escape the severe Canadian winters. I fretted about the birds getting cold until someone reminded me the Finches and Jays aren't cold so I let that worry sit on the shelf. In due time I got the photos, fed the geese, walked the shoreline at a low tide and had them around my feet. And I didn't get bitten.

Then in the grocery store one day I caught another goose story. I spotted an older gentleman I knew standing, chatting to a friend. Finding an excuse to speak to them, I launched into my recitation about the geese.

"Oh, my dear. They've been here as long as I can remember."

Of, course.

Then his friend started telling a tale of how his mother loved to get a goose to cook, so she could have some goose grease to apply to a chest when someone had a cold. Worked every time he pronounced. By this time two other men had joined the group, at first listening, then his eyes clouded over, he turned red and started to laugh. He laughed and choked and choked and laughed. Finally he got enough air to relate the story of goose feather pillows they had as children. By this time the third member was gearing up to launch into his goose tale.

I slipped away.

The winter solstice came and went. The weather was bitterly cold, the harbor iced up and still the geese stayed. I thought about the little sweaters like those made for the victimized sea birds of the Exon Valdez disaster, but then I came to my senses and realized that a goose dips under water, hence the little cardigans would get wet and freeze in the cold air. Then one day the geese were all gone, not one down near the wharf. I missed them terribly .Were they OK? Did anyone know anything regarding their location now? Were they getting feed? The only way to find out was to ask, so I did.

I inquired of the gas station attendant as he was filling my car if he knew where the Canada Geese had gone.

"No, I don't," he said. "But you go up to the garage and ask buddy and he can tell ya. He's into that kinda stuff!"

So I dodged into the garage.

Not seeing anyone, I called out, "Buddy, you in here?" There was a rattle of metal.

"Yeah, I'm down 'ere, what's the problem?" asked Buddy, who was attached to a pair of legs sticking out from underneath a car.

So I launched into the usual 'goose inquiry'. Yes, sure enough, they'd been around as long as he could remember. And he didn't see them go, but he knew they would be back, leading me to ask how he knew that.

"Cause they likes us maid! Matter of fact I saw them in Lower Clarenville this morning. They'll head for Shoal Harbour tonight. Love to be in the cabin wid a few of dem roastin'!"

I thanked him and left. So, I discovered, that is what they do, spend so much time in each place, near open low tide waters.

Two days later, on one of the coldest days in February I went to Bayview Road in Clarenville and found my handsome, stately gaggle. They were all over the place, slipping and sliding, their webbed feet unable to grip the shiny smooth ice surface, but they seemed happy. If one goose was sliding, he would stick his beak into the tail feathers of another walking by and get a good tow, there was evidence of them having been fed, but it was cold! I stood on the bank and asked them why they didn't go to a warmer place, they did not need tickets, it would cost them nothing, no baggage to lose and they could be somewhere in a farmer's field filling their bellies and soaking up the warmth.

Honk! Honk!

They wanted to be here. They were being fed, they were together, and they were quite content. When I went to drive away, I found my car stuck solid in a snow drift. I tried my best to dislodge it to no avail. Two strong men came and helped a damsel in distress. And of course I had to launch into the story of what I was doing there, how I once had seen a duck frozen to the ice and having to be rescued and how I feared for the geese. The duck that was saved had feet that took months to heal.

The older man just stared at me. Then he spoke, in what one could call a rant.

"The birds look OK don't they? Nobody got stuck, except you. I think, dear, that these are not just Canada Geese, they got a lot of Newfoundlander in 'em. They'll be fine. Now you just go and get warmed up yerself, the birds are gonna be just dandy!" And he walked away with his shovel dragging behind him.

He was right, so right. I love the geese, but nature does not need my daily undivided indulgence. We all play a part, share in the job of keeping an eye open for anyone or anything in distress and we all should do just fine that way.

The geese honked loudly as I drove away. I saw them in Shoal Harbor the next day looking handsome. So the little detour into the 'gaggle of geese' gave me tremendous laughs, I met lovely people and I learned so much. My photos are great reminders of that fork in the road. Our geese are still here as I write this and people are used to me with my camera now and tell me where something interesting or unusual can be found worthy of a photo. So chance encounters led to even more encounters, the geese are fine, and a random act of kindness led me to the geese and memories to tell grandchildren someday.

POPPYS' WORKSHOP

Tucked up in the bottom of Trinity Bay, Newfoundland, is a little harbor with very shoal water, hence its' name, Shoal Harbour.

Not too, far from the seashore, just up from the old railway bed is my husbands' childhood home. Just behind the house is an enormous woodpile, and just to the left of the woodpile is a little shed with a big window in the front overlooking the lilac tree and the land sloping down to the sea, and then a view right out over the water. The same view is seen from the windows at the front of the big house.

Everybody has their own special story of the 'shed' or 'Poppys' workshop' as it came to be known. The first little girl to call it that is in her mid-thirties now and she still calls it by the same name as she did as a child. The youngest little girl visited 'Poppys Workshop' this summer, just a year and a half old.

Poppy Lowe worked with the railway, known to his friends and family as Abe. But Poppy also had another line of work he enjoyed and is known by many for that work. You see, Poppy was a fine skilled carpenter, working his magic on the wood- always to perfection. From coffins to egg cups, Poppy could make anything with different kinds of wood. His inlaid woodwork is art and most of the family has a piece or two of his wonderful creations. The granddaughters have their jewellery boxes topped off with an oval of ebony. They are splendid, lined with red velvet with the tiniest of little latches to keep them closed. His work included special twirled candlesticks that grace the altar of the Shoal Harbour United Church, along with inlaid collection plates perfectly finished.

His other inlaid work included trays, vases, tables, picture frames, spice racks, and too many other things to list. The shed still holds samples of the woods he ordered from far distant lands, ebony, mahogany, ash, as well as our Newfoundland birch and pine-such smells and sights that it makes you close your eyes and savor it all. Poppy loved to show his wood samples, his tools, and his work. He would rub his weathered hands over the wood lovingly, explaining the way the grain lay and what his plans were for each piece. Yes, Poppys' workshop was the place to be and the place to learn. On a rainy day he would pull the chain of the bare lightbulb over his workbench and set to work. A nice place to be, the children all thought, as they took their places beside Poppy at the workbench, the stove making the shed warm and cozy.

I visited the shed this week, the first time for a while, and watched the bits of sawdust dance in the sunbeams streaming in the windows. The smell is the same, nice clean wood, paint and shellacs. The view of the water, the tool cabinet with an old Fathers' Day card still taped to it is all still there. The bare lightbulb, the sheets of sandpaper and jars of nuts and bolts are all the same as they were twenty years ago. The lathe and bandsaw are quiet today, but the little pile of fresh sawdust, and the cabinets that lie, in the process of being finished, across two work benches tell me it is not always silent in there.

A splash of red on the workbench catches my eye and I know without looking that is the handiwork of my daughter, from a time years ago when Poppy gave her some red paint and a brush, and she painted her initials on the workbench with '1982' beside them. My husband told me he found the childrens' rock people, and a wooden boat roughly nailed together, and many other things that are reminders of our yearly trips back to Shoal Harbour to visit Nanny and Poppy Lowe. They learned so much in that tiny workshop, probably more than we will ever know. I used to ask them if "Geppeto had Pinnochio made out there yet?" They would giggle with Poppy but the secrets stayed between them.

Poppy left his workshop and left us in 1982, not long after the red paint was used. Nanny lived by herself in the big house for many years and then she too left, leaving us with a legacy of knowing we were all loved.

But there is another Nanny and Poppy Lowe here now. Our ways are different in some things, much the same in others. The new Poppy Lowe fills the place at the workbench, working his skills on the wood, building cabinets just as painstakingly as his father before him. He walks like his father, has the same self-determination and humor and fills his fathers' shoes just as his father would have wished.

He is Poppy Lowe now, and his family, a son and a daughter, will come to Shoal Harbour to visit us, and they will bring their families in due time. The first little grand child was here this summer, just a year and a half old, and she visited the workshop for the first time. Was the magic still there as it was for her mother who used the red paint, of course it was! The imagination of a child, even so young, can go to far off limits while sharing a place like the shed with a smiling Poppy who loves you so and takes care that you do not get hurt. The little hammers, nails, and the inevitable red paint were all still there, just waiting to be held and played with.

Yes, of course the wonder and the magic are still there, left by a kind Poppy to his son and family. And Poppys' Workshop came alive again with the sound of a childs' laughter as she marveled at the thrill of being in this seemingly awesome place with the kind Poppy who loves her.

The little shed, in the little harbour, our 'round the bay' in Newfoundland-who would ever think what a castle it can be?

THE LITTLE PINK RUBBER BOOTS

What a spectacular summer day it was, with everything fresh and green, the little flowers bent with the weight of the raindrops from an early morning shower, but now the sun was shining, all was so quiet you could hear the bumble bees buzzing and then the laughter of a child from quite a way's away. It was time for a walk, a little stroll to the seashore in front of the house. My companion led the way down the lane from the house to the workshop at the end of the tree-covered alley way. She stopped now and then, picked a flower or two, passed it to me, and I did the same for her. And so it went, just a nice comfortable slow stroll taking in all of the beauty around us and finding all sorts of new things to observe. Every little thing my little friend saw was a reason to stop, every little sound a reason to look at me in wonder, and when the blue jay perched on a branch over our heads and started its' lecture to us, she squealed in delight, so full of the wonder of it all. An adventure lay ahead at the end of the walk, an adventure for her, but she was unaware of it while I anticipated great excitement. You see my little companion and friend was my tiny nineteen month old grand daughter, Kylee. She was a gift and a joy in our lives and had come to Shoal Harbour, Newfoundland to visit us on vacation with her parents. Her other grandparents lived in the Codroy Valley so she had quite a lot of new experiences, sights and sounds to see this summer. And lots of people to hug and love her every day. She had been a tiny baby, born a little early, anxious to get here I told my daughter, but she had grown, and was bright, healthy and smart. Every moment we spent together was an adventure for her and one heck of a memory for me. Kylee was interested in all things, and had many admirers, and she admired many in return. Today was a special day for Kylee. Today she had a brand-new pair of little pink rubber boots that her mom and dad had brought home from a shopping trip the evening before. Now this little girl had sandals that lit up when she walked, ankle boots for long walks, slippers galore, but these little boots took her fancy and were her favorite footwear since she first saw them. She figured out how to put them on, and she kept them on for a long time, in the house, in her pyjamas, until her mother could not take the 'boots on wrong feet's gait' that could only bring trouble. So the little boots were put away until this morning of our walk. And she strutted along in those little pink things, so proud of them she would stop and look down and point to her feet. Yes, Kylee had new boots. And it was perfect timing because this morning I, her Nanny, was taking her to the seashore. It was to be her first trip to the ocean, first time to see the little waves of Shoal Harbour, and walk on the beach and play where her Poppy Lowe had played many years before. As we walked, she would get tired, I would pick her up, and she would wrap her arms around my neck, making my heart practically burst with love for this little girl, this little part of me. Her boots would fall off, and she would giggle as we made a game of running back for the boots. She didn't want to lose those precious pink belongings! The wind ruffled her light baby hair, her eyes widened and she was totally quiet as we reached the water. In amazement she looked and looked, trying to take it all in, and then she saw the sandpipers and the seagulls, the little boats coming and going, and most of all the waves teasing the shoreline, tumbling over each other as if showing Kylee which was better, this wave or that. Her eyes sparkled in wonder and she squiggled out of my arms. Once on the ground she figured out in no time that she could walk in the water and her feet would not be cold, nor would her get wet, and she was enthralled by the protection of those boots. For half an hour or more I watched those little legs and those pink covers tease the waves, jump up and down, she picked up seashells and ran to give them to Nanny, and she was in love with the salt water, the salt air and the experience of the sea. Her cheeks were so red, her eyes so wide, her laugh like music to my ears. She loved the sea, just as her Nanny and Poppy Lowe did, just as her mother did when she was brought to play on Shoal Harbours Beach when she was just little. Kylees' Newfoundland Heritage shone through, and I was so honored to be the one who took her to see the ocean for the first time. The ocean that we took so for granted growing up in Newfoundland, but Kylee cannot see in Calgary. Lunch time came and I picked her up to go. She held on, her boots fell off, and I cleaned the sand off and gave them to her to hold, and she clutched them tightly as she looked back over my shoulder for a last glimpse of the water, with the sun reflecting off it like tiny lights.

Kylee wore her boots many times while she visited Newfoundland, did all her visiting, went to the seashore many times, and loved to walk in the water. Photographs are all we have now of her time by the sea, but my heart holds the biggest treasure of all, the special pleasure I was given, the honor of taking a little girl to see the Atlantic Ocean for the first time, watches those little pink boots running to and fro, running with her arms up to catch a seagull, running to tease the waves, running toward me with a seashell for my collection of Kylee treasures. My little grandchild is back in Calgary now, and still has her pink boots. And in time she will outgrow her boots, but she will, hopefully, somewhere in her heart remember the day she spent with her Nanny and the waves, and wore her little boots for the first time on the shores of Newfoundland. And one thing that is for sure and certain, this Nanny will never forget the time spent with Kylee, her pink boots, and watched the rhythm of the waves. A treasured memory for this grandmothers' heart, one that I will always hold as close as the little girl named Kylee held her Pink Rubber Boots! I love you little one, for always and forever. Come back again, and we will visit the waves, and maybe this time Nanny will find some Pink Rubber Boots to match yours, and find that childlike wonder once again, with a special little girl.

MY QUEST FOR

THE WONDERFUL PARTRIDGEBERRIES

Well, OK, the fishing was over, the blueberries were picked, and jammed or frozen, and even the awesome bakeapples (just a few) were in our possession. So now where were the partridgeberries that I so desired and had waited so long to start picking. I had waited patiently all summer for my special berries, their dark burgundy color and exquisite taste something I had yearned for in my years away from Newfoundland and Labrador..During those years away my kind sister-in-law had from time to time, sent me containers of those wonderful gems of autumn, but now I could get my own, but where? The berries sent to me while away would be hoarded and squirreled away by me the same way I would hide licorice pipes from my siblings during our childhood days, as if to say "They're mine, all mine!"Now that might have been necessary with the pipes but not the berries because nobody I knew around me loved them as much as I did so they were mine anyway. But I knew how delicious they were, knew how versatile and I was home, the first time for 34 years, for the partridgeberry pickin' season, and I wanted berries!

I asked everybody where I could find them, even asked the driver of the courier truck who said "Never mind my love, you'll get your berries after September 20th."

September 20th came and went, the world had gone mad with crushing blows being dealt between countries, the stock market was teeter-tottering, the News generally was not good anywhere, and usually I would be head first into three daily papers and reading and watching it all with a close eye. But not this time, because by September 20th the wait for the berry picking, the relentless questions that had no answers, had robbed me of all cognitive powers, all rational thoughts and I was on a stubborn headlong quest to find what I so longed for! This was serious business, this had happened to me before once or twice in my lifetime, and I knew how ruthless I could become, so I had a long discussion with myself and started anew.

However, that is easier said than done. In my little place of abode, Shoal Harbour, somebody must be able to tell me something. The place we had picked partridgeberries so many times on our Newfoundland Vacations was now a highway overpass, nobody seemed too concerned, and I could feel the familiar pins and needles of a Newfoundland rant tingling my tongue! The brilliance of the autumn colors, the deep blue of the Island sky, the smell of the junipers, the cool sweater weather was just making it worse. The end of September was fast approaching, and it was time to get serious, and when October 1st came along, the quest slipped into 'full speed ahead'. No more messing around, time was up, I would find the berries with or without help.

I sat on a rock outside the house and remembered days as a child on the Labrador coast, high on the hill with the winds a welcome part of the day. Sun shining and the women and girls all engaged in a day of berry picking. Us younger ones, maybe everyone, would have a small container called a 'picker' to fill, then that was emptied into the large flour sacks and we started all over again. What excitement it was to see that sack fill up, bulging at the sides, the red stains of the berry seeping through the cloth! What delight to have food and tea with the grown women, the lunch and boilup enough to get us through until we got home. Every now and then someone would ask "Is your bottom covered yet?" If the answer was yes, then you were doing OK. When the sacks were full the women would take them to a high piece of ground, where the wind was really felt and they would "winnow" the berries. They would take a clean flour sack and container by container of berries would be held high and slowly poured into the sack, the wind blowing the browse and leaves away, making the sack of berries just perfect, no unwanted debris would remain. It was time to go. And what magical days they were, we would all head for home, exhausted, sunburned, and our mouths stained with berry juice. The fly bites would itch. We would be thirsty but what innocent fun times. I saw a Newfoundland painting that I just had to buy that shows the children picking berries that was so like it was that I knew it had to be mine, and it is!

The frustration had peaked, and I finally approached my husband and asked "So what about the partridgeberries?",launching into the story of my Labrador berry picking days, and the winnowing and on and on.

"Well, "says himself, "I'll have to ask around again. We can find out where to go but you can't do that to them anyway."

"Can't do what?" I am crazed enough to ask, adding "see, I darn well knew you didn't know about winnowing and all that!"

"No, that's not it at all," he taunts, "I just don't know where you'll find flour sacks in this day and age!"

That did it! I had been had again. So I would find the berries myself!! And then it happened. I stopped at a local grocery store to buy fresh fruit, passing the bakery section salivating like Pavlovs' dogs, and what should I see but BAGS OF PARTRIDGEBERRIES, BEAUTIFUL MOUTH-WATERING PARTRIDGEBERRIES!

I made a mad lunge, right over my grocery cart and had three bags of those berries confiscated on the first grab! I wasn't sure how much they were, if I had money with me enough to purchase them, and I sure as heck didn't care. They were mine, all mine, finally! I was to put it mildly just plain "ethereal, "as I checked out and headed for home. Locked all the car doors and dared anyone to approach my berries. No sense of reasoning left at all, but so happy!

I plunked the bags of berries down on the kitchen table. Himself walks in and takes in the scene. "What in the name of heavens are you going to do with all the berries?" he asks.

Gloating by now, filled with an invincible ego, I said "Just watch me!"And I went on to say that there were muffins, loaves, jams, pickles, sundae toppings, and by then I noticed I was alone. I stood and caressed my bags of berries, not knowing where Himself went. Probably looking for flour sacks, but I didn't need them now. My quest was complete, and oh what a feeling!

But this year I need more berries, I ran out too soon. Does anybody know where the partridgeberry fields are in Trinity Bay, I have the flour sacks, and I am on a quest again? I just can't stop myself it seems!

IN SEARCH OF OCEAN JOY

Our little compact car had driven the distance from the highway to Jackson' Arm, passing tidy lawns, well cared for homes and wild rose bushes heavy with the blossoms and the scent that I so loved. And now as we reached the crest of the hill, and the ferry to Harbour Deep came into view. There was something very familiar about this boat, something bringing back a memory, a vague recollection of another time. And that feeling was so right, the ferry, although sporting another color paint and another name was in fact what my husband and I had known as the MP34, the "Fort Steele," a patrol vessel of the RCMP, a vessel he had sailed on and a vessel young wives detested because if the Fort Steele was the posting the trips away were longer. But it was all memory, and some good memories, now that it was thirty some years after the fact. So my husband got to set foot on the Fort Steele again, and I followed him, making the three-hour trip to Harbour Deep.

The little community of Harbour Deep is nestled under the hills, just waiting now for the time to reach the hour when it will be a ghost-like village or outport, because by October 31,2002, Harbour Deep will be resettled and the people there will begin their lives anew, in another less isolated area. It is bittersweet, but it needs to be, and it will be. The changes are beginning, boxes being packed, and plans being made for the future.

Our pilgrimage to Harbour Deep centered around a boat, a thirty-four foot, radar equipped, kitchen equipped cabin cruiser. Many boats had been inquired of, many photos and magazines searched, but the photos e-mailed to us from Francis Ropson from Harbour Deep, through the Community Access Program, kept pulling us back to the computer, until finally I printed them.

Yes, this boat had a special something, so Francis was contacted and the plans began for the trip to visit Francis and Bonnie Ropson, and try out the boat, whose name was 'Ocean Joy'.

Ocean Joy was sitting quietly at the wharf when the ferry arrived, and Francis was there too. In a few minutes we were aboard the much sought after cabin cruiser and , after a supper at Francs' place we headed out and around the harbour, seeing the eagles, Francis telling us about the area, his thoughts on moving out, his history with the Ocean Joy. Fog enveloped the hills of Orange Bay, a chill deepened, but inside the boat it was warm. This was what we wanted, a boat to keep us warm and dry, and a boat that could venture further out on the water than our little Kylee boat. But our Kylee boat is special too, being our little open Newfoundland boat that brought us so much adventure and fun last summer. The Kylee boat will stay with us too we said, and she is special too.

At Francis' house later in the evening we sat back and talked boats, resettlement, kids getting educated, and all sorts of topics got tossed around. Bonnie came home from work at the lodge, and immediately she made herself known to us, and made us feel so much at ease as she coiled up in the corner of the big sofa with her late supper and told us about the Goat Dance, about the Vinegar Tarts that are special to Harbour Deep, and discussed how she felt they would be OK. Francis is the 'Hydro' man there so they do not know where he will be posted, but she knows they will be OK. And she is so right. She and Francis are resourceful, practical and smart. Their kids are honor students, they all know it is time to go, and they know they will miss it, but they will adjust. No looking back for them, Bonnie says. Life will go on.

But what of Ocean Joy? She sits tied to the wharf, and a 'For Sale' sign in the wheelhouse window. She looks lonely and forlorn. And she is beautiful! My husband turns to me at one point and asks "What do you think?".Well, I am not a boat expert, but I answer quickly while looking at her through the window "I love her!".

Another bit of chat in the morning and we ready to make the

afternoon ferry ride back to Jacksons' Arm. By then the deal is done. We will take the Ocean Joy from Harbour Deep, and we will give her a new home. When arrangements are in place, navigation charts and supplies bought, the Ocean Joy will make the journey from Harbour Deep, or Deep Harbour to Shoal Harbour to start a new beginning.

And there is no trace of doubt, no hesitation, because something says this boat is meant for us, Francis and Bonnie will move on and so will their boat. And she will bring us joy, getting us closer to the magnificent Newfoundland sunrises and sunsets, cooking a special meal out on the water, and taking friends along for a day free of the bonds of land. Her name will stay the same, because it is perfect, she is perfect, just the way she is.

As we ride the ferry away from Harbour Deep, a glance back takes my breath away, a ray of sunshine has peeked through the cloud, and a prism of color lingers over the Ocean Joy, I wave to her. I'll be back little boat, and every time I board you I will think of the evening two 'Bonnies' sat in a comfortable room in a house in an isolated little community soon to be forsaken, and found common ground talking of family, cooking, work, and so many other subjects. And down sitting politely by the wharf a little boat called OCEAN JOY waited patiently, while her Bonnies' and their husbands made arrangements for her future.

Yes, we found our boat, and soon she will be here with us in Shoal Harbour, and the people of Harbour Deep will move on into their future. May they find pleasant lives and their very own JOY wherever they go.

GODSPEED!

THROUGH MY LENS

The hot sun, bright blue clear sky, icebergs lying offshore, the sound of the waves as they tickled the rocks, clothes blowing on the always full clothesline, and the baby carriage were all parts of a Twillingate August afternoon. I had one little sister, three years younger than I, and now we had a new baby brother born the past May. On this particular lovely summer day Mother had us all outside, she wore a sundress and sandals, topped off with her long thick dark hair tied back in a pony tail. We were having a picnic, and Father would soon be home to join us. I would push the 'pram' and Margie would hold the handle as we moved our baby brother around the yard, the first of many such walks over the upcoming years. Very important I felt in the early 1950s' with two younger siblings to care for and to play with. It was a fun day, and it makes a warm and fuzzy memory.

Soon Father was home, and then Mother appeared with something strange looking in her hand. It looked like a black box with glass in it. "Stand by Dad now, and I'll take your picture" she said.

Well now, what was this? I had never seen this thing before so I certainly was not going to follow any directions until I knew what that black box was, showing a rebellious streak even then! Mother explained that it was a camera, and it could take pictures to look at and save forever. It was called a Brownie Camera, and she let me hold it and look down into the view piece that was on the top of the black box. And lo and behold, there was Margie, and the baby, with Father standing in the background. This was nothing short of a miracle to me. I was four years old, and from the time I clicked that shutter button and took a picture with the little Brownie Camera I was totally, head over heels in love with cameras. My parents used that camera for a long time, and we grew to love the photos it took, photos of all our growing up years, of our parents smiling, young and fresh faced, of my long curls, and Margies' flaxen hair, Beryls' big smile and Davids' freckles. Yes, this camera was wonderful. And by the time Kathy came into the family a newer camera had replaced the little Brownie box camera.

Life was so busy, always studying, working, having a family of my own, that a point and shoot camera suited me perfectly. Yet more photos of my growing family, another set of photo albums to look at in future years.

By the time I reached my thirties I decided I need to 'blur the background', and move into creative photography. A promotion by Time magazine ended with me having a little 35mm Camera, and after that things were never the same. I was so hooked I had sleepless nights thinking of how to get a better photo of something, or setting up still life shots. I needed to know more about this photography business, so off I went to Mount Saint Vincent University two nights a week and learned settings, the effects of light and shadow, the way to bracket a photo and all sorts of great things a camera could do. I read and studied journals and books on the Art of Photography, looked at cameras all the time. assessed every photo I saw, photographed my co-workers' children, sought out different plants and flowers, and did a whole project on hands, healing hands, working hands, a mothers' hands, and yes, one could say I was slightly obsessed. I loved it, then and now. My two cameras are great friends, always with me, just in case a good shot comes my way.

Photographers historically have been categorized as people who can see outside themselves, I don't know about that, I always thought everyone had that ability. Humor helps, and there always seems to be something funny that happens when two 'shutterbugs' meet. I met one a few days ago and we were discussing the Flicker woodpecker in my bird feeder and I remarked that I was unable to get a good shot, only to be reprimanded by an older man behind us in the line up. We tried to explain but he was having nothing of that and stormed away from us, leaving us with our mouths open.

The famous photographer, Karsh, renown for his portrait work of Kings, Queens, heads of state etc. had a healthy sense of humor, one of his best kept secrets. The magnificent image he captured of Sir Winston Churchill was done by Karsh. He had spent considerable time with Sir Winston and felt that he was unable to really capture the essence of the man, so in the end he did something very differently. He set up the shot, then ran up and pulled the cigar from Sir Winstons hand, a click, viola, the famous growly look of Sir Winston Chuchill captured for the world to see for years to come.

So we learn, we watch, read and learn and then get to another level and the learning starts all over again. That is the way it is with the camera for me-and I only wanted to learn how to blur! If one of my cameras is broken, I am heartsick, If I fool up a shot, I am disgusted with myself, but I'll try again. I freeze fingers and burn clothes at boilups, I love sunsets, rainbows, babies and most of all I like to share it with others. A short time ago a young man approached me and asked me to do some photos of his rebuilt Elan snow machine, one that he had worked on for months. We did it, I matted and framed it and now he has a keepsake forever.

A camera can seize the moment, make you forget about turmoil and hurts in your life as you concentrate on what you see through the lens, and what you see is self determined, whether it be a rose or a pothole, always the choice to make is the photographer.

A passion indeed for me. My family gave me one of the later cameras that Mother and Father had used. They all decided I would be the one to appreciate it more, as I remember how hot the flash bulbs would get and how quickly they had to be changed. We have come a long way since those days.

While visiting my daughter a few Christmas seasons ago, her brother joined us at her home in Calgary. Of course all sorts of shots were taken of the new baby.

While my son was using his sisters' camera, framing his shot, I heard my daughters voice doing a perfect imitation of me saying "Now Jawn, this looks like it should be vertically framed, Yes, turn the camera around, now tighten it up, a little more, yes, that's it!"

Her hands on her hips and with my glasses on she was a second "Me." John looked at his sister and collapsed into laughter. "Perfect, "he managed to say, "just perfect!"

That's an OK, great laugh by all, but he took one heck of a shot and my daughter takes great photos too. Do you suppose it's a 'Shutterbug' virus that we have? It must be, but I'm surely glad I caught it!

" Say Cheese Please!"

HOPSCOTCH BY GOSH!

My eyes were fixated on the marks drawn in driveway near my home. I couldn't believe what I was seeing! It was a seven-block hopscotch game, outlined with the special chalk the children have now. Beanie bags were lying nearby, as if the game had been ongoing before the children were called to lunch. I was fascinated. I had not seen a hopscotch anywhere for many years. Often I had wondered if they still played it, and asking my sisters always developed into a conversation about our hopscotch days growing up around Newfoundland.

"Go outside. You're not hanging around here on a day like this!" our Mothers would all say as if they had a mantra they practiced. We were sure all our Mothers had some secret fraternity that made them all act the same way and enforce the same rules.

So out we would go. It was better to be out exploring and playing and getting into mischief than being home helping fold diapers, iron clothes or wash dishes anyway. The unspoken rule was "if you are hanging around doing nothing, I'll find something for you to do!" Another of our Mothers' criterion that was widespread.

Just as you headed out the door you would hear another command such as "And take your sister and brother with you."

"Why do they have to come with me?" I would ask.

"Because I said so, that's why!" was the prompt answer.

And another day of activities would begin. Hopscotch was one of the most popular games. We didn't have chalk. Our lines were drawn in the mud or gravel with a stick, common stones were our markers, no beanie bags were around in those days. We knew nothing of the fact that hopscotch began in ancient

Britain during the early Roman empire and that some hopscotch courts were more than 100 feet long. But we knew that we became more skilled the more we played and winning the next round was a victory. Our canvas sneakers would be scuffed and ready to disintegrate after many games of hopscotch, and there was always someone who wanted to start a game.

A few years ago I lived in a neighborhood for months and never realized there were many children living in the area. I only realized when school started and the brightly clad students stood at the bus stop that there were many children around. They have so many things to do inside now. So much technology, too many movies, and a stack of video games have taken over from the games of our childhood years. I still wonder why they never seem to be 'berry picking', something that was a joy for us as children, going home with blue or red mouths and a belly full of any kind of berry that was ripe.

In one day four or five, if not more, of us children would play hopscotch until we were exhausted, climb the huge rocks looking for a spot out of the wind to sit in the warm sun and tell stories, play games of ball with the red, white and blue rubber ball that sent you running forever as it bounced down the gravel road. Most of the time it would end up in the water, and so would the outfielder.

Everyone had their skipping rope tied around the handlebars of their basic, no gear, bicycles which we rode for miles, and if the urge to jump rope for an hour overtook us, then we would stop and do just that.

"Let's go fishin'!" someone would suggest after lunch (dinner we called it then). Then out would come the long bamboo fishing rods, lines and hooks, a few worms would be dug, and we would head for the pond. Usually our younger charges would be napping at home by then and we were free.

The fishing would soon get boring, the best part was the preparing and getting to the pond, so another plan would be hatched. That could be anything from having a fire on the beach, building a 'camp' in the woods, to tying string on an old wallet and placing it in the middle of the road for the sole purpose of yanking it away when the unsuspecting adult would bend to pick it up. We would run like heck toward our bicycles.

By days' end we would be scratched, cut, covered in fly bites, our hands filthy, our feet even filthier, but there would always be energy left for another game of hopscotch. Our legs would be so tired, our stomachs growling, but we kept going until the call came to come home. There was no issue of childhood obesity, we were as fit as the best of the triathalon athletes. And probably would never be as fit again in our lives. Our bodies got a cardiovascular workout every single day.

Going home, putting your bike away, and entering the house was an interesting exercise in itself.

"Before you come in take the clothes off the line for me," Mother would dictate.

The clothes would be reeled in, the reels squeaking all over the cove as every Mother, as usual, had their routine plot well rehearsed. Then Mother would notice just how dirty and dusty we were.

The usual "Wait 'til your father gets home!" was said but unheard. For us it was really was no threat as Father would just smile and ask what we did all day.

"Nothin'! Played hopscotch."

"Where did you go?" he would press.

"Nowhere." the common answer.

"Who were you playing with?" Father kept pressing.

"Same crowd." another pat answer.

Than Mother would declare that "tomorrow you aren't getting outside the door to come home in that state. What in the world is wrong with you that causes you to roll around in mud?"

That was totally ignored because we knew where there was a great hopscotch drawn, and we had our special rock, and after an hour of our antics the next morning Mother would be mesmerized and disgusted.

And it would start all over again.

"Go outside and play. You're not hanging around me all day! And take your brother and sister with you!"

We were ready, and right on cue the gang would meet at the hopscotch on our bicycles, anxious to start the game. Just as sure as it was used as fitness drills for Roman soldiers, it was our drill. Our younger siblings watched and learned.

Yes, hopscotch by gosh. We would jump, run and skip our way through the day, probably do a little berry pickin' or fishin' too, then get in a punt if we could get one and row around for a while. It was nonstop activity in those tender, fuzzy memory-making days.

It was a magical time in our lives. Carefree childhood days in a 'Hopscotch by Gosh' continual tournament. Hopscotch kept us fit, taught us teamwork, helped us learn to accept victory and defeat, and to move on.

I would not trade one moment of it, because I know of nothing that can come close in value to such a lighthearted childhood and the 'hopscotch days', and all that the game taught us.

Yes, the hopscotch drawn in chalk tells me it is still a game being played by the children. I wonder if they would play a game with a Nanny? I have my marker rock all ready just in case. . . .

A GIFT WITHIN THE GRIEF

Beautiful big, white bellied, bewhiskered codfish died in Smith Sound, Trinity Bay in April 2003. Thousands and thousands of fish met their fate due to the formation of ice crystals on their gills. The water was a few degrees colder than usual, and theories abound from the fishers and the marine scientists, as to exactly what caused the tragedy, however I will leave that to them to study and develop their various reasons as to how and why this occurred. For me it was an experience more on a personal level, mindfully aware that I was watching what most likely was the end of the fishery in Newfoundland, and awful aftermath this would cause.

During the week when the fish were discovered to be floating in icy water near the end of the ice sheet covering the 'sound', hundreds of small boats were launched, motors hastily mounted, and they headed out to recover what they could from this disaster, trying to avoid it becoming a total waste of a resource. And they came back to the wharf in Lower Lance Cove, Random Island, loaded with fish, the little boats' gunnels level with the water. And this happened for days and days in many coves around the area, the fish plants were opened to process the fish, and the trucks were loaded and took to the road with their precious cargo, heading for the various fish plants.

But my experience was a personal and nostalgic one. It brought a memory floating to the surface. It was the memory of seeing this activity before in many outports around Newfoundland when I was a child, taking for granted that scenes like this would always be there, would stay the same, would be experienced by my children and grandchildren. But it was not to be. The fishery was in trouble, bad trouble. And this was an omen of worse things to come, and everyone in Lower Lance Cove that April 2003 day knew it was the beginning of the end. For us in our fifties it is unlikely that we will ever have the gift of seeing Newfoundland the way it was ever again. And it is heartbreaking. Our Newfoundland is hurt, and we hurt with her. But what has happened is over, is done, and we have to move on.

I stood leaning on a fish shack on a stage head that day. Everyone was moving about quickly, trucks drove in and out, fork lifts loading them with huge boxes of iced cod. The fishermen unloading were talking excitedly, and those standing on the wharf getting ready to go out to salvage fish were asking questions about what it was like 'out there'. Motors hummed, the sea licked the little slip way where a few boats still basked in the sun bottoms up, the air was cool, the sun warm, the smell of the kelp and the sea was marvelous. Yes, it was truly a step back in time.

As if on cue the women would arrive with lunches for their men, bringing the children along with them. The colors of the bright life vests, the trim of the boats, the Canadian and Newfoundland flags flapping in the wind, the children's clothes, the sea and sky, and the mountain behind us seemed more intense that afternoon.

The men would unload, their fish boxes weighed, and then they would walk up to join the women and eat their lunch off the tailgate of their truck or the various stage heads. They had stories to tell in a way only the Newfoundlander can tell them in my opinion. And of course they all had their theories on this phenomenon. The children ran about, their laughter musical on the wind while they stuck their rubber boots into the edge of the water and played, building dams as we used to do. They watched the minnows, they studied the boats, and they knew this was different. Just as I knew it and the child within me was tempted to stick my feet into the water with the children. Music flowed from a trucks' open window, and more and more it was a scene from a Newfoundland of long ago.

Being basically curious I went out to the edge of the wharf and looked down into the little boats at the fish. They were beautiful cod, big and healthy looking, and while caught in a tragic circumstance, they were at least salvaged. The elderly gentleman who was a fish plant owner was there, just like me, savoring this special moment. The weigh scales clicked and clacked as the records keeper and a dockside observer weighed and recorded the cargo of each fisher team, and they were serious about their business. One young fisher told me he got ashore on the frozen ice sheet and cut a hole about six feet square and the fish just bubbled up through it spilling unto the ice, something he had never witnessed before, nor had his boat crew. The dockside record keeper had to make a new category on his record sheet. Categories of how the fish were caught were listed such as gill net, handline, rod, net, but there had been no place for 'gaff', but there was now. And that was so sad.

A splash of Newfoundland humor was present in the midst of it all as everyone turned to watch a little boat coming toward the wharf.

"Now look at that, that's a submarine for sure!" a young man announced, as the boat was level with the sea. The laughter of a dozen or so men sounded so pleasant as they watched and waited to view the catch, and ask the usual question "What's it like out there?"

And they always got the same answer. There were dead fish, thousands and thousands of dead fish, nothing like it had they ever witnessed before. Then they would unload, have a snack, and take to the sea again.

The afternoon of big boatloads of codfish, the laughter, music, colors, children' delighted voices, the women gathered around, one with her apron still on, was a step back in time, no doubt about it. And it was a scene that took place over and over during an almost two-week period. Then slowly it wound down, all the fish were gathered, and the ones 'coming up' now, they reported, were lively enough to get their strength and swim back down. So the tragedy of the frozen fish was coming to a close.

For me, it was an ethereal experience. Putting aside the meaning and outcome of it all for a short time and looking at it just as it was, closing my eyes and listening to the sounds, smelling the air, feeling the wind on my face, watching Mr. March fillet a cod that I had acquired, was really like being caught in a time warp. It was an afternoon of my childhood being played out as if it were a movie. But deep in my heart I knew it was not a movie, and it was not likely to be something I would see again.

The days that followed were full of media interviews of the fishers, theories of what had happened, and finally the announcement of the closure of the fishing of the Northern Cod stocks in Newfoundland waters. And with one fell swoop a way of life came to an end for many. And now they struggle to come to terms with the situation.

For me, I consider that Lower Lance Cove afternoon a gift, a gift within the grief. I will carry it with me always, because I may never see a wharf so busy unloading boatloads of codfish ever again. As sad as it is, it is so. The big beautiful codfish, the feeling in the cove, the women bringing food for busy fishermen, and the laughter of the children as they shared in the delight of the day, the fleet of little boats of Newfoundland working hard, will just be a memory now.

But for that afternoon, I was given a gift, and indeed it was 'A Gift within the Grief'. And I pray that God will guard thee Newfoundland and Labrador. May you find the courage to carry on, remembering, and telling the stories to the younger generation who will never know what those special days were like, and need to know their heritage. Yes, God guard thee our beautiful province as you move ahead into a confused sea and uncertain waters.

THE CAPTAINS NEW RECIPE

Our boat pulled gently away from the wharf in the small cove where we had been docked. The rhythmic sound of the diesel engine was hardly noticeable above our animated conversations, the activity of preparing our hand lines for fishing, and the Captain, my husband, was at the helm, as well as starting to prepare his speciality-'Jiggs Dinner with 'Pease' Puddin''-which he cooks so well. And that was fine with me. Thirty years ago he had told me how to place the vegetables in the pot, then at the end of a certain period of time I was to 'lay the potatoes gently on the top'. Since I had been cooking since the age of nine, I had taken offense and thirty years later I still enjoy his Newfoundland cooking, and hardly ever attempt it myself. I know my limits! He does it well, he has the patience for it, everybody loves his 'Pease puddin',including me. He is always the cook for the Newfoundland dishes prepared in our home. I did teach him 'Cod au Gratin', and he does a good job of that now as well.

It was a hot day in the middle of summer, 2002, and the food fishery was open. We had the tags, bait, lines, and our small boat in tow for going fishing while leaving the bigger boat at the dock. So anyone staying behind could be comfortable and in charge of housekeeping chores. It was a situation that worked well. We fished in early morning and evening, spending the time in between exploring isolated coves. The big pot would be on the oil stove on the boat, giving us warmth on chilly days, and drying our wet gloves and clothes. The smell of the food cooking, the sound of the music playing, the crackling of the marine radio all made for a delightful experience. And we shared it with friends who enjoyed it as much as we did.

The water of Smith Sound was truly a mirror on that August

day. The 'Ocean Joy' glided along smoothly, we all talked up a storm, bragged about our last big catch. The smell of the Jiggs dinner cooking wafted through the boat while the binoculars were in use looking for whales and eagles. My husband knows navigation and understands boats, and we all trusted his judgement. Our friend Gene, is an airplane pilot, and lifelong friend of my husband. He is always a good support when a consult on the radar or GPS was necessary. These two men were like a pair of synchronized professionals, and we felt no fear, safety was a big factor with them both. For Lorraine and myself it was time to catch up on the news, listen to a joke from one of them that we had heard and laughed at fifty times before. All was well with the world on that sensational day under the brilliant Newfoundland sky that I loved so much. It was exhilarating to be back under that sky, and out on the water after so many years away. Having friends we had a connection with since our youth join us made it all so much more special.

The Captain took a good look around, looked at the instruments, told me to take the wheel, keep her on course, and he bounded back to talk to Gene at the stern of the boat where he was preparing his fishing gear. Gene wanted the big cod, the huge cod, the biggest of all, and was determined to get it. The two men had somewhat of a quick conversation, Lorraine went back to join them, and the Captain came back to the wheelhouse and shut the power down considerably. I didn't ask why, I relied on his judgement. Then he went back for another few words with Gene, and came back to the wheelhouse where I sat controlling the wheel as if I knew what I was doing. The Captain reached for the controls and set the boat into reverse, and bounced back to the stern again. Now this was becoming a tad strange. However I was told that he felt we were over a 'ridge' according to the charts and it was a great place for Gene to catch his 'super-cod'. I stayed at the wheel trying to stay the course. Then I heard the bang, slam, shriek, crash, and I looked back to see my husband and my friend Lorraine sliding and slipping on the galley floor like a pair wriggling codfish! What in the world were they doing? Then I saw the pot that was full of the ingredients for Jiggs dinner and was slowly cooking on the stove, giving us its' great aroma.

Well, the pot was not on the stove any more! And the dinner wasn't in it either! Gene appeared from the back, and the three of them slid around frantically gathering up all the hot food that they could and throwing it back into the somewhat dented pot. And then I knew–the pot had flown off the stove! It just took a flying leap when the boat settled after going into reverse for a moment, and we ricocheted in our own sea swell. The pot smacked into the table, the food was everywhere in the galley and it was one chaotic scene! I couldn't leave the wheel, they were sliding, slipping, yelling, grabbing, and trying to hang onto each other as they skated through large green leaves of half-cooked hot cabbage. What a sight! I kept on the course, they kept picking up the food, finally putting the damaged pot back on the stove. Then the Captain took the wheel again. We proceeded to clean the greasy galley. I never in my life saw anything like it. I found the 'pease puddin' bag on the top of the cushions at the table, Lorraine had taken with a fit of laughter, Gene was awestruck, and the poor Captain had his meal ruined. Now this was a fine fix to be in!

One thing that is certain, he was not throwing that dinner out! He gave the wheel to Gene and came back to the galley, took wire and lashed that pot onto the stove, lashed the cover onto the pot, and by the look of this solution I thought the pot was there forever! By then we were all somewhat giddy over it all. And the Captain was thinking hard. I knew that look.

Then after twenty minutes or so the hard thinking Captain announced that he was adding the potatoes. He would finish cooking supper. It took longer to unlash the cover of the pot than it did to grow a turnip, but he did it and laid his 'potatoes gently on the top'! He then tied down the cover again and announced that all was well, and dinner would be ready on time. His face was saying 'don't ask me any questions'. So of course I had to ask a question just to keep my reputation for disobedience.

"How do you think we can eat that food? It has been on the floor for heavens' sake. Have you lost your mind?" I had the audacity to ask!

I stood there waiting for an answer, which, if you know the Captain, would not be long coming.

"Heat kills germs," he announced, "and we will not be having the Jiggs dinner as planned, we will have now a new special meal. Ever heard of 'DECK STEW? Well, that is what you will be having!"

It took ten minutes before we could catch our breath. We had such a reaction to the declaration of the Captain. He meant what he said, and 'Deck Stew' it would be. We all agreed, because on a boat the 'Captain calls the shots' as they say. So we continued on, Gene caught fish, we chatted and joked some more, and soon we docked the boat in Popes Harbour. OK, we would have the 'Deck Stew'. We never had anything else anyway. We set about to have our meal, a lovely glass of wine, a lantern candle, and lots of babble about 'the event'!

Actually the Deck Stew was rather enjoyable. The Captain asserted that 'no pot will fly off that thing again!'.And by the amount of wire he had in his hand we believed him.

We remained fairly under control from that point on, and got back to talking about our usual topics. Things seemed to be relatively civil.

That is until Lorraine held up a fork full of carrot, looked at me and asked "Do these carrots taste a little 'dieselly' to you?"

The gales of laughter started again, and the question never did get answered. The carrots were a tad 'dieselly', but they were good!

So our Captain goes down in the history of Smith Sound as the only Captain ever to come up with a new recipe for use at sea, diesel spiced and delicious. He had become a Trinity bay Gourmet!

And that is how 'Deck Stew' came to be an original dining experience in Trinity Bay, Newfoundland! Give it a try. Remember to 'lay the potatoes gently on the top', and various other spices may be used in place of 'diesel fuel'.

As the fine Captain said, "Don't knock it 'til you try it!"

PART FOUR

*Of family, friends, pets and all the other things
that make Our Lives—
A Wonderful and Interesting Journey'*

*Through the ups and downs, the good and the
bad—but always a journey!*

MY ATTACHMENT IS GROWING

The chores were done, and the house in order. I was ready to turn on my computer. The electronic computer enables me, as it does millions of others, to keep in touch with the world. There is unending information at our fingertips. It is just a matter of learning how to access it. Even those who said they never would learn to use a computer are learning, using and enjoying the experience.

My Personal Computer enables me to keep in touch with old friends, send greeting cards and letters, pay bills, and display my photography of the beauty of Newfoundland for others to enjoy. It also makes my writing much easier than using a typewriter. I cannot help but think back on the days before going to nursing school when I studied a business course and learned to type on manual typewriters with no letters on the keys. The keyboard had to be memorized, and like learning to ride a bike, it is something you never forget. My acquired skill of typing was always a great asset during my Nursing career.

Yes, I am attached to my Personal Computer, and my computer station is a place where I spend considerable time, writing, setting up photo albums, researching material I need for my writing, and communicating with the world. But even more so I am attached to an attachment. It arrives regularly, and gives me great joy.

For those not computer oriented let me explain that strange statement. First of all, when you open your computer mailbox you find a list of messages, some personal, some ads, the same as you find in your post office mail box. You have to filter through and discard what is offensive to you, the uninteresting junk mail, and then you get to the mail that you have looked forward to with great anticipation. A computer e-mail letter with an 'attachment' is the same as receiving mail through the ordinary means with a photo or other messages in the same envelope. On the computer, mail containing photos is marked with a little 'paperclip' drawing. When I see that my heart skips a beat and I go immediately to the message where I see my daughters' name, and the tiny paper clip that tells me she has sent an attachment.

My daughter, her husband, and little girl, and also our son, live far away in Western Canada. I miss them, want to be with them, to be part of their lives as they wish to be part of ours. But instead we settle for photos, cards, phone calls and of course our computer and its' e-mail. To see their names, and that minuscule 'paper clip' icon, means they have sent photos. And all of their photos are wonderful, giving us a window to peek through to see how they are doing, how their lives are progressing, what the new house they just bought is like, and for us our only grandchild, a precious little girl named Kylee. I click on the paperclip drawing to view and save the photos. Later I go back and make them bigger on the computer screen. My husband and I watch the photos as a slide show, admiring each and everyone. We are always quiet when we do this. Each lost in thought, each with our own special memories.

A few days ago I started a project. Our granddaughter will be three years old soon. I went back to her first Christmas when she was just a month old, and we visited her in Calgary. Neither my daughter nor I had a computer then, so the photos were all carefully placed in albums, and treated with loving care. When we returned home, we could see Kylee grow with each photo we received. Then she came for a visit to Newfoundland when she was about a year and a half old, and we took more photos of her various activities. So, yes, I started a project.

My project was to put these photos in an album on the computer, enabling me to share it with my family, and of course with Kylee. It took hours and hours, but it is complete now. Kylee has been shown the album by her Mom, and she wants to know who the baby is on the computer screen. She cannot understand that the tiny baby she sees is really herself.

As I did the project, I realized what an attachment I have to this small child who is, like her mother and grandmother, strong-willed and determined, creative and sensitive. I also realized that she is growing up so fast. One of the last photos to go in the virtual album was of Kylee helping make muffins. She is wearing a bib apron Auntie Joan made for her, and in that way she is so like me, her grandmother, who loves bib aprons. In another of the latest 'attachment' photos she is sitting back on her feet on her parents bed completely engrossed in a book, again like her mother and me. She is part of us, and part of her other grandparents in the Codroy Valley. But she is my 'attachment', both by lineage and by a computer 'paperclip' icon.

By the time I completed the project I had made a decision. I decided that I can no longer watch my grandchild grow by 'attachment'. I want to hold her, read to her, bathe her, take her to the park, cuddle her, make her laugh, take her shopping and be a real, bona fide grandmother. My 'attachment' is growing, she will be three years old soon, and she will not remember me when I visit. She will be a few days getting to know me and her Poppy again.

Something no 'paper clip' can provide is that human touch, that sweet smell of freshly shampooed hair, sharing of a ball of play dough, our hands working together to make small creations, the warmth of her body as she leans into me and listens to a story being read, hearing her giggle when something amuses her and the touch of the softness of her skin and curly hair. That is the true attachment. And that is what I am longing to experience.

I am a new grandmother, but I am unable to show my love to this tiny life that has enhanced mine. The computer keeps me attached with photos, and my heart keeps me attached with love. It is a love so intense that nothing less than holding Kylees' little hand will soothe the yearning in my heart.

So, we will visit Kylee in that place far away. I need and want to be with her, even if for a short time. And for that short time the 'paper clip' will be put aside, and we will be together, attached by a secure love, a love so strong that no computer can ever express it, but a Nanny can and will.

Until then I will look for the paper clips, and the photographs that cause my heart to dance as I see my 'growing attachment' on a computer screen.

THE GARDEN

The corner of a small magazine sticking out from under a pile of sleeping, aged, 'waiting room' reading material caught my eye. The green background of the magazine cover accentuated the bright orange color of the flowers I remembered so well. I gave the corner a little tug and there it was-a seed catalogue of several years ago, but still full of rich vibrant colors, colors of all sorts of flowers, fruits and vegetables that grace our lives through the hands of wonderfully gifted gardeners. It didn't take too long for my eyes to focus on the big, orange, perfect petals of the ''tiger lilies'. Although called by another name in the catalogue they were 'tiger lilies' to me, and they were called that by Grampy Bud too. And Grampy Bud was the best darned backyard gardener I ever knew so I'd go with his name, regardless of what someone else would call them.

'Grampy Bud' and 'Nan' were not related to our family, other than through friendship and sharing. They lived a short distance from our house, and his grandchildren were good friends of my son and daughter. Shelly and Michelle lived in the same house as his son and family, and because of that my children grew to know him and he was called Grampy by all the children. His daughter Becky was a good friend of mine, and throughout the years we all became connected through community activities, Girl Guide outings, school events and all the things that make up our lives. I could drop in and see Becky on my way home from work and moan and groan, Becky would listen, and I would always leave her house feeling better.

This older couple were surrogate grandparents to my children who enjoyed that kind of relationship because their own Nanny and Poppy lived far away. Nan would call my son, John, and tell him his fresh bread was out of the oven and he would jump on his bike and head for her house, devouring practically the whole loaf of bread on his way home. They were kind and generous to us, and we shared in turn if we had anything special to offer.

'Embert' was Grampys real name, but one time when he was a boy somebody called to him saying "Hey Bud!", and the nickname Bud stayed with him after that. He had retired when we met him and devoted countless hours to his garden.He was totally immersed in growing any thing you could mention. And I was awestruck at how a tiny piece of land could yield so much food, and of course thousands of beautiful flowers. He had Hummingbird feeders everywhere and you could sit on his step and watch the little birds for hours while Bud worked in his garden, keeping weeds out and the rows neat and straight.

The rhubarb always started the spring run of goods. Followed by everything you could name. Peas, beans, squash, carrots, savory, chives and with it all the beautifully colored flowers which he seemed to be able to get to grow so prolifically Tiger Lilies, peonies, roses, tulips, magnolias, just to mention a few. I was always attracted to the Tiger Lilies the most because as I rounded the corner near his house I could see the big orange lilies waving in the wind. And it was a magnificent sight to see after a long day at work.

Autumn would bring the corn and pumpkins, but the in the middle of summer I would get my raspberries. He would have them placed in their little paper containers and would call me at home or at work and tell me "Your favorite berries are ready."

I'd buy the vanilla frozen yogurt and that would be my supper. I love raspberries, and when Grampy Bud gave me half a dozen boxes I would hoard them, hiding them from everybody, and that always caused Grampy to say that I didn't need to do that, lots of berries were still to be picked! And he would laugh heartily at me over the raspberry issue.

Buds' grand daughters were always pulling one stunt or another, and my daughter would be right in there with them. She adored Grampy and Nan, as did my son. They would hide the garden tools, the lawn tractor, the bag of fertilizer and anything they could to try to irritate Grampy. But it would just backfire because Grampy soaked in the circle of attention he was receiving. Gary, his son, was the worst tease of all.

But Gary never won either! One day Gary, for some unknown reason, decided to plant tulip bulbs. He planted them at the end of his house and told everyone he knew that he was 'into the flowers like Father now.' Bud stood back as grandfathers do and rubbed his head and said "Well, well, well!" Enough said.

A few days later Gary walked out of his house, past where he had planted the bulbs and there was a row of tulips, in assorted colors. Grammy had made wooden tulips and placed them near each tulip bulb spot. The whole village knew about the prank by lunch time and Gary gave up farming for a time, that is until his tulips did really bloom.

The summers passed, the children grew into teenagers, the days of raspberries and yogurt, fresh bread and jam went on, but most of the time the kids were off on some other escapade, job or summer study course. TheTiger Lilies were more gorgeous than ever, but one day Grampy announced that he would have a smaller garden next summer. He was having a bit of pain he told us, and not being one to complain it was clear that something was very wrong. His family and friends convinced him to see a doctor, and he did. In less than a year Grampy lost his battle with prostate cancer, and we were totally devastated to lose him. His garden looked forlorn, Nan hung the hummingbird feeders, and Becky and I carried on our usual chats while we sat on the step and watched the birds and discussed our issues of the day. We would talk about all the food, the beautiful bounty, that came from such a small piece of land, and the Grampy who had shared what he had with those he thought should have it. Everything was different then and it would never be the same. We moved on with our lives, getting the offspring off to University and working, stopping for our talks, Nan joining us often as she was so lonely. The wooden tulips faded in the hot sun, and Garys' tulips grew beautifully.

On a weekend home from university I noticed my daughter was wearing unfamiliar pyjamas, I definitely had not seen these before and asked her about them because clearly they were a mans' pyjama set. She asked if I liked them, and I told her that I did.

"Well, Mom," she announced, "these belonged to Grampy Bud. Nan gave them to me after he died, still in the package they were. They make me feel good and bring me lots of good memories." I couldn't believe it. It had been three years since her special Grampy had died.

"Remember his garden Mom? And remember how he had all those Tiger Lilies you loved so much. You should plant some, you'll feel better!" I didn't know that she would notice that I was not feeling better. It was a deep sadness I was experiencing, because just one day short of a year since his fathers' death, Gary too passed away. It was such a difficult time for Becky and Nan .And for their friends too.

It is many years later now, I think Heather still has the special pyjamas that make her 'feel good', even though when I saw them last they were threadbare.

We are living back in Newfoundland again. I saw enormous Tiger Lilies in a garden last summer, and this summer our new house will need to be landscaped, and splashes of colored flowers will be placed here and there. I have chosen my flowers, no matter what the proper name the seed book calls them, in my garden they will be 'GRAMPY BUD LILIES'.

It is a truth, now I know, that to live in the hearts of others is not to die. And I remember with fondness and gratitude the special grandfather gardener that touched our lives and shared his 'garden of life'.

JOHNS' JOBS

The clunk of the bicycle against the steps leading into the house, followed by the fast footsteps, and mumbles of a male voice, led me to believe that our son John had arrived home. And he was not happy! This six foot tall seventeen year old had a summer job that he despised more than he could express. He left in the morning on his bicycle, was gone six or seven hours, and then returned in the afternoon in a state of angst that would scare anyone who didn't know him. He was disgusted with the world and everything in it, no doubt about it.

In the heat of the Annapolis Valley summer I could hardly blame him for his anger. However every summer John and his sister would have a summer job of some kind. Making cotton candy, babysitting, taking the census, and other jobs along that line were his sisters' challenges, but John always seemed to have a job that engendered physical distress and one heck of a bad mood.

When he started high school my tall, gangly son was determined to have a job during weekends and summer holidays. Usually he worked helping the farmers with the haying, then at the Christmas tree farm, shearing and pruning the trees in the summer, his height a great advantage for that type of work. He came to know trees, how they grew, which were good Christmas trees, and what not to have as a tree. The workers would tag trees, each color tag meaning something different, a code to the Christmas Tree farmer. Then as the end of November approached John would be called to work as they started to harvest the Christmas trees for shipment to far away places. This was brutal work at times, cutting, bailing, and loading the trees onto a tractor trailer in all sorts of weather, on cold windy days, and then snowy days. But this all encouraged John to pursue his education. He said over and over again that he would not do this for a lifetime. And of course nobody expected he would.

Because of his quiet manner and brute strength he was always wanted for the Christmas tree work, but there did come a summer when he worked with a construction crew, doing labor work, and loved it, making life much more agreeable in our household. Another summer he worked with an electrician, as he was, by then, in college studying for his Electrical journeymen' papers. Well, some good days were to come our way that summer, but when the electrician had a contract to install a fire alarm system in the towns' theater which required six foot four inch John to crawl under a building and be in there for hours on end, life at home when he arrived there was, shall we say, quite tense! He hated it with a passion that he could not find words enough to express his despair.

He despised the theater after that job was finished, and he had gone through two or three lunch kits, having thrown them away or stood and stomped on them, or just plain put them in a dumpster. John just could not come up with the 'perfect' job. He would arrive home, go straight to his room, then to the shower and them stomp off to pitch a softball game. And his mood was not good, and he was not approachable. And the hotter the weather got, the meaner he got, and the meaner he got the more determined he became to get a good education. If nothing else, it encouraged him to work hard, and eventually he graduated from Kings Technical College, winning an award for 'Perseverance', and he really did deserve it.

Not too long after his graduation John David moved to Calgary. The quiet boy had become a young man with a burning desire, and a steel-like determination to finish his electricians' journeymen papers. There was no work in Nova Scotia that would allow him to do a proper apprenticeship, so he loaded up his red pickup truck, found someone who wanted to go with him, and drove across Canada. He arrived in Calgary one day, and the next day, armed with only the newspaper want ads, he walked into a company, told them who he was, they sized him up, and told him he had a 'JOB'-and he was in 'electrical heaven'. He found a place to rent, sharing with friends, did a certain number of hours, then went to the Southern Alberta Institute of Technology for the next level, and continued this until he was a full fledged Electrician. He worked hard, and now is a foreman with an Instrumentation diploma to accompany his Journeymen' papers and works with a company in Fort Mcmurray ,after spending almost ten years in Calgary. He is dedicated to his work, takes it very seriously, and is proud of his accomplishments, as we all are. And he finally is doing work he likes to do.

For John to succeed he had to work hard. In Grade Twelve he developed Hepatitis and was very ill and we came very close to losing him. However he did graduate and never looked back. He worked jobs nobody else would do, he also will always have the perfect Christmas tree, knowing just what to look for, and remembering his days of shearing them in the hot sun, fighting off the flies, and bailing them in the winter with the icy rain freezing on his face.

When I saw the e-mail pop up on the computer screen, saying "I Got it!", telling us he had received his promotion to Foreman, I could not hold back the tears. He is a man of 32 years of age now, but he is still my boy, the boy who threw the bicycle against the step and stomped in through the house mumbling unrepeatable words as he went to the shower. And I especially remembered that particular summer job that upset him so much when he mailed us that day, because that was the summer that he had the very worse job of all! He had the daily gross job of cleaning the lab for a researcher who was studying giant sea snails! In the basement of her house he would have to clean their tanks, change the water, and tolerate the smell. He hated, despised, berated, yelled, kicked, jumped up and down, and generally became someone we didn't know on the day he came home and reported that overnight the snails had all crawled out of their tanks and were all over the beams and walls of this so-called research lab. And he had the obnoxious job of collecting them all.

But he learned that one has to work, to learn, to be dependable and prompt, to observe and to apply yourself to the best of your ability, that if you are expected to do a job, then you do it, and do it well.

I just don't ever want to be around if he is ever offered 'escargot' as an appetizer, because I know, and fear, that he will become one giant enraged man as his mind fills with the memory of the 'summer of the snails' and the time they got away!

THE PERFECT PROM DRESS'

The six o'clock news was almost over when I heard the reporter talking about graduations and careers. Then I realized the focus of the piece was on 'prom dresses, and finding the perfect prom dress. A group of graduating girls, filled with the vitality of youth and the thrill of success, talked excitedly to the young reporter about the absolute necessity of finding the 'perfect' dress for the prom dance. Of course they were excited, and filled with the bittersweet emotion of moving on, leaving their school mates that they had spent years with, and with whom they had developed strong friendships. Now they would go their separate ways. One young woman expressed it so sincerely as she said "I want prom night to be really special, because we may never all be together again." Yes, she was so right, and to have a special prom required having the special dress or the special tuxedo for the boys as they celebrated one of life s' milestones.

Ah, yes, the perfect dress indeed! They were each searching everywhere for the elusive proper dress, and I had done so as well, although it had been many moons ago. In 1964 my prom dress, for graduation night at Grand Falls Academy, in Grand Falls-Windsor, was a white chiffon knee length creation with a trace of pastel yellow brocade on the bodice. Oh, it was divine, and so was the prom.

The search for that apparel took me all of ten minutes, then the shoes were chosen, that was a good five minutes, and that was that. But I have been through this drill many times since, and the time is never that short it seems. Today proms are high fashion, glittering lights, limousines, and special dinners. The music and dancing goes well into the night and most proms have the 'after-prom party, and that often is a weekend event.

But one year, in the early nineties, the search for the prom dress for my sweet daughter came close to causing my demise. 'Death by dress', not a good epitaph, but it would be so true. My dear daughter had a picture of the 'most divine dress Mom' in her head, and was determined that it would be hers if she rubbed Aladdins' lamp often enough. In this case I was the lamp.

My son had graduated four years before her and he casually rented a tuxedo, got dressed and off he went. This was not, and is not the case for a daughter. Ask any mother of a graduating daughter how she is doing and her eyes glaze over as she becomes transformed in front of your eyes into a stressed, tired, overwhelmed, distraught woman. There is no way to describe a mother's dismay during the search for 'the perfect dress', it is something that has to be experienced first hand.

However, we go back to the graduation of my daughter, a girl that played rugby, was a member of the school band and cadets', rode a mountain bike, was on the downhill ski team for her school, and generally followed no gender guidelines. She had been known to escape from her bedroom window as quietly as she could talk on the phone at three in the morning. Now she was in the market for a dress yet to be created. I was dragged, driven, pushed, pulled, pleaded to, and finally gave in just for the sake of finding mental stability again. I let her buy the 'divine dress' when she and a friend eventually decided that this black, strapless, sequined, short little dress that could be had for a mere two hundred dollars, was found. By the time the dress was cut to a length an inch shorter than it had been, fifty more dollars had been spent, but she was enthralled, and I was actually beginning to think peace was in the air. Never did I bring up the fact that my wedding dress only cost eighty-five dollars. That would just bring a remark suggesting that my wedding immediately followed the invention of the wheel, not in an obnoxious way, but her quick wit was so well known. So I said nothing. It was her time to celebrate her achievements so I would ride out the storm. One of my friends who was experienced in the ways of graduating girls and their mind set, having been through the rigors of it all, came to visit one evening. She asked my daughter if she could see her prom dress. So my dear daughter brought forth the zippered garment bag containing the precious dress. Then she stood there with a bicycle helmet on, soccer cleats on her feet, and gingerly unzipped the bag. My friend was allowed a glimpse as if the crown jewels were somewhere in that zipped bag, and that was that.

We just shared glances of 'whatever', the look that mothers' share in times like these, and settled back for a chat. We didn't settle for long before Miss Rugby/Skier/Bicyclist walked by on her way to her game. And it was then I had the moment of temporary insanity and asked her if she had yet chosen shoes to compliment the dress. After that question, and its' answer my life became a mindless blur, and I walked around with that stuporous look that I see on other mothers' faces now.

"Oh, Mom, I forgot to tell you I guess, but I'm not buying shoes."She said over the mouth guard sticking out of her mouth.

"What do you mean, no shoes?" I just had to ask.

"Well, I'm wearing sneakers, one black and one white," she explained, Melanie and I are buying two pairs just alike, she's buying white and I'm buying black, and we're gonna wear one of each color. We take the same size.

Neat hey?"

My heart turned over, my palms filled with sweat, my friend stared straight ahead, and my daughter prepared to leave the house. This was too much, I could feel the rant coming and I couldn't stop it."You have lost your mind young lady. Do you mean to tell me I paid two hundred dollars, and fifty more for alterations, for a prom dress for you and you are wearing sneakers with it? I suppose you'll carry a grocery bag as a purse will you? And why not get some face paint while you're at it? And top it off with some Halloween earrings. Indeed you will not wear sneakers, as a matter of fact you may not be allowed to wear sneakers at a prom!" I blabbered on and on.

Finally I could hear my friend laughing, my rebellious daughter had a game to attend and I was in shock. She went out the door and I continued my rant.

Friends are good in times like that, they listen, and very often they empathize, and they help you regain sanity and go on living. I was advised to leave her alone, and she wouldn't do that anyway, was my friends' opinion. But I certainly knew my daughter and I knew she would do it. And she would be all that more determined if she knew it was upsetting.

I promised myself not to mention it again. And I didn't, and I don't know how I didn't, but Divine Intervention was the key I think.

Prom night came, the girls were back and forth each others' homes all day, and by six o'clock they were ready to go to dinner, followed by the dance. The sneakers were on, little beads strung on the laces, the hairdos were as stiff as steel wool, and the smiles were contagious. They had hired a limousine, and when it arrived they all went running toward it, laughter filling our whole neighborhood.

And I never mentioned the sneakers. I was so very proud of myself. They all looked beautiful, I did their photos, the other moms came by, and it is a fond, fuzzy memory now. They were little girls, dressed as young women, that is until you got to the feet.

They all had dates, and they all had dinner, and they all arrived at the dance around nine p.m. But not before they persuaded the driver to go through the 'take-out' window at the golden arches. One of them had a cell phone and had called to describe their meal and how nice it all was, and laughter and giggles could be heard in the background. I did the usual 'be careful, have a good time,' speech and they entered the school gym for their dance.

Ten o'clock our phone rang. It was my sequined, tulle, and bicolored footwear daughter.

"Mom, I'm sick of this now. Can you come and pick us up?" she whispered into the phone. Of course I would. And I did. They had only rented the limousine for four hours, after that the parents were the chauffeurs.

So the two hundred dollar dress was worn for four hours, she had a new pair of sneakers that she wore doing her summer job of making cotton candy at the fair grounds, and she had a graduation diploma. As for me I had gone into the overdraft!

Now, she has finished University, has a good job, a handsome husband, and a little two-year-old girl, the love of our lives. And to this day I have not mentioned the sneakers or the craziness of buying an expensive dress and wearing it for four hours, coming home and changing into camping gear and leaving to go camping, returning covered in flanker holes and totally exhausted.

It is a tender memory now, and has caused many a good laugh between us, and the sound of her laugh makes it all seem worthwhile. And the best part of it all is that she has given me a delightful little grand daughter who is rebellious, wears what she wants, when she wants and she is only two and a half year's old. If her boots are on the wrong feet, she wants them to stay that way! If you brush her hair she will immediately mess it up and memories of her mother at that age come to mind.

I hope I live long enough to see what her mother has to say when her prom time comes. I really hope I am there, if only to finally get to tell her about the darned mismatched sneakers! But until then I have a word of advice to suffering 'prom moms' and that is to ride it out Let yourself have the joy of a warm, sweet memory to tell your grandchildren. Because I sure as heck am gonna tell mine!

SIMON, MY CHRISTMAS CAT

I have always had a cat in my life. For those who are not cat oriented there is one rule to learn-a cat is not owned by you, you are owned by the cat. If you leave a cat for a day or so, or give it a scolding, it will turn its' back on you and punish you for your unsuitable behavior. Right now I am owned by a Tonkinese cat named Simon. His coat is a beautiful beige color, with a grey face, paws and tail, and he has blue eyes. Simon is mellow, has made friends with a Labrador Retriever, and looks at birds with an expression that says "Why bother?". He considers himself Royalty. He captured me, and knows he is fortunate. If you take his favorite chair he will stare at you until you move. If you displace his dish or give him food he dislikes, he will walk away with an air of disdain.

Simon likes Christmas, and turkey is his favorite food. But one Christmas in particular, Simon became a celebrity and people still talk about him with fondness.

We lived just up the street from a little Baptist Church, which always had the most delightful Nativity Scene, with flood lights shining on the Babe in the Manger. It was endearing, and the chimes playing Christmas music always added to the festive atmosphere of the neighborhood. The church was on the other side of an intersection but I never worried about Simon in traffic because he did not venture outside. One cold evening, with air that would freeze your breath, the wood stove was inviting, and we were all inside, thinking Simon had found his favorite spot of the week, and was safe and warm. Then the phone rang.

"Is your cat home?" a neighbor asked. I told him yes, but he insisted I check to see if he was indeed home. We began the search.

No, Simon was not home. Panic set in. How did he get outside? I went back to the phone and fearfully asked my neighbor why he was inquiring, expecting to hear that Simon had been hurt. But thankfully that was not so.

My neighbor lived directly across from the church and was in the habit of sitting in his cosy chair by the window, watching television, while keeping an eye on the Nativity display. He thought he saw movement in the manger, and it looked like a real baby moving around. Then he remembered that I had a beautiful beige cat. He got the binoculars, and he and his wife decided that it was indeed Simon in the Manger. He went and verified that it was indeed my Simon. His fur was warm from the hot floodlights as he snoozed next to the figurine of the Baby Jesus.

I rushed out to fetch my cherished cat. He wasn't pleased about leaving the manger and the warmth of the lights, but I cuddled him, and went home.

So Simon became a celebrity that Christmas. He had slept in the manger with the Baby Jesus, surrounded by shepherds, wise men, Mary and Joseph. My precious cat became part of Christmas in our village. He never tried that again, because Simon knows what is good for him, and what is bad. The warm Manger was good, but the busy highway was bad.

Every Christmas since when the Nativity Scene is built, the story of Simon, the Christmas Cat in the Manger, is told with fondness. My fugitive cat had stolen their hearts.

Merry Christmas to you Simon. God understands and loves all the little creatures. It reminds me of the childhood hymn we sang, "God sees the little sparrow fall, it meets his tender view." And Simon, if God so loved the little birds, I know he loves you too.

IT'LL BE GOOD FOR YOU, YOU'LL LIKE IT!

As an adult, with two children, and as a family unit, camping was one of our favorite activities. Year after year we would drive through Nova Scotia, take the ferry to Newfoundland, and camp overnight any place where it was convenient. With a van, a tent, and lots of camping supplies, the trips were peaceful and so much enjoyed by our children. The campfires at night were always the big highlights before settling for the night.

But my introduction to camping was not quite the same as those trips. The summer of my twelfth year, living on the Northern Peninsula in Port Saunders, with all types of daily activities on the beach, and in the ponds, and the pool parlor and lots of jukebox music, I was quite content to spend my summer enjoying those things, and caring for my younger siblings. However this one particular summer it was decided that two weeks at the girls camp at Kildevil Lodge in Lomond, Bonne Bay, would be first of all 'good' for me and secondly I would so 'enjoy it'! So the gear was gathered up, the registration forms sent, and in midsummer I found myself carted off to camp with another girl from our school. I half heartedly went along, determined to make the best of it.

When we arrived at the camp, there were numerous large canvas tents set up, little flags flying from the tent center poles, the sun shining, the eagles soaring over the high hills, everyone so friendly, and I thought maybe it won't be so bad after all. And it wasn't, for one night!

The first morning of ten or so such mornings found us having breakfast, then dispatched to various assigned chores. Four girls to a tent, each of us responsible for a different chore every day.

That wasn't so bad. We always passed tent inspection, and then the daily activity schedule kicked in.

Swimming lessons were an absolute requirement. After shivering through morning after morning until the end of camp, I managed to pass beginners. And that's what I have today-a beginners! I despise having my head under water except for the shower, and have never progressed beyond that stage and never will. My love of boats astounds people who know of my fear of water. So that was one aspect of, the 'it'll be good for you'!

Then the competitive team sports started. I was kicked, pushed and shoved, cut and bruised and learned to despise team sports if it included me. I didn't have the "I want to win" mentality when it came to team sports. I really didn't think winning a volleyball game in the hills of Bonne Bay would impact on my life in any sensational way. And to this day, while competitive with spelling tests, knowing facts etc. is and has been a big part of my life I never ever let another bunch of athletic girls beat me around. And at the age of 54 years, it will never happen! So much for that!

The campfires were the favorite part of my day. I learned to love that aspect of camping. Every tent, every camper had to participate at campfires. We had skits, wrote poems to be read, wrote short stories and songs, acted and impersonated our leaders and had a free reign over our creativity. That was the best and most popular part of the whole two weeks to me because that part of the camping experience was absolutely heavenly. Different regions were represented by the girls and everyone put their heads and their talents together and we were worthy of Academy or Emmy awards at those campfires, wonderful!

The fly bites, the cuts, the hives, the earaches, was all treated by the camp nurse, and someday, now that I am retired I want to do a summer camp, and be the camp nurse. She was lovely, kind and courteous and very understanding of the adolescent girls' angst.

When we broke camp and headed home I looked forward to returning to my friends, and with my wet sleeping bag, itchy head, dirty clothes and filthy sneakers I finally got back to Port Saunders, so looking forward to seeing my friends that night. That was until a mother headed me toward the bathtub, and as she was preparing my bath she called me to come closer to her.

My hair in pigtails, with the scalp showing between the elastics, seemed to be her area of interest. She examined me for a few minutes, picked through my hair and then gave a loud shriek! I had brought back, in my pigtails and ponytail, a few thousand lice! Mother was frantic, the doctor was consulted, treatments begun, hair was cut, and in a few days I was given a clearance to be around other people. That was the end of my camping experience, and I mean the END!

After that, all through my life, when somebody would tell me that something would be 'GOOD FOR YOU' or 'YOU'LL REALLY ENJOY IT', I get itchy, suspicious, and downright determined that they're wrong! I smell the delousing shampoo, feel the fine tooth comb, the cold water covering my face, and my heart rate triples.

But the great part of it is that I also remember those campfires, those wonderful skits, the roasted wieners, with mustard, the stories I was allowed to write and read to the group, the smell of the campfire blankets, seeing the flankers bouncing from the fire pit, and my heart soars again.

Ah, yes, camping! The good and the bad, the wet and the dry, the warm and the cold, but always making memories.

NO CHANGING SCHOOLS FOR ME!

There was definitely something very strange happening around me as I fooled around and babysat my siblings, went fishing, and generally learned how to pocket a billiard ball after naming the pocket. Oh, yes, life was fine, the weather sunny and hot, lots of activities, including getting stuck in a raspberry patch and eating our stomachs full of the sweet berries, while the mosquitoes munched at our necks. We were a mess, but that was just fine with my friend and me, as long as we were together we were happy. Port Saunders was the place to be that summer.

We had attended the same one room high school for two years now, and although it really wasn't a school, but rather a big room in the parish hall beside the Roman Catholic church, it was a room we knew as school. Never mind the frost on the inside of the windows, never mind the old wood stove that was so slow to warm the big room, we were in school, together, all of us knew each other and loved it. It was even more special in the spring after the freely roaming sheep sought shelter under the old parish hall all winter and the warm weather caused an unbearable aroma, and school was out for a day or two while the men attended to the mess. Oh, it was a grand place!

In that little Newfoundland outport where I lived for four years, the experiences I had really did shape my life. And one of the best things of all was going to that little school room and being with friends. Passing notes, having a spat and running out of the school room onto the ice and literally pounding at each other, leaving us both startled at what we had done, and then carrying on as usual, after some stern lecture from the parents, teacher and priest of course. It was truly the place to be.

However I knew something strange was afoot this year! Word

was around of a new school being built at the other end of the community, much further away from our school. Because at that time Newfoundland had a denominational school system, this new building would bring me unprecedented anguish, and also a worry for my younger sister. We talked about it at night, and fussed to ourselves, nothing yet had been said, but we knew something was about to happen and we weren't going to like it.

Finally the word came. Yes, we would be changing schools in September, or October, as soon as the new school was ready. Oh, is that so now? Why is that? The questions were asked, and the answers given. We were attending a Roman Catholic School and the new school was a Church of England School, and we were Church of England children, so we had to change. Nothing made sense to me after that. My life came to a complete halt! How silly it all was, why would they do that, did it really have to be, and my mind was in a state of angst and misery, shared by my best friend, who was Roman Catholic, and would be staying in our Parish Hall School. My little sister did not seem to be too upset, she was too young and very quiet and accepting but my rebellious spirit started to spin into high gear.

Wherever Dad was stationed, no matter what, we attended the school closest to our home. Religion was not a factor, accessibility was the key word, and here we were having to go further to school. Promises of rides in the jeep, consolations by our parents, bribing even, did nothing to change the situation, I just was not going to change schools in Grade Eight. The Roman Catholic School didn't care if we stayed, so what was up with that, as the kids say today. But school opened and I managed to go to the new school, walking past my friends at the old one, and hating the new one more than words could say. I am sure I was totally obnoxious, but I was still in the other school.

So I had three or four days of this foolishness, missing my buddies, missing the same teacher we had for two of the past years, and the time came to just throw caution to the wind and commit the final act of rebellion. On a gorgeous fall morning I left with my sister for school, and when we reached the Parish

Hall School, I walked in and took my seat, just as if I had never left. And we all tittered, giggled and laughed, and waited for the bomb to drop. I don't recall what my sister did that morning though I think she stayed at the new school as she had friends there of her own age. The teacher arrived, there was an air of expectation, like the floor was about to collapse or something, but he just said his good mornings, sat at the desk and did his name calling for the record, with each person sticking up their hand in turn and saying "Present Sir!" And down the list he went and we were in terror, then he called "Bonnie Jarvis," and I stuck up my hand and said as always "Present Sir!" He marked on his register, I guess his check marks to say I was present, then he launched into the days' school work. Not another word was said, not that day nor the remaining days of the school year, or the year after that. It was simply accepted that I was going to be where I wanted to be. No parental punishments, no remarks from the teacher, although I am sure they must have conferred, but for me life went on as usual. Back with my friends and my teacher, and cold floors and lots of skits and concerts, writing essays on topics I loved, and best of all getting the "Manure Day" off, and going fishing! It was blissful, but to this day I do not know how I got away with it, I think they probably just gave up on me, and that made life a whole lot more pleasant for all concerned. Sometimes it pays to 'JUST DO IT'. It sure worked for me!!

MOMS' SPECIAL COOK BOOK

Growing up in a family of five siblings, and living in small communities around Newfoundland gave me opportunities, probably because I was the oldest of the group of rascals that we were, to experiment with all sorts of cooking and baking. Mother never minded the mess, and she taught me the basics of baking. After that I was on my own and Mother had many a terrible mess to clean up after my culinary exploits. Many years later, while living away from Newfoundland, a friend was visiting me, and I was baking muffins, huge muffins, to use as lunch for work. There happened to be six muffin spaces in the muffin pan and I was finishing up, so only had enough mix for four muffins. I just filled the empty muffins spaces with water, to keep the pan from burning. My friend watched as I did so and finally asked "Where did you learn that water trick, I always get burnt muffin pans, you must have got that from Home Economics." She received a strange look from me, and then I broke into uncontrollable laughter!

"No, my dear, there was no Home Economics where I went to school" I managed to tell her as she looked at me with a bewildered look, "My home economics was my mothers' kitchen, I do the things she taught me, and I passed it down to my other siblings over the course of ten years or so before I left home."

"I don't believe that for a minute," she went on to say. I convinced her by telling stories of making fudge, cookies, loaves, taffy candy, birthday cakes, all with my mother as my guide. Although finding it hard to take, she did get to the point of believing me. And I, of course, had to tell her of the time I made the fudge too hard and had it on a foil or plastic plate, and took the knife to cut it into squares, and to my dismay, the knife went through the fudge, through the plate, and into my hand, with the sharp end sticking out of the back of my hand. Impaled on a plate of fudge, now that caused quite a stir around our house, but it did not stop my baking all sorts of new and different things. Just got two new scars!

I visited my mother and fathers' house some time ago, and of course the big thick cookbook is still there in Moms' collection of cookbooks. Taking the book from its' resting place I sat and browsed through it. It is a good cookbook, and every recipe I ever used can be readily noted, as those pages are messy, covered in stains, and quite used looking. Yes, I learned from my mother, and this great cookbook. Page after page, stain after stain, the memories came streaking through my mind. And I thought of all the messes I must have made and yet I don't recall hearing a mean word. All my father would have to say was "Now, Bonnie my dear, why don't you make your dear dad a treat?" And out came the book, and all the ingredients for some special cake or cookie that he enjoyed the most. Hence the story my family holds over my head about the "Blue Cookies." Saying I should have published the recipe, and how in heavens' name did I think people would eat Blue Cookies-well, Dad did! How I managed the blue is more than I can say, but my siblings cannot pass up the opportunity to comment on the special color cookies I made.

Over the years, I conquered the basics of stuffing a turkey, preparing Jiggs Dinner, making cheesecakes, loaves, muffins, fish dishes such as Cod au Gratin, and finally became a half decent cook. But I could never catch up to Mom. She would make biscuits, and I would ask what page they were on in the 'the book' Mom would say "Oh, they're not in the book, they're in my head." So I would get her to tell me and I would write it down, and some of those childhood notes are still in the cookbook, Mom kept them all those years. I am 54, and started in the kitchen at the age of eight or nine so that's a heck of a lot of tested recipes. And a lot of dirty, sticky messes to clean.

Still she never complained. Years and years ago she told me that I should never use a metal spoon on a metal pot, because it would scrape the metal off the pan or pot, and she would give me the proper wooden spoon. Then there was the trick of not reversing anything you are stirring in a bowl to make a cake, keep stirring the same way she told me because your cake will be fluffier if air is stirred into it, reversing the stirring action would cause air loss. Oh, yes lots of things to learn in Mothers Home Economic Class! However no matter how hard she tried, I could not conquer pies. And to this day I have not achieved the ability to make pies. Nothing she told me helped nothing I read helped, but I was determined that someday I would find the trick to making good pastry.

After I married and moved away I would often, when home on vacation, take 'the cookbook' and write off recipes. My sister came up with a Christmas gift one year of an empty book, with 'BONNIES' COOKBOOK-FROM MY KITCHEN' written on it and I loved it and still do. That book is filled with Moms' recipes. And it is also becoming stained. Then I got the surprise of all time when I found a recipe for pie pastry called "Brides Never Fail Pastry" in a cookbook, and I wrote it down.

When my young husband and I returned home after our vacation, I set out one day to bake a Nova Scotia Strawberry Pie, using the 'Brides Never Fail' pastry.

I had flour everywhere, and when I finally got the finished product into the oven and heaved a sigh of relief. And of course I forgot all about the pie, and it burned a little, giving it a rim of black around the pastry edges. Woe was I! But I cut a section out and ate it and it was quite good, and I was pleased as punch as they say.

My husband arrived home, hours later, and of course, immediately went to the refrigerator. He stood back, looked, then looked some more, then looked at me and asked "WHO OWNS THE CLUTCH IN THE FRIDGE?" Needless to say I was devastated, he said he was joking, I didn't believe him and although he ate it, I promised myself, "NO MORE PIES!"! I still have no interest in making pies, and am not going to try it again. You have to know when to quit, and I did know, and I did quit!

Baking, cooking, making meals and serving them, and knowing how to serve them well, came from my Mothers Home Economic Class 101. Moms' book has been stained, the pages worn, but I quit the pies. In due time my daughter will inherit a book of mine with stained pages, and stored memories. And I have kept her notes, and her funny quotes in the back of the book, like Mother did for me.

So I can cook, and I can bake, but not pies thank you! For the most important lessons of all I learned in Moms Home Economics, was knowing when to quit, and don't waste supplies.

Yes, Home Economics is a good class, even better when the teacher is your mother, and you have free reign of her kitchen, and her special, faded, stained cookbook, worn from the years when Mom was able to teach, and I was a willing student. And when the "Brides Never Fail" pastry recipe did fail, it was Mom who said

"Do it my way."

"And how is that?" I asked.

"Oh, I don't know, its' all in my head"she answered!

And the pastry recipe ,and many other recipes, in her special cookbook never failed , in the stained and faded one, or the one she kept hidden in her memory.

But I failed 'Pie making', but all the other things make up for the one failure, at least that's what Mom says!

TEENAGERS, YES, TELL ME ABOUT IT!

When, and if, and it will happen, someone looks you straight in the eye and makes that silly statement "My kids wouldn't do that," there are just two ways to react that will give them the message "Oh, yeah?"First of all you can burst into loud hysterical laughter, or you can just mutter something to the effect of "We'll see won't be we!" Because any parent who makes such a remark is vastly out of touch with the innovative and subversive mind of the teen, boy or girl.

Having been a teenager myself many moons ago, I know that teens are forever planning a coup d'etat, some parents are away party, or a 'just plain don't like you' event or activity. Anything that can cause worry, sweat, tears, money spending, or doubling up on daily prayers, a teen will do at one time or another. Like silent creatures of the forest they lie and pounce when you least expect it. I know I did it, my kids did it, my siblings and their offspring followed the same pattern, my sons' friends, and my daughters' friends all engaged in those same activities and you may be well sure the person who says they won't is going to be very shocked and upset someday.

Those little rebellions are usually quite innocent, easily handled and still they will never be forgotten. There are the other big rebellions that cause tears to flow, heartaches that hurt deeply, and are painful to all involved. Thankfully the latter type of action is, truthfully, the kind that happens less often than the little actions of the first type. The little 'messups' are remembered, lessons learned by all, and life goes on. In later years those same teens, now young adults, talk with their friends, parents and teachers about the petty rebellion and laugh their heads off, usually joined by their audience.

My son is thirty-one now, my daughter is twenty-seven, and they have admitted to things I am amazed they pulled off under our noses. Having a policeman for a father you would think they would be caught, but nosiree, they were good! Activities such as escaping through bedroom windows after we were all settled for the night, wearing our clothes and us not noticing, hooking off school on Friday afternoons especially, that was the favorite of my son.

Having three sisters and a brother I, thankfully, had sense enough not to make that famous remark and say they would not do this or that, because I knew they would. They had bright sharp minds, quick wits, and were active and healthy teenagers, so expect anything at anytime was my attitude, and the same attitude was adopted by my husband. Dents in the car, lost hub caps, a beer stopper in the pocket of a pair of jeans, strange magazines found in a closet corner, resulting in me being banned from a bedroom in my own house, were all experiences that caused me great concern for a time, but put in perspective, I took the necessary actions to curtail such behavior and life went on.

That is until the day just before Christmas when I was to pick my daughter up at a friends' house after I left my work. I did pick her up, and the fact that she was wearing a T-shirt on her head did not even make me blink an eye, she was known for her creativity in dressing and wearing odd things at the age of fifteen. The next night my husband and I were hosting a Christmas party, so I made many stops on my way home, my daughter happily following along, still wearing the shirt on her head. It was pulled back like a hair band at the front by the time we arrived home, she helped me unload the car and ran off to her room and her phone.

"Why does Heather have that stupid shirt on her head?" asked her nineteen-year-old brother. "She drives me nuts sometimes!" He didn't really expect an answer but I did say that we were certainly not the Brady Bunch so forget about it. And we did for an hour or so.

And then it happened! It caused my heart to come as close to a full stop more than anything I had ever experienced. I was making those silly, party munchies when Heather walked by me and chatting away she pulled a soda pop from the fridge, and turned to return to her room. And it was then I saw 'IT'! She had half her hair, or was missing half her hair, however one thought of it! The whole back of her head was shaved, and she had about an inch of bangs in the front!

I cried, pleaded for her to tell me why, threatened to send her to a hotel room for the night of the party, phoned her father, asked her brother to come home, but what could anyone do? She said they started cutting and couldn't stop while at her friends' house. I was paralyzed with anger and misery. What a mess of a head I cried. It was then she set me straight.

"Now, mom, are you upset about my missing hair, or the fact that your precious party guests will see me?" she demanded to know.

Upon reflection for five minutes or so, I realized she was so right! I knew the hair would grow back, it wasn't hurting anyone, it was just injuring my pride in my lovely daughter. So I stopped crying, let her do her thing, explained to nobody, the hair grew back, life went on and she grew up, and to this day has a beautiful head of thick dark hair.

The young fifteen-year-old girl was so correct, so insightful, and so confident. Her hair was not a big concern to her, but she knew it was to me. She knew I needed to introduce a 'perfect' daughter to my guests, but what I needed to be taught was that she was just fine, just perfect, hair or no hair.

It was I who learned the lesson, and it is I who passed the lesson onto others.

"Don't be too hard on them, don't sweat the small stuff, love them anyway, and they will remember you for it, with love and not bitterness!"

So you think you have a big problem, think about it again, maybe it's like the hair, just a small blow to the pride. Let it be!

DO ANGELS MAKE PICKLES?

When my daughter was beginning her second year at St. Mary's University in Halifax, Nova Scotia, she moved from residence life to her own apartment, sharing it with a friend. We had found the perfect apartment building, close to campus, and very cosy and attractive. It was located at the end of a street that was lined with huge oak and elm trees, making it a pleasure to walk to class. She loved it.

Her parents concerns were of no consequence as we asked her about coming home from class after dark, walking down that very beautiful tree lined road was a different story when darkness fell. Anyone could hide behind the very trees and shrubs that were so beautiful in sunlight, but an excellent hiding place for anyone who wanted to pounce and assault the unsuspecting walkers. We were assured that all would be OK, because St. Mary's University has what is called the 'Husky Patrol'. This is a program that the popular St. Mary's Huskies football team members and other students had developed. They worked in teams of two, a football player, or senior athlete, and a senior female student would made up each team. The 'Husky Patrol' would walk with the student if they lived off campus and had to return home after dark. It is a terrific program and worked well for the off campus students who needed the service. Heather assured us she would use the Husky Patrol when necessary.

However, one evening it was not quite dark when she headed for her apartment building with her backpack and books, feeling quite sure she would be safely in her building before it was really night. But it was late October, and evening came quickly. She soon found herself on the dark street, alone and scared. Halloween decorations were everywhere and in looking at them she had wasted precious moments of daylight.

Then she had a feeling of being watched, she would turn to look, and all she would see would be a shrub or tree limb moving. When she picked up her pace the watching eyes, now accompanied by the sound of shoes on the dry autumn leaves, would pick up and move faster as well. Consequently she regretted leaving campus alone. She knew she was being followed and became terrified.

Heather, right from a very young age, was a problem solver. She never failed to come up with a solution to problems and obstacles that she and her friends would encounter. And she did not fail now. She knew she had to seek shelter, and get off this street as soon as she could. Assessing the situation, her heart pounding, and her knees weak, she noticed a small, cottage style house just a few doors up from her location. An inviting overhead light was on over the quaint entryway. She moved quickly toward the tiny house, still hearing the footsteps behind her. Mustering all the strength her athletic soccer- playing legs could conjure up, she walked smartly up to the house, turned the doorknob and found it was not locked. She opened the door and walked in, closing it behind her. Near tears by now she leaned back against the door. From her vantage point she could see three very 'grand-motherly' looking ladies in a small kitchen, each one very intent on her task. And that task was making pickles. The smell of vinegar and dill, the warmth of the little house and the reassuring presence of the ladies, calmed the upset young student.

"What can we do for you dear?", one of the women approached and asked. The lady was not at all surprised or perturbed at having somebody just walk in the house. Soon the three ladies had her sitting in the kitchen, and she told her story of being followed, her scare, and her need to find help. They listened to her story with rapt attention. Then they offered her a hot chocolate, and continued to reassure her that she was safe now with them and they would take her home.

When the pickles were all done, one of the women took her by the hand and led her outside to a late model car. She kept reassuring the frightened young woman, and drove her safely the rest of the way to her apartment tower. Heather was very grateful and said so many 'thank yous' that the adorable, elderly lady said she must be 'thanked out by now!' And they shared a laugh. The once terrified student left the car, and waved to her chauffeur as she reached the inside of her building. The lovely shiny car then drove slowly away.

The weekend arrived and Heather came home for Halloween. Of course she never told us the story until she was good and ready, but she did tell us. She knew the lecture she would get about not staying true to her word and using the 'Husky Patrol'. After that was dealt with, she decided she would buy a gift box of the famous Annapolis Valley apples for her rescuers. These boxes are beautifully presented, each apple with its' colorful paper nest in a box of forty-eight small cubicles. She attached a bow and a thank you note and took it with her when she returned to Halifax and her classes on Monday.

But the strangest thing happened. She located the quaint cottage house, but no car was in the driveway. As a matter of fact, what she thought was a driveway was just a little path leading to the front door. Several times she took the box to the house, but could never locate the endearing 'lady picklers'. Finally she left her gift on the step, hoping they would find it. She would talk to them when she could.

My daughter went on to graduate from St. Mary's University. She never did find the kind ladies, never knew their names, and there was never a new car at the tiny house. She could only hope they had found her gift. During a discussion with another student one day she was bemoaning the fact that she never got to say 'thank you' in person to her kind helpers. The other student remarked that she had never seen anybody in or around that house, and she had lived on that street for five years. Needless to say we were all dumbfounded by that disclosure.

So, we have come to believe that she found angels that night.

Angels who wrapped her in comfort, soothed her fears, and took her safely home. As for Heather, and me, her mother, we will remain convinced, always, that ANGELS DO MAKE PICKLES!

THE MARIPOSA AND THE BOSSA NOVA

The blazing sunshine was stinging my shoulders, my feet feeling as hot as the pavement beneath them. I had been walking the main street of town for over an hour, exploring the markets, enjoying the Latino music that seemed to be all around, admiring the crafts on display, but it was time to take a break. In a very short time I found one of my favorite street cafes, and it was so inviting. The shade, the comfortable blue chairs, and little round blue and white tables looked like an ad setup for cold soda pop, so I entered the ad and ordered the cold orange soda. Then I chose a table with a great view of the busy street and sipped the tangy cold liquid while taking in the sights, sounds and smells of the busy morning. Water dripped from the frosty can, and it was cool to the face. The flavor of the orange soda here reminded me of the Gadens' Orange soda I loved so much during my Newfoundland childhood. My pack back on the chair beside me held my book but I didn't reach for it, I wanted to soak up the day instead with full attention.

I was in Cuba, a country I had been drawn to many times before, loving the sea, the beautiful Mariposa blooms, which were everywhere it seemed. The Mariposa is the National Flower of Cuba, the Royal Palm is the National Tree, a tall straight tree with enormous beauty. Then last but not least was the quiet acceptance of the Cuban people who worked so hard, the fast melodic Spanish and Latin music they enjoyed so much was always playing, and their musical voices all combined to take me back to another time, to remember friends of childhood days, to wonder where they were, how they were, and if I would ever cross paths with them again.

An hour would pass quickly as I soaked up the rhythm of the

day in the busy commercial area. The big smiles, unusual motorbikes, vintage cars and just plain fatigue would keep me sitting longer than planned but I decided it was time to move on. Just as I stood to go, I saw a little truck pull up and out of the truck jumped three or four schoolgirls in their red jumpers and white blouses, with sparkling white socks and sneakers. They were in their early teens and the laughter skipped across toward me as I stood riveted, frozen by a memory of two Cuban girls of my childhood days. I focused my lens to capture the moment and as I did I heard a sweet voice call "Hola, Evita!" and two young friends ran to greet each other.

And I remembered so clearly another Evita, one that graced my life so long ago when my family was living in Port Saunders, Newfoundland, in the early 1960s. A revolution had forced a Cuban family out of their country, and the father, being a physician, came to Canada and was now in Port Saunders working. He had a beautiful wife who was sad, so sad, and two young daughters, the same age as my sister and me. Evita, known as Eva, was my age, Katrina was younger, around my sisters age. The country and climate were so foreign to them, but they worked hard to adjust, having left everything behind except their high spirits and determination. They struggled to learn our English, and because we lived next door we became good friends. Somehow we conquered the language barrier and shared each others lives. Eva was emotional and full of boundless energy, her sister Katrina was quiet and controlled, almost a mirror like image of my sister and me.

Eva would tell me how our English sounded flat, and many words she could not find in the dictionary, but we learned together. We laughed, talked, told stories, had picnics, went fishing in the ponds, and played the occasional game of pool. Their father worked, their mother kept the home going, and gradually their mother got to know my mother and life was good. Katrina was sad many times but Eva plowed through life like a threshing machine. She had no intentions of being beaten. She had lost everything but her spirit she told us, and they would not take that from her. They all came to understand they were safe in our country as opposed to what they had suffered during the revolution in Cuba, and they grew to love our activities, our carefree days and the awesome sense of security.

In later years I came to know more about Cuba, the Bay of Pigs, the Cuban Missile Crisis, the Cold war, the United States Embargo, Che Gueveras' death and so much more. But at the ages we were in Port Saunders for four young girls politics was not a major issue. Our music and little collections of 45rpm records took up much of our time as we danced and sang, picked mussels and cooked them on the beach, did each others' hair, Eva announcing a four letter unmentionable word that grounded us both, exploring the shoreline, teaching them to row a boat, and the time they spent teaching us a Cuban board game, led us to having very full lives and too many adventures to recount.

After we left Port Saunders I lost track of my Cuban friends, although my parents kept in contact with them for awhile. Eva eventually became a physician like her father, Katrina became a health professional but in what area or where we do not know. I learned their father had passed away and Mrs. Aude had possibly moved to the United States.

I gathered my things and left the café, and someone else immediately sat where I had been. I realized as I walked away that regardless of who sat there they would not leave carrying the special memory I was carrying, the memory of two young girls dancing. It is the surreal memory of two dark haired girls, Eva and me, in the front room of the doctors' house in Port Saunders in 1960, the sun streaming in through the large windows and reflecting off the shiny hardwood floors, the harbor water calm, the sound of little boats skipping in through our open window, and the two of us in bobby sox, pony tails bouncing, as we wove, skipped and twirled, our feet slipping on the smooth floor, and the little record playing "Blame it on the Bossa Nova, the Dance of Love" at high volume. And what a dance of love it was, crossing all boundaries, all language barriers as the Bossa Nova carried us away to a land of happy moments, and the sweet dreamy place of childhood, and childhood dreams.

If I could talk to Eva now, I could tell her that I have been to her beautiful country, walked on the warm sand of the Bay of Pigs, seen the destruction of war, but experienced the kindness of the Cuban people and was humbled by it. And every Mariposa I saw and photographed made me think of her and her family. And I then would remember the Bossa Nova, and what a dance of love it was!

THE KEEPER OF THE ISLAND LIGHT

A Sunday afternoon drive to Bonavista to visit the icebergs, say hello to John Cabot, and visit all the little bays and inlets was always such an enjoyable experience. Spring was coming, so many nice things to see, such as the little foals and lambs sunning themselves, people out pruning bushes and uncovering precious shrubs, men mending nets and piling lobster and crab pots on various wharves, getting ready for the upcoming week, and it all would add up to a delicious awakening of the senses.

The grass was gradually getting to be a better shade than beige, and the icebergs that were being much admired, that held a persons' gaze for so long, had that tinge of blue that I remembered seeing so many times before while growing up in Newfoundland outports.

All along the way there are little lighthouses, some are actually functioning light signals, others are lawn ornaments, but the big lighthouse in Bonavista, so much photographed, sits precariously on the high rocky cliffs as if it had just poked up through the rock and kept on growing. What a grand sight that lighthouse is, especially to those who see it for the first time.

The lighthouses always remind me of a special uncle of mine, Uncle Enos Yetman, who was a light keeper on Saddle Island, off the Labrador coast. Uncle Enos kept the light there, lived on the island with his wife, my mothers' sister, Aunt Winnie, and they raised their family there. During special times or harsh weather Aunt Winnie and the children would go to Red Bay, but Uncle Enos rarely left the light. He worked day and night, through all the seasons, and quietly went about his tasks as it he were born to do just that, and maybe he was. Saddle Island was barren, as is the coast of my beloved Labrador, but it has its' uniqueness, and with the Northern Lights helping out from time to time, I'm sure many a ship made a safe journey because of that little lighthouse and the lighthouse keeper who was so dedicated to his work, knowing the importance of it, having grown up on the coast himself.

Uncle Enos told me many years ago that he did not set out to be a light keeper, or anyones' hero, he just happened to be. As the story goes when World War II began Enos was already one of a group of young men who went out to Saddle Island and pounded on empty oil drums, warning the ships with the noise that they were too close to land, the fog was so thick they would never have seen land, night or day. So eventually, through all the red tape that goes with such things, it was decided that Saddle Island definitely needed a lighthouse, and the foghorn too. Navigation had increased ten fold, so Enos took the job and worked the light for thirty-five or forty years. He came ashore when necessary but I, as a teenager, was thrilled to get a visit to Saddle Island and my cousins. I thought it was the most spectacular place to live, taking a boat to go to school, having a lighthouse to climb up the staircase for the divine view of the ocean, eating Aunt Winnies' wonderful home made goodies, and exploring the island and berry picking with my cousins, yes, I thought it was perfect, absolutely perfect! That lasted until a foggy night came and the fog horn rang all night, and the next night, and by then I knew it was not the place to be in anything but sunny, summer weather.

Years later Uncle Enos was almost deaf, a result of the damage the continuous noise had done to his ears. He was almost ready to retire, but not before he needed a hearing aid device, which he absolutely hated, he figured the deafness was just fine, now he didn't hear the foghorn! However his family got tired of yelling and kept him wearing these various hearing aids. He wore them to make people happy but most of the time they weren't working. He would be off in the boat oblivious to the noisy engine, he wouldn't answer a direct question and was driving everyone to distraction as they dragged him to doctor after doctor, buying one device after another. Finally it was time to retire, and he did. He was lost without his lighthouse, and his foghorn, living around so many people, and the adjustment must have been difficult for him. But one day someone mentioned that he seemed to be hearing better now since he was off the Island, the lighthouse computerized, his family all grown by this time.

Yes, he admitted, he could hear better. Nobody pursued it any further. As long as he was off the Island, staying healthy, things were OK. , Don't rock the boat they said.

But the time came for the checkup, the visit to the hearing specialist, and that brought him to St.John's. The specialist was amazed that the device Uncle Enos had now was lasting so long. He couldn't fathom what the previous problems could have been.

My dear Uncle Light keeper looked at the doctor with a sly grin, and of course the doctor asked him what was so funny, and did he know what the problem had been over the years with his hearing aids.

"Oh yes," Uncle Enos said, "I always knew that, nobody ever asked before!"

"Well, what was it?", asked his perplexed doctor.

Being a man of few words, Uncle Enos just looked him in the eye and said, 'RUST, SALT WATER CAUSES RUST!!!"

The light keeper was right, just that nobody had asked! And that is the true story of my special Uncle Lightkeeper who did so much and said so little!

LEST WE FORGET

Every year for many years, in November, we have a garden of red poppies spring into our lives, and into the lives of our communities. The stunning combination of the red and black of these small flower symbols on lapels, caps and in car windows draw your eye, and you cannot help but remember for what reason they come into our lives. These brilliant red poppies are very significant, and each and every one is worn in remembrance of lives lost, battles won, the gratitude we feel for those who gave their lives for our country, our freedom, and our way of life. They also honor those who served and came home badly scarred, both in body and spirit. This symbol of the poppy also honors and remembers all those that were the backup teams, the people who worked in factories, ran our transportation systems, knit warm socks and caps for those on the front lines, and those who supported their loved ones in the cause they were so desperately fighting for and wanted to protect. And that cause was our freedom, a country free of anarchy and chaos, and a better life for their children. We will always, and should always, remember them.

So we pick up our poppy from the immaculately clad Legion Veterans at their little kiosk and tables, chat with them, and marvel at the wonder of such a country as Canada. In good times and bad, the red maple leaf flag flying high above our heads, symbolizes all that has been fought for, the way of life we lead in our country, our political right to vote, and our freedom to worship as we so choose. All this came at a very high cost. We will never forget that. Nor should we.

Most of the men who served our country are now grandfathers and great-grandfathers, and also the women who served have moved into the same role, the tender role of being a grandmother and great-grandmother. So most of us have, or have had a 'Pop' or 'Grand-dad' or 'Poppy' of our own now. And surely we all have a 'Nanny' in our lives, or in the lives of our friends.

A few years ago, in a larger center, I attended the November 11th, Remembrance Day Service at the War Memorial. All through our growing up this Remembrance Day Ceremony was part of our lives, and it continues to be. Because you see, I have a father who served in the British Royal Navy overseas during the last World War. I have a Dad who is a 'Poppy' to my children, and to my grandchild. Wearing a poppy is a special thing to me and my offspring because of that. We love and honor our Poppy. And thousands of other people do the same thing all across this massive country. That day, after the Memorial Service I watched as the cadets and the local people took off their poppies and stuck them in the ground near the memorial.

And when I glanced back it looked like a sea of precious blood. The red was everywhere as hundreds of red poppies were bright under the noon time sun. It symbolized to me what the surgeon, Dr. John McCrae, a Major in the lst Field Artillery Brigade, saw beside the field hospital at the Canal de l'Yser, just north of Ypres and its' horrendous battles. Dr. McCrae had lost a friend a day before he penned his verse. He wrote 'In Flanders Fields', then decided it was not a good piece of work. A colleague retrieved the paper, and submitted the poem to a publication in England who published it, and it is a well known piece of verse to this day. It was written in the midst of seventeen days of horror, on May 3, 1915, and was published in the English magazine on December 8, 1915.

My father rarely spoke of his wartime experiences. And we could not get him to talk about it. But when I think back, we had small glimpses into that world. He was a seventeen year old boy when he joined the Royal Navy, Newfoundland was a British Colony, and he left Belloram, Newfoundland, for what was to become four years of hell. He became a man through all that, a strong man, but troubled when he came home at first according to my mother. He was sad, with wild eyes and bad dreams. The sights, the frights, the cold, the torpedoes, the sea seeping into his bunk as he caught his 'forty winks' on the Corvetter he was stationed on, all haunted him.

We knew he had scarred legs, scalded by a blown boiler, and we knew he, although a policeman, wanted 'peace and quiet' as he often says. And one incident stands out that told us so much about Dad and his terrible memories.

My brother, in his late teens, arrived home, shall we say, chock full of 'liquid courage'? He was ready to take on the world in his courageous state, and my mother was determined he wasn't, but he would punished, that was a given.

"Go to bed now," Father said to Mother, "when I was his age I was fightin' a war!" And that was the end of that. It said a lot when you really analyze it.

This past summer Dad showed me a photo my brother had found of the Corvette he sailed on. He showed it to me, so proud of his ship. So I took the plunge and asked "Dad, what was your worst, very worst, experience during those days?"

He shocked me by answering, I really did not expect he would.

"The Invasion of Sicily." he revealed quietly.

And he went on to tell me his experience. My heart ached for this young Newfoundland boy, caught in the midst of death and destruction, trying desperately to return to his ship. And it aches now as I tell you about it. He is a 'Poppy', and he loves and is loved in return. I am sad that he had to go through that misery, but at least he came home. His drive to give his kids a good life, combined with his wife and childrens' love for him, became his port in all of his storms.

Yes, we will wear our poppies proudly, and we will remember them. All of them, those who have left us and those we are overjoyed to still have in our lives.

Wear the poppy, read Major McCraes' verse, remember and give thanks for the freedoms won with blood, sweat and so many tears. Always remember them, not just on Remembrance Day, but every day.

If you do not have the words, I will share a few of them with you. Beautiful words written by a young man who had seen too much, lost too much, but would not quit.

'To you from failing hands we throw
The torch; be yours to hold it high.
If ye break faith with us who die
We shall not sleep, though poppies grow
In Flanders fields.

A MEMORY FROZEN IN TIME

Anybody whoever owned and wore a 'Mary Maxim' sweater years ago when they were all the rage, can tell you very quickly, and with a certain amount of pride, what color their sweater was, who knit it, what the pattern on it consisted of, and was it buttoned or zippered. It was just that way! We had those lovely handknit sweaters and were so very proud of them. I clearly remember mine being a beautiful burgundy color, a favorite color of mine to this day, and the pattern was that of curling rocks and brooms and it had a big zipper up the front with a wide collar. I can almost feel the collar brushing my face as I describe my sweater to you. I was around twelve or thirteen years old, and just beginning to be clothes' proud.

My one brother, in a family of four sisters, just five years old at the time he had his special sweater, knit by my mother while she was recovering from an injury, sported a beautiful blue model with caribou on it, in white. His had a zipper and it was a battle to get him to keep his sweater on and stay warm.

After our school day, during that hour or two of the day that still has a twilight, before supper, in the Northern parts of our Newfoundland,

It would befall to me to get home from school and get David outside to go sliding or skating, or just occupy him until he ran some of that energy off and was cooled off enough to go back into the house. Our school room was chilly some days but once we got out, gathered our things, including David, we were certainly not cold.

David marched to his own drum. Still, does in fact, and I would gladly stay in school and clean erasers all night sometimes rather than have to face this quick and fiery five year old.

He had a will of iron, loved everything and everybody and never stopped, he was in constant motion. But forty years after the event I can still see that little blue sweater with the caribou, and my little brothers' sled go right under a car, just as slick as hair gel! My heart, I am sure, came to a complete standstill, and then the fracas began!

All of this was my fault, I just knew it, I was supposed to be caring for him and he had buddied up with Dennis Lowe, one of his favorite friends in Port Saunders, and they were going up and down the hill beside the pool parlor. Many children had gathered at the hill, using all sorts of materials, canvas, cardboard, tin, plastic and some had real sleds, like David.So David and Dennis could go faster than anyone else. Even those using old barrel staves couldn't keep up with those two speedsters. After two or three runs down the hill, the clacking of the pool balls inside the warm pool parlor was too much to resist, and I ducked inside, just in time to see my school mates starting a game. Deciding in my adolescent mind that I could care for David from the window at the front of the parlor I took the pool cue and started playing a game I loved, and still do in fact. The kids seemed fine, I was warm, we were having a great game when I casually glanced out the window only to see that precious little sweater disappear under a car. The car was driven by one of Davids' teachers, as David had started school that year, not too taken with it, but it beat staying home he figured.

I was as panic stricken as my thirteen-year-old mind, body and soul had ever been. I should have known, if I had used common sense I would have foreseen that you could not leave David for a minute, but at that age common sense is in short supply sometimes. And now this! My inattention was the cause of this, and Mr. Teacher was a wreck as you can imagine! I adored my little brothers and sisters, what if he were dead. I got down on the ground, tried to crawl under the big car, digging snow as I went, calling his name. I have no recall to this day how I got from the pool hall, down the steps to under the car, must have been the supernatural! Calling his name did not work, no answer! Dennis, his friend, was in tears, I yelled "Go get Dad!" and kept clawing at the snow.

By this time some men had arrived and sized up the situation as men do, and determined how to jack up the car, but all that is a blur to me. Dad arrived, tried to get me out from under the car, no way, no how, I wanted David, or I wasn't going anywhere but over the head of the wharf! Soon I could hear mumbling, and all of a sudden a little voice said "It is really dark in here BABA!" his pet name for me. I started to cry, and when I see that sweater now, it is still at my parents' house, the tears could very easily come again as I remember how closely I came to losing my little brother, my little charge that my inattention had allowed circumstances to hurt so much.

By this time Dad heard him too, knelt down in the snow and talked to him as the men did whatever they had to do with the car. Poor Mr. Teacher was so upset, Dad was upset ,but as a policemen he was always cool, and I was a babbling teenage idiot! As luck should have it the car was going slowly, the snow soft, and the sled hit against the front tire, those three circumstances combined saved my brothers' life. For years I would wake from dreams of seeing that little sweater disappearing under that car. I could never, ever forget it, and I still can't!

They took David by Jeep Land Rover to Bonne Bay Hospital, all he had was a broken bone in his foot, a fracture that healed a lot faster than my broken heart.

Yes, Daves' Mary Maxim is still with us, as is Dave. Thank heavens! He is the father of three children of his own now and is very safety conscious, as am I. Dave still marches to his own beat, and calls me 'BABA' from time to time, and he is still adored by many women, his mother, four sisters, two daughters, three grown nieces and that's just for starters. And may I also say he never wears a blue sweater if he knows I am going to be around, he can't stand the tears!!

HOOKED ON COD CANDY

Childhood is a time when a person is developing their own personality, exploring their world, and getting an education. Well, I did all of that. However, I am somewhat odd in the area of the personality development. As a child and a teenager I was constantly jumping back and forth between being riddled with anxiety, and being the one who had no fear, disobeyed, and incessantly tried breaking barriers, and it is still the same to this day. Of course now I can conclude that the latter aspect of my personality caused the former! If I would be told not to do something, that was the challenge to do it. And I cannot stop! While working as an Operating Room nurse, the nurses were told they 'HAD TO WEAR' scrub dresses, only the doctors could wear the pants. Well, that changed after six months when I got sick of the double standard. A female surgeon joined our staff and scrub pants and shirts were delivered for her, so I wore them too. Nobody said a word. The nurses before me would never dream of doing that, but the barrier was broken, and everybody was into pants and tops. They were easier to work in, and life went on. That was a simple thing, and no big deal after all. The boss knew I would do it, and I did. They also knew they couldn't get rid of a skilled Operating Room nurse over such a silly thing. Another win for me!

But breaking barriers, disobedience, and being, as my family has been known to call me 'HEADSTRONG AND FOOLISH', is not always that simple. I do not know why I intentionally disobey. I just do–and it brings me pain, physical pain, and sometimes emotional pain, and I just keep walking into it.

Let me tell you about my experience of last summer. My husband and I had our boat docked in Popes' Harbor. We were the only people there, when usually there was always another boat or two. So we went fishing early, in our little open boat, came back with our cod, and my husband proceeded to clean them.

Now, for two days I had been watching some type of fish breaching across the harbor, within walking distance of our boat. I really had to know what they were. They thrashed and swirled the water around from time to time, and I just could not stop myself from investigating the whole phenomena. I took the handline and still with my rubber gear on, I started out for the little pond. My husband glanced up, shook his head. He said later he expected trouble right then and there, but didn't want to waste his breath on lecturing me, knowing it was futile.

I reached the little pool, no fish to be seen, so I sat on a rock, still holding my handline and hooks. The hooks were large, and each had a 'cod candy' attached. For those who do not know, the 'cod candy' were little rubber fluorescent squid, and the cod loved them. They came in different colors, and mine were sort of a pale green. Lovely little candies for the fish they were. I had caught a thirty-pound cod with the cod candy.

Then I saw a fish, just a little one, but figured the school would be soon coming into the pool. And some did. I picked up the handline, tossed the lead weight into the pool of fish, and then I felt pain, bad, awful, wretched pain in my hand. And the handline was not unraveling to follow the lead weight. So, following the pain to my middle finger I saw what I had done, and I knew I had trouble, big trouble! Sticking out of my finger was a large hook, it had pulled with the lead weight, and because of the way I was holding it, the hook could not move and had imbedded itself in my finger, in one side and out the other. So here I was, bleeding, in pain, with a fluorescent squid sticking out of my finger. And I felt the anxiety, big anxiety, worse than the pain. I gathered the line up, and made it back to the wharf.

My husband took one look and said "I knew it, I knew it! When I saw you going with that I knew it!" So, OK, now what do we do? I was in tears by then. A few tears might lessen his anger I figured.

So he cut the line, leaving just the squid and hook sticking out of my finger. He gathered the first aid kit, and decided the four fingers had to be immobilized, and thank heavens he knows first aid. He saved the lecture, had to untie the boat, and get us out of there without his first mate. He gave me something for pain, made up a bed in the wheelhouse, and we headed for Petley, Random Island. The pain was incredible, but I did OK. And the good captain got the Ocean Joy to her berth, docked and secured, and I was helped into our vehicle and taken to the hospital.

Saying I felt foolish lying on a stretcher in Emergency with a squid sticking out of a bandaged hand is an understatement. I knew the lecture on disobedience would come, but for now the doctor had to work on freezing the finger and dislodging the huge 'cod candy'. My husband watched the procedure, I thought that might make my talking to even less harsh, and it did!

I had a week of not doing dishes, three days of miserable pain, two new packs of cod candy not opened, and a month left to fish. I had to talk myself out of this one. And somehow I did, got allowed back aboard the boat, and was instructed in no uncertain terms to 'do as you are told', and I did manage it somehow.

Now I don't know how I got hooked on 'cod candy', other than that I have an addictive personality, addicted to disobedience. And I thought I may as well come clean and tell the story because I know if I don't he will, every time we board our boat this summer. But this summer I won't have my cod candy, or my cod, but those fish are still in Popes Harbor, and I have a fishing rod now. I despise trouting, but I love to fish so I have to like it. And if I have to turn away from my cod candy and go to bobbers and bait, then I will.

So, I truly was 'hooked on cod candy', the same as I am addicted to peppermint knobs. And the Cod Candy made great tree ornaments at Christmas time. My finger healed, and I was told to look for a place that teaches 'Obedience Classes' to adults. Now, I don't think I am going to obey that one at all!

And yesterday I found a whole new package of cod candy, unopened. I hid them, because I am still hooked on the little squid. If he finds them, he will take them, and I hate withdrawal from anything.

Now, did you ever hear the like of that–and it is an absolutely true story, written by someone who cannot seem to obey –and is unlikely to change at this point in my life. Now, where is the fishin' rod? I can rig that up, maybe catch a whale -you never know!

FOR THE LOVE OF BOATS

Boats have always been in my life, in one form or another. I entered the world in Marys' Harbour, Labrador, just six months prior to Confederation of Newfoundland and Labrador with Canada. I was taken from the Nursing Station where I was born, back to Port Hope Simpson by the 'KYLE', a steamer or coastal boat as it was called, and that was the beginning of my relationship with boats. And that relationship continues to this day, whether it is a big boat, a small boat, a ferry, a cabin cruiser, or anything bigger or smaller, there is always a boat in my life somewhere. I actually wait anxiously to step onto a boat when it is the way I am traveling.

I cannot swim. I just trust boats. Foolhardy, maybe, but that is how it is. I do not understand it and probably never will. The smell of the boat is unique, the movement through the water effortless, the ocean kissing and caressing the hull, the trail of foam in the wake of the propeller, and the bow cutting through the ocean is all ethereal to experience. The sunrises and sunsets seen from a boat are magnificent, the rocky cliffs that appear to reach out to touch the bow are like old friends, and the sound of the ocean swishing against a rocky shore is music for the soul. Yes, I do enjoy boats. However I will never be talked into going on a large cruise ship, of that I am certain.

And sometimes it is much to the dismay of others who love the huge ships, but I am not interested whatsoever in traveling on a gargantuan boat of any sort, although I do admire them. Boating is being near the water, not three stories up from the waterline. Boating to me is being with just a few people, pulling into a little cove or harbor and getting off the bigger boat into a smaller one to go fishing, or tying up to a wharf in a little place no longer inhabited. In that little place I can feel the wind on my face and hear the sound of the waves around the wharf and on the rocks. They are the same sights, sounds and smells that people long before me experienced in that little Newfoundland community, and I then know why they shed tears when they had to go. Visiting there is like visiting them, seeing where they lived and imagining how they felt as their tears fell on leaving day. And of course these little communities, now vacant, are accessible only by boat, having been settled for the sole purpose of the fishery, and having a place to call home. When I go ashore and sit on a hilltop, I can visualize the bustling little community, their presence seems much more realistic when I smell the food cooking in the galley of our cabin cruiser. The silence is broken only when the gulls cry, or a fish breaches to make the water ripple for a short time.

During my growing up years in Newfoundland we always had a dory or a little punt to paddle around in and we learned the art of rowing a boat. Travel to visit relatives was always by coastal boat, or steamer, with names like the Northern Ranger, Springdale, Burgeo, Baccelieu, Bar Haven, and many others with names that became familiar household names as the steamer report came to us by radio several times a day. These ships with their small cabins, shiny cutlery, stiff white sheets, narrow ladders for disembarking, all stand out in my memory as if it were yesterday. Those boats were part of our lives, part of us in those days long ago. Coastal boats were a necessary part of life in outport Newfoundland.

Then at one point when my parents were on Bell Island and I was a student in St. John's I had to take the Bell Island ferry when I wanted to visit my parents. The most familiar to me was the Kipawo, and two things you could always count on is that the ferry would be late, and that you would meet somebody you knew on the journey.

Books on ships, small boats, disasters at sea, yacht races, the mysterious 'Marie Celeste', the boat found with nobody on board, but the table set for a meal, as if the crew and passengers had been plucked away in an instant, the loss of the 'Florizel', the 'Patrick Morris' and the 'William Carson', the amazing story of the first 'Caribou' that was destroyed in 1942 by a torpedo from the German submarine called 'The Laughing Cow', resulting in great loss of life, although there were survivors. Any books about the sea, ships, and the drama of the ocean, would engage me in a reading marathon. And it remains that way for me. Later years found me living in Nova Scotia, and for thirty-three years the drive to North Sydney to board the ferry to Port aux Basques, Newfoundland was a yearly pilgrimage, and not always an enjoyable trip with small children to keep safe and by the hand. The ferry trip to Port aux Basques, the drive across the island, a three-week stay with family, then reversing the travel to return to Nova Scotia was an exhausting exercise worthy of a Survivor series in itself. Many times I would vow never to set foot on a boat again, and many times the sunrise and the motion of the large ship would rock me to sleep. All was dependent on weather patterns, wind changes and the children s' ages and behavior. But I did it, and I would not change it. Those trips have given us as a family so many memories, good and bad, but memories all safely stored and pulled forth for a discussion from time to time.

Living in Lunenburg, Nova Scotia, so near the sea, we just had to have a boat. The young, Newfoundland couple, with a little boy and a baby girl, would not be complete without the little green boat with the Acadia gas engine going 'pik-a puk, pik-a-puk' as we cruised around the Islands of Mahone Bay with the baby in her travel bed sound asleep. That little boat was lovely. Green and white, with the 'pik-a-puk' motor and two little bunks up in the cuddy. Oh, it was bliss, and our little boy, now a tall man of thirty-two loved to take the wheel with his dad as we motored along, often taking friends with us on summer afternoons.

After moving to the Annapolis Valley accessing boats was more difficult. So on Sunday drives we would gravitate to Chester, NS, and watch the boats, go to the wooden boat festival in the summer, and walk the Halifax waterfront once in awhile just to 'see the boats'.

I am back home now, back to stay. And owning a little open Newfoundland boat named 'Kylee', after a special little granddaughter, and a cabin cruiser that came with the name 'Ocean Joy' is like living a dream. The 'Ocean Joy' is my cruise ship, and the 'Kylee' my special little open boat. Frank and Dolores, good Nova Scotian friends who visited us last summer, gave us a plaque for 'Ocean Joy'. It reads 'M V OCEAN JOY- RECOMMISSIONED 2002-Captain- A .J. Lowe, First Mate, Bonnie Lowe. It is a beautiful gift, a thoughtful gift, and it will be mounted in the wheelhouse when 'Ocean Joy' is launched this summer. She is our special ship. The waves will kiss her hull to greet her as she reaches the water, and she will settle gently onto the ocean, where she is meant to be. And I will wait with keen anticipation for the Captain to steer her out into the bay. Then the log book has to be written up, the binoculars ready for a closer look at an eagle or a whale, and I will have music playing. The bright green of the radar screen keeps us transfixed at times if we are nearing a shoal or if fog is enveloping us. It is all part of a special, unforgettable time as we begin our boating season.

Yes, I am a Newfoundland girl with the Newfoundlanders' love of boats and ships, of the outdoors and the sea. And with that love comes a great respect for what the sea can do, what dangers we can encounter, and what rules we have to follow. But it is still marvelous to know that we can explore Newfoundland in our own little thirty-four-foot ship, the same way our ancestors explored to find places to call home in this 'Newfounde-lande'.

And I remember then two little boys, one my brother, and one my son, shaving a piece of wood with their pocket knives, making it into the shape of a boat, sticking a nail into the tip of the bow, tying some twine on to hold it, and getting me to take them to a pond or brook so they could play 'boats'. I enjoyed it as much as they did.

So, it is a great love I have, for boats great and small, from the pieces of wood of the little boys, to the majesty of the ocean liners, boats are special. And what better name could a boat for me have than 'Ocean Joy'? Because that is what she gives me — sensational ocean joy, and a sense of being one with the sea.

It will always be that way–it is my heritage, the longing to be near the sea, to be on the sea, and to feel part of the universe. May we have fair winds and sun drenched days, may we be able to ride the waves in our ocean joy, and may the experiences we have bring renewal to our spirits and pleasure to our lives. And may we also be able to share it with others. That is the best part of all!

Yes, I love boats, I always have and always will. As a line in a song I heard some years ago said "We are nearer to heaven by sea," and indeed it is so, it is a piece of heaven for me to ride the waves in a boat called 'Ocean Joy'.

THE END

Or is it? Did I ever tell you the one about…

A JARRING EXPERIENCE

I was standing in front of a mirror in my parents' house, while home on vacation. Mother walked by me, turned around and came back, and stood looking at me with one of those 'Mother caught you' looks.

"What did I do now?" I inquired. Of course I was only 45 years old after all, and whatever I did I should have know better etc. Such was the conversation I expected. But that wasn't it at all!

"What is that dreadful chemical smell?" Mother asked.

"There's no smell here, I'm just putting my moisturizer on." I answered.

Still, she stood there. Finally she inquired as to what kind of 'cold cream' I was using. I told her it was the stuff in the blue jar that she had used on all of us for sunburns, face cream and taught us how to apply correctly! I've been using it all my life I told her, and she had introduced me to it at a very young age if she cared to recall!

"Oh, that stuff! No wonder! I despise the smell of THAT STUFF!" And she turned to walk away but I followed her.

"But Mom you used that on us all our lives. You must have been through gallons of it, what's the problem now?" I was fool enough to ask.

"Yes, I used it on all of you. But I never ever said I liked it, and I don't! It smells like burnt wool!" and she turned and stared at me, making me feel like a five-year-old. I was shocked but I persisted and tried to make sense of this 'cold cream jar' conversation, but to no avail. She had said her bit and that was that. Although she did recommend some 'nice new creams' that were on the market now.

I picked up my blue jar and carried it to my bedroom. I felt leaving it in the presence of Mother would prove disastrous!

I couldn't understand it and I never will. But when I mentioned it to my father he seemed to think that it had something to do with the fact that at a very young age, I had taken a spoon and eaten a goodly portion of a jar of this cream. After that when Mother used it she thought of the unending laundry that little prank of mine had caused her and after awhile she banned it from the house, some ten years later. I didn't know it had that effect on her. I thought she was more upset the day when I was five years old and took the family record for eating a dozen oranges in one sitting. Now that must have been a laundry nightmare! But oranges weren't banned!

I don't understand it, and never will. But lately I have had that incredible urge to dip a spoon into my same blue cold cream jar, and have a taste of it! It just might be good with oranges?!

QUITTING THE COLOR BOTTLE

Yes, I do go on rants, and darned good long rants from time to time. I don't know who listens or cares but I still rant. Let me tell you about my rant of this past winter. I don't care who likes it or doesn't but my hair is totally devoid of color, it is snow white. As a matter of fact my daughter, when she saw a photo taken recently, during the winter, made the the crack that "You gotta hand it to ya Mom, it is a great camouflage in snow!" That did it! I have listened to stories about hair, hair coloring, questions about why I do not color my hair anymore, why I let my hair go white after coloring it for twenty-five years and every other foolish question that a human can come up with. That does not bother me. I know there are all kinds of products out there and I can have any color hair I want, but I do not want it. Can't anybody understand that?? I guess not! My mothers' family had a trait of the men going bald at an early age, my fathers' side has the trait of prematurely grey hair. And at the age of 17 I was going grey. So, I took to coloring my fine long locks, and it was a procedure that took two bottles of hair color because my hair was long and thick. And of course I did not want to be grey as a teenager, or as a young mother, so the coloring continued for years. When I worked in an Operating Room and my head was covered all the time, I finally, about five or six years ago, quit the bottle. I wore shorter hair, more becoming, and more convenient for my lifestyle. And I wore a much shorter cut. I was darn sick and tired of spending a fortune to have a someone color my hair, having to sit still for an hour or so, of me doing it, getting it all over the bathroom and it would not come off the walls if the splatter hit them, and I was too busy fishin' when I came back to Newfoundland to sit still for that long- so I quit. I had suffered through every color hair in the book, including 'Accidental Green' or 'Streaky purple' and enough was enough. So that was that. My friends grew to like it, I became a grandmother and I write. So white hair and dark frame glasses gave me the tad of eccentricity I wanted. Good enough, if you're with me this far I will tell you the final straw regarding this mop of mine. I was sitting at the picnic table on the wharf in Shoal Harbour, Newfoundland, (where I live) waiting to photograph the geese when they honked in, so I was basically just killing time. Then an elderly gentleman pulled in beside my car and got out to have a conversation. After a few minutes, he squinted at me through his cigarette smoke and said, "Fine head 'a hair ya got dere!" I said thank you, and tried to ignore him. I was not in the mood to discuss the pros and cons of Lady Hair Color with him or anyone else!! There was a few minutes of silence, then the old gent walked around to the front of me, leaned over and stared at my mouth. Before I could ask what the heck he was doing he came out with the zinger, and this is the truth! He continued to look, squinting over the smoke of the second cigarette, leaned in closer and asked, "YA STILL GOT ALL YER OWN TEETH!!??" That did it. I marched back to my car with all the self-control I could muster, jumped in and drove away! I could see him staring at me and had the crazy desire to go back and knock him off the wharf, but I managed to keep controlled. He must have been quite surprised to see my late model car rather than the 1924 Model T, a beautiful treasured vehicle about town. Now, isn't that something? I was insulted, and really, really angry!! Just because I have white hair does not mean I am 90 years old, or that I have a full set of dentures, or wear a medic-alert bracelet. It is only hair for heavens' sake!! "Got all yer own teeth?" Indeed I do Mister I thought to myself, and if I gave in to the way I feel right now I would bite your ankles! And you are just lucky you caught me on a good day or you would be over the end of the wharf!! Did you ever hear the like of it?? Oh, me Nerves!! And all over a head of white hair!! Your own teeth-Indeed!! And that was my rant for this past winter!

HOW MUCH COLD DO YOU WANT?

The air outside the hospital was frigid, the doctors' coming and going through the large sliding Emergency Room Door let a blast of the ice crystals escape into our Nursing station from time to time until one particularly verbal nurse put a stop to that. They could use another entrance, thank you very much. Yes, that was Barbara,the one who went around muttering about how she was getting out of this and taking a job as a Walmart Greeter, until someone told her she would have to change her attitude, and she decided she didn't want to do that either! She was a genuine character who afforded us many a story, some would make you pull your ears over your mouth!We loved her,who wouldn't?

The ringing telephone got Barb off her story as she swirled her chair around to grab 'the thing' as she called it. Two of us listening to her story were called to do something, and then down the hallway comes Madame Barbara, "Do you want to know what that call was?" she asks, hands on hips, not a good sign.

"Not really", answers June, "but we're gonna hear it aren't we?"

Barb ignores this completely, and turns in my direction, mainly because, I discover later, we were two Newfoundlanders working in a Nova Scotia institution and had heard our share of 'Newfie' jokes,and neither of us appreciated them,but tolerated them.

"Well, yes you are," she says to June. To me she says "Umph,and they talk about Newfoundlanders! That woman on the phone said that Dr. Stone told her to wrap her daughters' ankle in ice this evening to get the swelling down and she didn't know what to do because she defrosted her fridge today!"

I was a useless lump of laughter, and even moreso when June asked "What's so funny?"

"See what I mean?", says Barb, "every idiot in this county knows it's permafrost out there tonight. Now where would you go to get ice June? Don't ever tell me another Newfie stupid JOKE!"

And she never did!!!

PATIENCE PATIENTS!!

I was in the process of adapting myself to a new department in a little rural hospital. Of course, for the staff members who had been on the unit for some time, it was no problem for them to know every patient, their families, and their special circumstances. But for me, it was a struggle trying to familiarize myself with the floor plan, let alone all the faces, names and desires, not to mention the routines, of thirty-three patients.

One early evening stands out in my mind as a 'watershed moment'. A young lady walked up to me and asked "Nurse, can Dad have something to eat?" My mind raced- "Who is Dad?"

In an effort to clarify who 'Dad' was I asked where he was. I carefully chose my words and asked "And your father is . . .?"

The little face looked up at me strangely and said softly,"HUNGRY."

THE SURGEON AND MY 'SEEMORE

As your children often do, mine had done. My daughter acquired two Guinea Pigs, a male and a female, and they were beautiful little creatures. They were named 'SEEMORE' and 'SEELESS', a play on the names 'Seymour' and 'Celeste' I suppose, but who knows the mind of a teenager?

They were, of course, finding their way into my heart. I went to the mill for shavings, bringing them home by the trunk load in large bags, I bought special food, I shampooed and groomed them, cuddled them and taught them how to kiss. Because you see a few months after acquiring these Guinea Pigs my daughter become aware of creatures much more interesting 'BOYS'! And Mom got the pets!

I talked about these little animals, I loved them, and in some peoples' view, maybe just a bit too much, seeing as how they were thought of by some as rodents, but not by me .Those tiny pets were the best cared for in the province of Nova Scotia I am sure.

Then tragedy struck, and Seemore became very sick. The staff I worked with were sick to death of me and my obsession with these creatures but they would hear me out and let me vent. It looked like Seemore was dying, and he did in fact die and broke our hearts. I called the Unit and told them I would be a little late as I had to stay and tell my daughter about Seemore, hear her sobs, and do the necessary things, before I left my house.

Dr.C., our surgeon of the day, had arrived shortly before I did that morning and she was told that 'Seemore passed away in the night', and of course she was told in a somber, whispered tone. She was sympathetic and suitably solemn, but in fact she had forgotten who 'Seemore' was.

Finally she went to one of the other nurses, and in a soft, concerned voice asked "Which one of the maintenance men is Seymour?"

The nurse told her there was no such person in our institution.

"Well, who is 'Seymour' that died and everyone is so sad about?" she inquired.

"Oh, that 'Seemore', you remember him, he's Bonnies' Guinea Pig she goes on about all the time!" my co-worker explained with a smile. Dr. C. decided to drop the sad face, and pick it up again when I appeared, which she could not do. All she could do was blush and tell me how she had embarrassed herself.

"That's OK, he had good Palliative Care and knew us right to the end!" I informed her seriously, knowing how easy she was to tease about things.

She looked at me, blushed again, and we headed toward our days' work.

But Seemore was gone, and I couldn't help but think how he would love how Dr. C. had mourned him for ten minutes!

I still had my 'Seeless' though!!

JUST CALL IT THE I/V

First when I left Newfoundland I, of course, took the colloquialism, pronunciations, and accents of my Island home with me. And being young and interested in so much more than accents, did nothing to hide how I spoke. I knew the grammar was correct so that was all that was required.

However I soon became aware that my accent, such as it was, was being the subject of coffee time humour, but not behind my back. The staff talked and teased me constantly until I thought the time had come to do something about it.

All of the intravenous fluids that hospital used, and in fact most hospitals up until the 1980s' or so, came in bottles, bottles with a hook for hanging. That was fine, until I realized that every time I said the word 'bottle' or 'kettle', snickering would occur. Finally I asked what seemed so funny? I was a trifle annoyed by then.

I was told that those words are not pronounced with a 't' but rather a 'd' in them. Well, pardon me! As far as I was concerned it was designed with 'ts' and should be said with those same 'ts'.

But to stop the fracas I practiced saying 'boddle' and keddle' day after day on my annual vacation. I finally had it right. By the time my vacation was over I was ready to go back to work with my new phrase 'the I/V boddle' and surprise everyone.

Imagine my surprise when I arrived early in the morning to start work and was told that the I/V fluids were now coming in 'BAGS'!! All that practice for nothing.

But guess who would ask every chance she got if anyone wanted the 'Keddle' put on to boil for tea??

Ya gotta win somehow!

POOR TIMING OR NOT??

As in any profession seminars and workshops are held on a regular basis to keep members informed of the changes in the work place, the new equipment or policies, and such is the way it is in the Nursing Profession.

However one particular workshop stands out clearly in my mind. There were three jam-packed non-stop days, ending on Friday afternoon.

The last session for the afternoon was a guest speaker who was to speak on 'DRUG AND ALCOHOL ABUSE IN THE NURSING PROFESSION' and everybody was expected to attend.

Further down on the Program was an announcement that the last speaker and lecture would be followed by 'A WINE AND CHEESE PARTY' for all those attending!

Poor timing, poor judgement or good planning??

Go figure!

WHERE'S THE KEY?

Computers had just been introduced to the unit where I worked. They were not being used by the nurses, although of course the nurses had their hands on them, experimenting just to see what they were all about. I never did know a nurse that could leave anything alone!!!

We did learn some things about the computer, the special dot. com language etc. Our ward clerk was increasingly frustrated by this 'darned computer' as she called it! Instead of helping her in her work it was causing her untold grief.

One day while we were at lunch an announcement came over the PA system asking 'Would the nurses from 5A please call their unit'. So one of the nurses did just that. She came back and related the hilarious conversation she had just gone through with our ward clerk.

"What's wrong?" the nurse asked.

"It's this bloody computer thing," an obviously very distressed woman said, "It erases everything I put into it and says to press 'ANY' key to correct the problem."

"OK," said the nurse, "No problem ,do that then!"

"Well, it is a problem," yelled the ward clerk, "you come and tell me where you see a key that says 'ANY KEY' ON THIS KEYBOARD!!!"

THE PERCEPTIVE PATIENT

My friend Alison now works in a Day Surgery Department, and she runs it with a strong hand, everything has to be done correctly, and she is as hyperactive as she has always been. The patients love her.

The first few years I worked with Alison we worked together on a medical unit that had many cardiac patients. Alison was a relatively new graduate and was doing everything by the book. She is built strong – in body and in soul. Alison knew the cardiac routine as well as she knew her signature, and she would make her patients comply no matter what. If they wanted to get well they had better listen to her, she was their nurse, and she told them so. She was always lecturing them about crossing their legs, always telling them to take their arms down from behind their head to lessen the load on the heart. Yes, she was and is a good nurse and I would put my life in her hands any day. She does her work well, and is admired for it.

Sometime during our first year of working together a man was admitted to our unit who had suffered a heart attack, and a rather severe one at that. He was a hard driving businessman who did not stop asking for a telephone and a television (things the acute care cardiac patients are not allowed), and he wanted more salt, he wanted to go home, he would not admit to having pain, and was just plain noncompliant. He managed to break every rule of our Cardiac Care routine.

But one day he crossed the line. This had gone on long enough for Nurse Alison. She jumped up, headed for his room and closed the door. We could hear voices, loud at first, then at a more reasonable level, coming from behind the closed door. But after that we had a compliant patient. We could only imagine how Alison had turned him around. We still do not know.

The mans' doctor arrived the next day to make his rounds. He emerged from this gentleman's room laughing. He could hardly tell us his story because his laughter was so breathtaking.

Finally he said that the now very compliant patient had asked him, "Who is that nurse out there who is built like a Green Bay Packer and thinks she's Hitler?"

WHAT WAS SHE THINKING?

One very nice retired nurse that I know tells the story of how just after she became an RN, she had to take charge of a large ward, and she had student nurses under her charge. But one evening the situation was too hectic to do much more than touch base with the students from time to time, leaving them considerable time to explore alternatives, sometimes a good thing but sometimes not so good!

She nearly collapsed when, at the preparation for bedtime hour came, a student walked up to the RN, with a washbasin full of dentures! She thought she would collect them all and then give them a good cleaning, and get them back to their owners. However, she had discovered that her idea had a great stumbling block, how does one identify dentures??

They found a solution, but only because they had a great group of patients, all elderly people who had been there, done that and seen it all! And this just relieved their monotony.

But what in heavens' name was she thinking??

And then my friend says she knew for certain that "the Road to Hades is paved with Good Intentions!"

RETIRED ARE YA?

My husband and I came home to Newfoundland to retire, having made the decision to retire early and pursue other interests. Being only fifty years old I found it very difficult to say the word 'RETIRE', and avoided it at all costs. I have no idea why- just a foolish quirk!! I guess it conjured up images of much older lifestyles and just plain made me feel redundant and much older than my fifty years.

We acquired a boat the second year we were back in Newfoundland and we spent a lot of time boating and exploring, fishing and having beach picnics or 'boilups' as they are called here. I loved spending time boating, and spent an extraordinary length of time preparing food and goods, and waiting at the wharf for my husband to bring the boat in off her collar, or buoy.

One day I was enjoying the summer sun, the lady was selling strawberries from her truck, and boats were coming and going like the Newfoundland of years ago that I love so much. Two women appeared, and started a chitchat, the Newfoundland style, saying "Some day on the bay today!" I agreed. It was wonderful. Then my husband appeared with the boat and joined in the conversation with the three of us women.

Then he turned to me and said, " Look at her ring, it's the same school ring as yours!" Of course then we realized we were graduates of the same school of nursing. And the 'nurse talk' started as my children used to call it. Who was in your class, what floor did you like best, what year did you graduate etc.

The nurse I had just met looked at me with a puzzled expression and asked "But you are not working here?" I said no, I was doing other things.

"Retired are ya?" she asked laughingly, "who else was in your class that's retired by now?"

Before I had to engage in the 'RETIRED ARE YA?' question that I hated so much my smart husband spoke up and yelled to her from the boat "THE ONLY OTHER ONE IN HER CLASS THAT'S RETIRED IS JOHN CABOTS' SISTER!"

We had a great laugh, and once again proved his Newfoundland wit was alive and well!!

RETIRED ARE YA INDEED!

WHO WAS SHE?

Just a short time before I capped off my nursing career in the year 2000, I had the sweet pleasure of working with a fresh faced young graduate named Susan. Sue, as she was called, had a positive attitude, an alert and bright mind and most appealing to me was her friendly approach to people and her ability to problem solve. I have always admired people who can take a different angle, work it through and come up with a solution to a seemingly unsolvable issue. Such is the type Sue was, always solving little problems, and I knew someday, I just knew, she would be a big problem solver, it would come with experience. She has a good future as a nurse, and many patients will be happy to have met her.

Sue was the same age as my daughter, so we certainly had an age difference but it didn't seem to matter. Nursing was our common ground and we worked so well together. Naturally I always enjoyed shocking her with some bizarre story and seeing her blush, and it would be followed by a great laugh and a cold soda pop, just getting through the tough stuff sometimes.

On a particularly hectic day I made my usual remark that "I'd like to have Florence Nightingale by the ears today for starting this nursing racket!" Sue looked at me over a mound of paperwork we were wading through and asked so calmly "Who was she??"

"Well, SHE, My dear, is the woman who started all this nursing stuff, the Crimean War, Soldiers dying, aseptic technique and all that, you know!!" I answered without looking up, knowing I would laugh.

A period of silence followed, no further comment from Sue. I looked up to see her lost in thought, trying to figure this Florence Nightingale thing out, and running questions through her mind. I knew that expression all too well!!

Than she caught me studying her, and she turned toward me and asked a question that collapsed the whole staff into a useless group of laughing hyenas, characters who were rendered helpless indeed. And Nobody had the answer to the question either.

"Well," says Sue, "where did she graduate from??"

THAT DID IT! OH, ME NERVES!!!!

REMEMBER YOUR HELMET

I am a Newfoundlander, a member of an elite group. On this big rocky Island in the North Atlantic called 'NEWFOUNDLAND AND LABRADOR' there are half a million of us, and we are all members of the Newfoundland and Labrador fraternity. Our favorite cuisine is salty, and our beer is the best ever made.

For those who do not know our culture some ways of the Newfoundlander are as hard to understand as the diverse dialects that abound on the island. Talented musicians, artists, writers, theater groups, and quick witted, resourceful, practical people make up our culture. This practicality was necessary for two middle-aged men when they were stopped by the police while driving their four-wheel all terrain vehicles into their cabin. The policemen checked them on the old woods' road, and told them that they had to wear helmets riding these vehicles. The men agreed to do so and continued on.

A week later it was time to leave the cabin and travel home. However, the 'helmet' issue was a problem. What would they do, how could they overcome this police decree and get out to their vehicles on the highway when they had no helmets? So they checked around and found the solution. Using what they had available in the cabin they designed their helmets, put them on, started up their four-wheelers and headed to the main road.

Imagine the surprise of the policeman, who was there again doing his road checks, when he saw those two resourceful individuals driving toward him with one gallon beef buckets on their heads. They had cut holes cut for eyes, and the handle of the bucket was the chin strap. They had created 'designer' helmets. The innovative mind of the Newfoundlander came through again!

Because one thing that is sure, where there is a Newfoundlander there is a 'SALT BEEF BUCKET'!

A MAJOR BUM CHECK

In one little 'Mainland' town I lived in during my long time away from Newfoundland, I had gotten to know many of the people in the town through my work, and also got to know many of their lives' situations-the good and the bad. At one particular time the buzz around town concerned the middle-aged lady who owned the bookstore. I frequented her store quite often and knew her fairly well. And I, too, had heard the story of the young man who came to do redecorating on the shop and a romance developed between the owner of 'BETWEEN THE PAGES' bookshop owner and the handsome young man. The whole town was tuned in, as most small towns would be, to the unfolding drama of this May-December romance. On my way home from work one day I dropped into 'Between the Pages' to pick up a book I had planned to buy. The lady wasn't there, but the young man was in charge it seemed, handling the cash register like a pro. I paid for my purchase with a check as I always did and left to go home. When I pulled into my driveway a few minutes later my two teenagers were hanging out the door, and yelling for all the world to hear that "The man from the bookstore called and your check is no good!" Well, thanks kids, now the whole neighborhood knows I pass out bad checks. I immediately turned around and drove back to 'Between the Pages', wondering what in the world could be wrong with my check. Imagine my embarrassment when the young man passed me my check and there in my very own bold print I saw that I had made it payable to ' BETWEEN THE SHEETS!' Thanks Dr. Freud, wherever you are!

THE SHORT EXPLANATION!

The 'tailgate conferences' are what I call the odd occurrences that take place when a group of men gather around the back of a pickup truck, babble for long periods of time about 'nothing', and laugh their heads off occasionally about 'nothing'. It is a mans' domain, and it is of little use for me, or any other woman, to try to join, understand, or explain exactly what the 'tailgate conference' means to the participants, but obviously they are of great importance because they take place everywhere.

In our little town a large tailgate conference was taking place at the wharf, and growing as the afternoon wore on. Boats were coming in to tie up and the men would be out of the boats and leaning on the truck in two minutes flat!!

This day the trucks' owner was a tall man, a gentleman everyone knew, and he was often called 'Stilt' because of his great height. Stilt was presiding over the conference around his truck when a fellow named Sammy arrived and joined in. Sammy was quite short in stature, and his head hardly reached the top of the back of the truck. Of course immediately Stilt started to tease him about his height, even going so far as to pick him up and sit him on the side of the truck. Sammy was a pleasant man who was quite used to this, and laughed at it all himself.

"How come you're so short anyway?" Stilt asked Sammy. The conference crowd laughed and waited for what they knew would be a witty answer. It seemed that one of the requirements of being part of a 'tailgate conference' was that you could be witty and make fun of yourself.

"It was me boots!" announced Sammy.

"Now, that is the most foolish excuse I ever heard!" one of

the men commented. "What would your boots have to do with your height?"

"Well, it's like this," explained Sammy, "I had no boots and had to wear me older brudders that was too small for him, so fadder stuck straw in the toes of the boots so I could wear 'em and not be falling around."

"Yeah, so???" asked Stilt.

"So," says Sammy, "the 'Calfs' of me legs went down to me boots, ate the straw, and never did come back up-and that's why I'm short. Me calfs are gone!"

The tailgate conference was adjourned due to uncontrollable laughter!

A MOST EMBARRASSING MOMENT

My lifes' work and passion was that of being a nurse. However even if passionate about something, you can make a major blunder that you remember forever and wish had never happened.

In one particular hospital, on one particular unit, I was the 'new kid on the block' as they say. I knew absolutely nobody in the town, my husband and I had just moved there six weeks or so before this most embarrassing incident. We were newly married, my husband was away quite a bit so I decided to get myself a dog and a job, and I did.

The little hospital had a large male ward, a medium sized female ward and private rooms. The nurse in charge told me to look after the private room patients and turned me loose. I went around and met my patients, all very nice people, and one man in particular was very jovial and interesting. He had been a patient for a long time and was perched up in bed quite happy to meet a new person, something to break the monotony of daily hospital life.

A few hours later the gentleman called and asked to be assisted to get out of bed, seems that was his evening routine. So off I trotted to help him. Wheelchair at the ready, he knew his special way to do things, and he patiently chatted away while I undertook a thorough search of his room. I could not find two slippers, one slipper was there, but I sure as heck could not find the other one. Finally I was on my hands and knees, when what should I see but the patients head upside down looking at me as he draped himself over the bed and peeked to see what this new nurse was doing down there.

"Whatcha doin' down there dear?" he inquired of his red-faced nurse.

"I'm looking for your other slipper," I managed to reply.

"Oh dear," he says, "I don't need another slipper."

Never one to give up I asked him why he didn't need his pair of slippers.

"Well ya see dear, it's like this, I only got one leg!" he yelled.

I climbed out from under the bed, the patients' laughter brought all kinds of other staff members to his room, where I stood, suffering the worst humiliation I had ever suffered.

I never did live that one down, and never could forget it. After that the patient would call me 'Lady Slipper', and we became good buddies for the remainder of his hospital stay. And in retaliation, I named him "Mr. Foot!"

Sometimes you just have to give in to it all.

MIXED MESSAGES

The Salvation Army Thrift Store is a place I frequent often, challenging myself to see if I can find something better than I did on my previous visits. And because it supports a good cause, I am happy to buy things and help one of my favorite special groups, the Salvation Army. All through the years the Salvation Army has had and continues to have, a great supporter in me. My father told me when I was quite young that the Salvation Army saved his life during World War Two, and he has always been a faithful supporter of them, instilling that need and wish to help them into his five offspring. Mother felt the same way. Then I did my Nurses training at the Salvation Army Grace Hospital in St. John's, Newfoundland, so the 'Army' has really played a big part in my life. The bonnets they used to wear, the sound of the band at 'open air' meetings reaching so many people, the tambourines and brass instrument music dancing out over the water on a calm summer evening, is a cherished memory indeed.

Recently I dropped into our local Thrift store, which is a veritable basket of unique items. Great used clothing and books for next to nothing prices makes that little store a true treasure chest. From skates, to pots and pans, to warm fleecy jackets, it is all there. And when I find a special sweater or blouse, wear it, and have it complimented, I just smile secretly to myself, knowing that only I know that I came to have this gem in a special way.

On my latest visit to the store I had a delightful collection of items and treasures and I held them tightly as I approached the man at the checkout, who happened to be a Salvation Army Officer. During our conversation I commented that he must be starting a new career in sales, and we had a short conversation about all the wonderful things surrounding us.

Then I noticed a small sign and collection can sitting on the counter. The sign read 'Support our Organ Fund'. Being in the medical field all my life, I decided without hesitation that I certainly would support the organ fund. I told the officer that organ transplants could save so many lives it was a shame that more people did not know or realize the need for funding, for having organ donor cards signed, and it seemed more public awareness was certainly necessary.

I continued to chat, while gathering coins from my purse, rattling on about organ donations, ending with "I really don't understand what the problem is with the organ program."

Then I looked up and noticed the officer eyeing me rather strangely. He appeared to be somewhat ill at ease.

Then it happened!

In a quiet voice he said, "I don't understand it either ma'am, but I do know that our church organ has the keys falling off one by one, and we really do need a new organ as nobody seems to be able to fix our problem," and he smiled.

I just stared blankly ahead, picked up my purchases and bid him farewell. I could not get to the car fast enough! What was that all about? Then I came to realize that we were on totally different wave lengths, but both well-meaning. A definite case of Mixed Messages!

I just got the wrong organs! Or I got the organs wrong! I really don't know, but what I do know is that I had an attack of 'the wrong rant syndrome'. And a kind Salvation Army Officer smiled and understood, as they always do!!

I CAN'T BELIEVE I DID THAT!

In every type of employment there are days that getting a break or a bit of time to grab a snack or some meals are total impossibilities. This is especially true of the job of a nurse. There are days and days, or at least one can expect days and days, of rushing around and the tasks and demands are endless and you wonder why you feel so terrible, then realize you have not eaten, and you are ravenous by then.

Such was the case on our Medical unit many days but one day in particular stands out as one of the most embarrassing of my life, but also proves that nurses will eat anything, anywhere when that strong hunger sets in.

From 6:45am to 1:00 p.m. on that fateful day, the Unit was like a beehive, no time to stop, no time to have a bathroom break, no time certainly to consider food. But by 1pm it had settled down enough for a couple of us nurses and doctors to realize we had to feed ourselves, and we skipped off to the cafeteria together.

Everybody had a sandwich of sorts, a cold drink, and since we had a great pie baker in our kitchen, we all had the lemon pie. It was a feast for us, and the pie was just marvelous. The only thing wrong was that the pie was sitting on a cheap paper plate, and had been there for some time, but that didn't deter us, our hunger was too great.

We ate, did a debriefing of our morning emergency, and then chatted about other things. During this time I happened to notice one of the other nurses starring at my tray, and then they were all staring at it, and then I looked down at it. I couldn't believe my eyes-the whole bottom was gone from the paper plate! The obvious answer to that strange looking vision was that in my hunger and talking and gulping food, and I had eaten the pie, and the plate, leaving only the rim!

The group laughed so hard, no way I could swear them to secrecy, and from then on when I was on duty someone would always say 'Bonnies' at the plate!"

WANT A REFERENCE?

My daughter was born and raised in Nova Scotia to two Newfoundland parents. After University she moved to the Great Canadian West, where she met a young man from the Codroy Valley in Newfoundland. They married, and eventually started their family.

Of course having a child meant having a babysitter so one was sought, checked out thoroughly and hired. She was a great babysitter but she grew restless and wanted a job outside of her home so she resigned,,asking my daughter and her husband if they would give her a reference.

"Sure",they said.

My son-in-laws' phone rang for him while he was at work a few days later. It was someone asking for a reference for Julie the babysitter.

"Yep,she'sgood," said my son-in-law "to tell the truth it sickens me to lose her!"

His Newfoundland brogue was on fast forward that day. Finally he got the message across. Then more questions, finally he said

"Look why don't you just hire her and find out for yourself just how good she is!!"

The gentleman said his thanks and that was that.

My daughter called Julie to tell her that they had called for a reference so the company must be processing her application.

"Oh," said Julie, "I got the job. I start tomorrow. It was really fast hey?"

Yes, it was fast. But not quite as fast as the reference she had been given by Lance who was rushed and therefore spoke even faster than usual.

Fast Indeed!

HOW WINDY WAS IT ANYWAY?

My brother, David, is gifted with a healthy dose of humor and wit, probably an inheritance from one of our legendary Labrador uncles, and Newfoundland father. He has the uncanny ability to catch a person off guard at times, something he revels in as he has his laugh.

From time to time David has to travel the province of Newfoundland and Labrador on work related matters, giving him ample opportunity to gather material to use on some unsuspecting characters in his life.

Some time ago he was on a lengthy trip down the Northern Peninsula of Newfoundland, an area he loves, having spent part of his childhood there. When he returned, I asked him during a phone call how his trip was. He answered in just one word, "WINDY!"

Falling into his trap, I asked how windy it was. For him to comment on it I knew it had to be really bad.

"Well," he said, "it was so windy that I was in a community for ten days before the wind died down and I realized that the Canadian flag on the pole outside the school wasn't made out of plywood! Now, is that wind or what??"

I had to admit, through my laughter that, yes, that was WINDY!

And I became another name on his list of 'humor victims'.

NURSING RESUME

Yvonne Frances (Bonnie) LOWE
88 Balbo Drive,
Clarenville, NL, Canada A5A 4A8
1-709-466-7022
lowe@superweb.ca

Personal Data: Birth date: November 20, 1948
                Marital Status: Married
                Place of Birth: Marys' Harbour, NL
                Citizenship: Canadian

Nursing status at present: Retired in June, 2000, hold inactive Registration in the province of Nova Scotia and the province of NL & Lab.

Educational Background: 1969- Graduated from Grace General Hospital School of Nursing, St. John's, NL as a Registered Nurse. Did extra work in this three year Nursing program in Operating Room, Labor and Delivery and Emergency Room Nursing.

Oct/69 - Jan/70	Staff Nurse	Grand Bank Cottage Hospital, Grand Bank, NL. Primarily Medical-Surgical, EmergencyDepartment, Clinics, plus Obstetrics and Ambulance duties.
Jan/70 - Apr.70	Staff Nurse	Grace General Hospital St. John's, NL Second Floor high risk pregnancy And Post Partum Unit.
Jun/70 - May/72	StaffNurse	Harbor View Hospital Sydney Mines, Nova Scotia Rotated through Medical, Surgical And Pediatrics/monthly basis.
Oct/72 - May/74	StaffNurse	

	Casual basis	Float team, Victoria General Hospital Halifax, Nova Scotia
Jun/75 - Dec/76	Staff Nurse Casual basis	Fishermans' Memorial Hospital Lunenburg, Nova Scotia
Mar/77 - Jun/85	Staff Nurse Casual basis	Hants Community Hospital Windsor, Nova Scotia Medical department and Out Patients. Did much ambulance nursing during This time frame, transferring trauma and Cardiac Patients to Halifax.
Jun/85 - Feb/95	Staff Nurse	Full time staff nurse in Operating Room and Recovery Suite. Was instrumental in developing a day Surgeon program, and became very skilled with laparoscopic surgery and keenly interested in its' development. Became very proficient with the use And care of endoscopic equipment. Also assisted with C-SECTIONS, and Colonsurgery on a regular basis.
Feb/95 - Jun/00	Staff Nurse	Medical Surgical, Palliative Care and Cardiac Care. Retired in June of 2000 At Age 51.

Mar/77 - Jun/00 were all spent at Hants Community Hospital, Windsor, Nova Scotia. Retired while working Palliative care and Cardiac Care at this hospital.
Successfully completed both BCLS and ACLS courses.

Member in good standing of Reg. Nurses Association of Nova Scotia
Member in good standing of Association of Registered Nurses of Newfoundland and Labrador.

Past member of Nova Scotia Nurses Union and active on the local executive.
Past member of the Operating Room Nurses Study Group.
Past member of the National Alzheimer Society.

Past member of the Board of the Victorian Order of Nurses, Hants County, Nova Scotia.

Have attended many courses, functions and seminars of the Operating Room Nurses Association, and Nova Scotia Nurses Union, ie. study groups, labor school, teaching sessions etc.

Attended Mount Saint Vincent University In Halifax, Nova Scotia, took courses in Sociology, ie: Women and Aging, Death and Dying, and then turned to the arts and studied courses in Photography and general interest. Did well in any courses I studied.

Now as a Retired Nurse I devote time to writing, photography, family and community issues. I feel I have a lot to offer and will always be a NURSE! It would seem that a lot of jumping around took place in my life, that is not due to being irresponsible or indecisive. I married a member of the RCMP and we were subject to transfers. We were fortunate to have been in Windsor, NS for so long. During that time he was transferred to Halifax but could commute daily. Nursing almost killed me at times, at other times it saved my life, but it was always like a dream, to be a NURSE, and I have three sisters in the field, in varying specialties. I like to think now I can be their big sister and confidante. And through the written word I can share the world of the 'nurse' with others.

Yvonne Lowe, RN. Rtd.
(Pen Name —Bonnie Jarvis-Lowe)

ISBN 1412018218